HOW TO SAVE OUR TOWN CENTRES

A radical agenda
for the future of high streets

Julian Dobson

First published in Great Britain in 2015 by

Policy Press
University of Bristol
1-9 Old Park Hill
Bristol BS2 8BB
UK
t: +44 (0)117 594 5940
pp-info@bristol.ac.uk
www.policypress.co.uk

North America office:
Policy Press
c/o The University of Chicago Press
1427 East 60th Street
Chicago, IL 60637, USA
t: +1 773 702 7700
f: +1 773 702 9756
sales@press.uchicago.edu
www.press.uchicago.edu

British Library Cataloguing in Publication Data
A catalogue record for this book is available from the British Library

Library of Congress Cataloging-in-Publication Data
A catalog record for this book has been requested

ISBN 978 1 44732 393 8 paperback

Cover design by Soapbox Design, London
Front cover image kindly supplied by Julian Dobson
Printed and bound in Great Britain by CMP, Poole
Policy Press uses environmentally responsible print partners

In memory of Victor,
and for all who believe in better.

*To be truly radical is to make hope possible,
rather than despair convincing.*
(Raymond Williams)

Contents

List of photographs

All photographs were taken by the author

About the author

Julian Dobson is a writer, researcher, speaker and commentator on towns, cities, and social policy. He is director of Urban Pollinators Ltd (www.urbanpollinators.co.uk), which shares creative solutions to the challenges of place.

He co-founded *New Start*, the magazine for regeneration practitioners, and previously edited *Inside Housing* magazine. He is a fellow of the Royal Society of Arts and a board member of the Centre for Local Economic Strategies.

Acknowledgements

This book has been influenced and improved by many people who have opened my eyes to the state of our towns and cities; who have steered and challenged my thinking; and whose actions have inspired and encouraged me.

Thanks in particular are due to those who work tirelessly to improve the towns and cities they live in, and who have convinced me that this book is worth writing. There are too many of them to acknowledge here, but I would like to pay particular tribute to the group who worked with me on 'The 21st century agora', a submission to the Portas review in 2011, which was the starting point for this particular journey. Mark Barnes, Joost Beunderman, Eddie Bridgeman, Euan Mills, Mike Riddell, Dan Thompson, Chris Wade and Pam Warhurst have very different perspectives and backgrounds, but a shared passion for creating better places.

Along the way others have stood out in terms of their contribution to action and thought. I have discussed, debated, supported or disagreed with them over several years, and they have helped me form the views I express here – sometimes in strong opposition to their opinions! Among them I would particularly acknowledge Joe Barratt, Martin Blackwell, Eileen Conn, Ed Cooke, Bill Grimsey, Neil McInroy, Mary Portas, Leigh Sparks, Jess Steele and Paul Turner-Mitchell.

I am grateful to all those who have asked me to share my thoughts and knowledge in advisory forums, events and conferences in recent years, especially the Royal Society for the Encouragement of Arts, Manufactures and Commerce (RSA) and Mainstreet Australia; and to the many more who have engaged in conversation and debate in social media.

Thanks are due to those who set aside time to be interviewed or to facilitate my visits, especially Jibunnessa Abdullah, Anthony Blackburn, Tessy Britton, Chris Chalkley, Mehul Damani, Simon

Danczuk, Michelle Denton, George Ferguson, Malcom Fraser, Stephen Hill, Andrew Heyes, John Lewis, Annemarie Naylor, Frances Northrop, Liz Peace, Ann Petherick, Chris Sands, Leigh Sparks, Neil Stockwell and Paul Turner-Mitchell. Reducing many words of wisdom to a handful of pithy quotes was one of the toughest challenges in writing this book.

Those who read drafts of the text and provided comment and encouragement deserve special appreciation. David Boyle, Leigh Sparks, Martin McNally and Samer Bagaeen have all helped to improve the content and argument. Stuart Mason provided invaluable research assistance at a crucial time, and I am especially grateful for his input. Many thanks also to Emily Watt and Laura Vickers at Policy Press; and finally to my family, for their constant support, patience and encouragement. Needless to say, all errors and omissions are my own.

Preface

When I began writing this book, the 'high street' was high on the political agenda in the UK. Politicians and pundits queued up for slots on prime-time TV to pronounce on the future of our town and city centres. Each had their particular bugbear: business taxes, planning rules, parking.

From the start I was clear that something different needed to be said. We have had enough experts from the retail and property trades offering shrivelled visions of the future, in which nothing shakes the interests and institutions that currently dominate our communities. Nobody needs a book explaining how broken systems can be preserved.

If we are serious about creating places for people, we need to delve below the minor crises of particular retailers or high streets and ask how town and city centres currently function, why they fail and who benefits from their successes and failures. In doing so we discover that the free market is anything but free, and competition is anything but fair. An agenda to save our town centres must involve addressing inequities and articulating a broader vision for the places at the heart of our communities.

This book is an attempt to set out such a vision for the long term, building on what is already being achieved in the UK and around the world. The perspective is primarily from the UK, but the issues it grapples with will be pertinent to readers worldwide. It looks at town centres as places of trade and commerce; places of leisure and sociability; places to live in and enjoy. It explores how the failing 'me towns' of the early 21st century can become 'we towns' where all share in a flourishing society.

I hope this vision will remain relevant and helpful for years to come. For that reason I have avoided including long sections on some of the issues of the moment, such as the intricacies of UK planning law or the opportunities that may or may not be offered by particular technologies. They are important questions, but will soon be overtaken by events and politics. Even when referring to particular examples and incidents I have tried to keep an eye on the long-term value of the illustrations I have used.

Any reading of economic, cultural and social issues is inevitably framed by time and geography. Aspects of this book will date, but my hope is that readers in years to come will still be informed and inspired by its content.

Julian Dobson
Sheffield, August 2014

Part One

Today

by particular technologies. They are important questions, but will soon be overtaken by events and politics. Even when referring to particular examples and incidents I have tried to keep an eye on the long-term value of the illustrations I have used.

Any reading of economic, cultural and social issues is inevitably framed by time and geography. Aspects of this book will date, but my hope is that readers in years to come will still be informed and inspired by its content.

Julian Dobson
Sheffield, August 2014

Part One

Today

1

It took a riot

The night of 21 April 2011 witnessed a first in the history of Britain's biggest supermarket chain. Tesco, the corporation that had grown from humble barrow-boy beginnings in London's East End 92 years earlier to control almost one third of the UK's grocery market and billions of pounds of household spending, was attacked by rioters in Bristol.

Eight police officers were injured in the disturbances in Stokes Croft, a neighbourhood just north of the city centre popular with artists and students. Several hundred people joined battles with the police after a heavy-handed raid on a squat known as Telepathic Heights. National media immediately labelled it the 'Tesco riot', linking the troubles with a vociferous local campaign against the company's decision to open a Tesco Express convenience store in the busy Cheltenham Road.

Four weeks later Prime Minister David Cameron announced a review of the state of England's high streets, fronted by the retail guru and TV presenter Mary Portas. Whether or not the so-called Tesco riot had influenced his thinking when the review was announced, a wave of rioting across England later that summer inextricably entwined the mayhem of street violence with the state of the nation's traditional shopping streets. Suddenly the high street was not just ailing, but dangerous. The boundaries between shopping and looting seemed to vanish in five days of madness in early August.

During those feverish summer nights nearly 15,000 people were caught up in a surge of disorder, starting in London's suburbs and spreading rapidly to Birmingham, Manchester and smaller towns. Five people died. Many more lost their businesses. Hundreds were fined or jailed as a result of the estimated 5,000 crimes committed that week.

What connects high streets and riots? At their heart, both are about the future of the places we live in, and where we base our everyday lives. The decline of the shopping street and the rioters' willingness to trash their hometowns both illustrate and expose the disturbed and often dysfunctional relationships people in 21st-century Western societies have with the places they call home.

The August riots began, as many English riots have done, with a protest against the police. A young black man, Mark Duggan, had been shot by officers in Tottenham while they were attempting to arrest him. But the protests rapidly became something very different, and commentators were quick to seize on them as evidence of their favourite bugbears: moral decline, poor parenting, poverty and inequality, and the effects of the austerity programme imposed by the government the previous year. David Cameron lost no time in absolving himself of the latter charge, declaring: 'These riots were not about government cuts: they were directed at high street stores, not Parliament' (Cabinet Office, 2011).

The stores may not have been the cause of the rioters' wrath, but there was no doubt they were the target of their revenge. The independent panel set up to investigate the troubles found that in addition to protesters and those seeking to fight the police, the rioters included a large number of 'late night shoppers', individuals seeking the latest goods and gadgets.

Some of the comments the investigators recorded were revealing. "I nick a radio and the world comes down on me, bankers take a million and nothing happens," one said. "The pressure to have the latest designer items is immense," complained another. "It wasn't political – it was shopping," one victim commented. It was as if a nation obsessed with bargains and deals had suddenly discovered the biggest bargain of all, instant access to what one called "free stuff" with a minimal risk of getting caught.

Some of the biggest brand names were ruthlessly targeted, with electronic devices, televisions and expensive trainers the favoured booty. As the riots inquiry panel observed:

> The desire to own goods which give the owner high status (such as branded trainers and digital gadgets) was seen as an important factor behind the riots. In addition, the idea of 'saving up' for something has been replaced by the idea that we should have what we want when we want. Levels of personal debt are in part a scary testimony to this. When asked why he rioted, one rioter responded simply 'greed'.
>
> In our conversations both with rioters and with young people who did not riot, it was clear that brands and appliances are strongly associated with their sense of identity and status. In these riots certain brands and products were repeatedly targeted. (Riots Communities and Victims Panel, 2012, p 104)

If some of the Bristol rioters wanted to destroy Tesco because it was a symbol of rampant capitalism, it seemed many of the August 2011 rioters just wanted a fast track to the rewards of rampant capitalism. A contemporary study of 100 British adolescents by researchers at Manchester Business School found that consuming 'the correct possessions at the right time' was essential in achieving social acceptance, and the poorer a teenager's family background, the more important it was to own the more expensive brands. The researchers described this as the 'commodification of self-esteem' (Isaksen and Roper, 2012, p 117).

Yet the brands and corporations that may have inspired anger or envy proved better able to weather the storm than the many small business owners who also suffered. The story of the House of Reeves furniture store in Croydon, which survived the Blitz of the Second World War but was burned to the ground on 8 August 2011, came to symbolise the destructive violence of that week. Shopkeepers and business owners were traumatised not only by the riots, but also by the task of negotiating with dilatory and obstructive insurance companies many months after the event. "Watching our whole life in flames haunts us every day," a couple from Salford told the inquiry panel.

Something else happened in England's high streets that week, and it was nothing to do with envy or grabbing the latest gizmo. Hundreds of people formed what were soon described as 'broom armies', using social media to summon friends and well-wishers to clean up the devastation. Thousands more expressed their support and helped to spread the word. It has been estimated that 90,000 people were involved in various ways. Photographs of local volunteers, brooms held aloft as they assembled at Clapham Common in South London, become the obverse of the week's images of burning and looting. There were similar scenes in Manchester, with scores of volunteers wearing 'I love Manchester' t-shirts.

One of the main instigators of the riot clean-up was Dan Thompson, an artist and activist from Worthing on the south coast. Worthing, in keeping with its genteel reputation, was untouched by the troubles. But the clean-up demonstrated the power of the internet to mobilise people: from his laptop Thompson, already a passionate and persistent advocate of creatively reusing empty shops, helped to coordinate the broom battalions. He described the clean-up as anarchy at its best: 'hundreds of individuals who, without leadership or state intervention, took to the streets and worked out a new way of doing things' (Thompson, 2011).

The long death of the high street?

The events of 2011 put the high street centre stage. These ordinary streets, used and abused with scarcely a second thought most of the time, were forced to the core of the nation's consciousness. How had they turned into such apparently dangerous and frightening places? It was hardly surprising that Britain's soul-searching over the riots became conflated with angst over the state of our town centres. Combine that with a desperate hunt by political leaders for actions to blunt the edge of austerity and stimulate economic growth, and a pall of malaise and distrust fed by scandal after scandal in the UK's financial system, politics and the media, and the result was a heady potion. As consciousness of the importance of our high streets was raised, so were expectations.

Boris Johnson, mayor of London, announced a package of £23 million of support for Croydon, one of the areas worst hit. 'The devastation of the August riots is a reminder of the urgency of investing serious sums into this potential economic powerhouse,' he declared (quoted in GLA, 2011). Smaller pots of cash were announced for other areas scarred by the disturbances. In Croydon, much of the money was to be spent on improvements to the public realm – the roads, pavements, street scenery and transport hubs.

Not once in the rush to help did political leaders stop to question whether these high streets had a future, or what sort of future they should have. The hurry to return to business as usual clouded any understanding of the changing nature of the places where the riots occurred, and of the public's relationship with these places. The fact that the riot clean-ups were coordinated from a place dozens of miles from the scene of any violence sent a little-noticed signal about the way human interaction with physical places is changing in a digital age.

The relationship between people and their town centres is complex and ambivalent, and not only in the UK. The US has led the trend towards sprawling out-of-town malls and retail parks, and most of the Western world has followed. The rapidly developing economies of India, Brazil and China are leaping on the bandwagon, unaware of the wreckage it leaves behind. News reports in mid-2014 spotlighted Nigeria and Indonesia as emerging markets, with strong shopping mall growth from Spain to Singapore.

Many, particularly among major retailers, property companies and academics, argue that the high street, the traditional meeting point and marketplace at the heart of our towns, is dead or dying, and nothing can stop it. They point to the rise of internet shopping on top of the 30-year advance of out-of-town malls as evidence that not only are the public turning their backs on town centres, they no longer care what happens to them. A leading British academic, Alan

Hallsworth, says the car-based food superstore has already become the 'hegemonic retail format' (Hallsworth et al, 2010, p 135). And as we desert our town centres, some say ghost towns or worse have become our just deserts.

Others, entrepreneurs and activists, have reacted to the apparent cynicism and despair with a passionate defence of traditional high streets, mounting imaginative or hectoring 'shop local' campaigns, celebrating and championing independent retailers, creating exciting and quirky 'meanwhile' and 'pop-up' enterprises to fill vacant spaces, and fulminating at the lack of help from government. High streets are not dead, they say – and they would be so much livelier if only the competition were fair.

Political leaders, meanwhile, have been quick to pick up the popular angst, if not to respond with any degree of wisdom. The choice of Mary Portas to head the 2011 review of the UK's high streets was designed to send a clear message to the public that the government cared. Ministers knew she would generate headlines, and were not disappointed. A packed House of Commons debate in response to the review continued for more than six hours before legislators ran out of time.

Presenting her findings in December 2011, Ms Portas certainly ruffled a few feathers. 'The days of a high street populated simply by independent butchers, bakers and candlestick makers are, except in the most exceptional circumstances, over,' she announced at the beginning of her report (Portas, 2011, p 2). And if by that she meant the traditional Victorian high street as immortalised on a million Christmas card illustrations, she was right.

For most of human history, buying and selling has been intimately connected with living and socialising. The agora, the souk and the marketplace have been the places of connection and exchange, friendship and rivalry, gossip and scheming. In the 20th century that began to change. Business became bigger, more efficient and more profitable at the expense of being trusted and personal; interaction became an inconvenience. For every nostalgic view of the high street as a place where every trader knew every customer, there are miserable memories of shoppers lugging heavy bags from one store to another in the rain, or of circling frustratedly around town centre blocks in search of a place to park. The motor car that made towns accessible also made them aggressive and congested; the supermarkets that made shopping convenient also killed its diversity and humanity.

The meltdown has been a long time coming. In 1938, long before the concept of 'clone towns' was popularised, the editor of the *Architectural Review*, J.M. Richards, wrote:

> In many places the personal and local character of the shops is disappearing. This is because many shops are now only branches of the big multiple stores, which for convenience are made all the same, and because of the use of ready-made shop fronts and fittings. But it is no use regretting the coming of the multiple store and the standardisation of shop fronts, as these are part of our modern way of organising business and do, on the whole, make better goods available for more people. Even if they do make towns look more alike, and therefore duller, it is a convenience when you are travelling to find branches of a shop you already know. (1938, p 8)

Fifty years later Professor John Dawson, of the University of Stirling's Institute for Retail Studies, wrote in the *Geographical Journal*: '… there is a concern that the High Street shopping environment to which society has grown accustomed, whether as shoppers, investors, employees or entrepreneurs, is changing and we are not sure whether we will like either how it will change or what it will be changed to' (Dawson, 1988, p 2).

Around the same time the UK government, led by Prime Minister Margaret Thatcher, commissioned a report, *The future of the high street*. Introducing its findings, Ann Burdus, chair of the Distributive Trades Economic Development Committee, commented on the signs of decay already evident in many town centres, and the effects on surrounding communities:

> A decrease in the economic importance of a High Street has considerable social implications. Visiting a gradually deteriorating and derelict High Street is not an attractive proposition for most customers, particularly if many of the goods they want to buy are not available. High Streets of this type may have lost their function as meeting

places because few people have an incentive to visit them; even fewer linger for social purposes. The crucial point seems to be that competition and market forces do not overcome problems associated with declining High Street shopping areas. (National Economic Development Office, 1988, p iii)

Several of the report's recommendations bore remarkable similarities to those of the Portas review 23 years later. The fact that they had to be repeated more than two decades on bears witness both to the continuing public concern over changes in our town centres and the inadequacy of the actions intended to address them.

The physical hearts of our communities have always suffered periodic palpitations. What is different now is that – with a few notable exceptions – familiar activities are disappearing without a stream of new ones to take their place, or being replaced by activities of doubtful social and economic value. The legacy of economic recession, technological change and shifts in the way we shop and live are combining to hollow out the centres of places that were once bustling.

In 2008 the UK's Competition Commission presented a snapshot of the decline of the independent high street grocer. The numbers of independent butchers and greengrocers fell from more than 40,000 each in the 1950s to one quarter of that figure in 2000. The number of bakeries fell from around 25,000 to around 8,000; the number of fishmongers from 10,000 to 2,000 (Competition Commission, 2008).

By early 2013, the failure of retailers in the UK since the onset of recession in 2008 had cost around 198,000 jobs and nearly £1.5 billion in lost rent for landlords (Ruddick, 2013). By December 2013 just under 12 per cent of all shopping was online, with British shoppers spending £675 million a week on the internet (ONS, 2014). Not only the shops are going: many of the institutions that once anchored town centres, from churches to libraries and adult education classes, have disappeared or diminished. The activities that brought people into town in the 19th and early 20th centuries are often no longer there, and sometimes no longer anywhere. As Gertrude Stein famously said of Oakland, California, there is no 'there' there. Richard Susskind, author of *Tomorrow's lawyers*, recently predicted the end of the high street law firm (Legalfutures.co.uk,

11 January, 2013). Even the rats, some might say, are leaving the sinking ship.

The driving forces for these changes are complex. They include the growth of out-of-town shopping and the planning regimes that have facilitated it; the gobbling up of market share by large supermarket chains; property deals which have left many towns saddled with unviable and unnecessary shopping centres; mergers and acquisitions that have lumbered retailers with unsustainable debts coupled with demands for higher profitability; and not least, the growth of internet shopping which has made much of the physical space provided for retail in the last few decades redundant.

In the US the phenomenon has gone a step further, with out-of-town malls now succumbing to obsolescence and a burgeoning interest in revitalising 'greyfield' malls by bringing in a mix of new uses. First the shops desert the community; next, it seems, the community has to be drafted into the malls to save the shops (CNU, 2005).

Should we blame the internet giants, the malls and the supermarkets for the economic sinkholes they leave behind them? We can argue that they should trade fairly, pay their workers a living wage and pay their taxes like everyone else, but that will not revive town centre bookshops and music stores, or the many other specialists whose goods you can now buy more conveniently online or with the weekly groceries. Fairer competition may provide a stay of execution for the traditional high street, but it won't prevent its decline any more than ratcheting up fuel taxes will revive the use of horses and carts. And while some might view a proliferation of convenience stores, betting shops and coffee shops as signs of the high street's 'adaptive resilience', such optimism bypasses the long-term challenges about how these places work and who benefits from them (Wrigley and Lambiri, 2014).

The issue is what to do with the holes: how to turn the gap-toothed relics of our town centres into places that will thrive again through better uses and activities. As Steve Bentley, President of Mainstreet Australia, put it: 'The world, our customers and community expectations have moved. Our challenge is to understand what they want and to be prepared to be flexible; to adapt and change so that we remain relevant and meaningful to them' (Mainstreet Australia, 2014).

That is the starting point. But as well as adapting and changing, there is a need to lead: to demonstrate how town centres can become better. To do that effectively, we must look deeper into our past and into our societies, and further into the future and into ourselves, than government reviews or expert inquiries are ever likely to do. We need to wrestle with the challenges of how the places we live in can be fit for an uncertain future, and how as individuals, communities, workers and citizens we choose to relate to them.

A warning from history

A place that works well is a place for people. Not just one that is occupied by people, or where they pass through on their way to somewhere else, or where they disappear into curtained rooms to interact with the world via their electronic devices. It is one where people feel connected and where they care. The anxiety we feel about the state of the high street is less about the loss of a Woolworths or a Jessops or the shock of a riot than about its abandonment by the people who used to populate it, and a sense that we are the ones who might be left behind.

In 1960 the urbanist Jane Jacobs wrote in her seminal work, *The death and life of great American cities*, of the 'intricate sidewalk ballet' of a well-functioning neighbourhood. Family, school, commerce and conversation all played their part in the comings and goings of the day. She described the rituals of the morning in Greenwich Village, New York:

> ... Mr Halpert unlocking the laundry handcart from its mooring to a cellar door, Joe Cornachia's son-in-law stacking out the empty crates from the delicatessen, the barber bringing out his sidewalk folding chair, Mr Goldstein arranging the coils of wire which proclaim the hardware store is open, the wife of the tenement's superintendent depositing her chunky three-year-old with a toy mandolin on the stoop, the vantage point from which he is learning the English his mother cannot speak. (Jacobs, 1993, p 66)

Half a century on, it is hard not to smear such a passage with a patina of nostalgia. But far from glossing Jacobs' street with a lacquer of wistfulness, she was describing the everyday life she could see from her front window. Hers was a ballet of movement and exchange, but it had other qualities that are disappearing from many town centres. Jane Jacobs' Hudson Street was a place where people lived and raised their families, where they drank and met their friends, where they sent their children to school. It was a street where businesses were run by family firms or local entrepreneurs, and where traders looked out for their neighbours as well as their margins because business was about personal standing and reputation, not just the financial bottom line.

Few local residents look from their front windows in today's shopping streets and there are even fewer children playing on doorsteps. The ballet is less intricate and less leisured, less sociable and less connected with its local context. In some towns it is a dance of death, the fleeting and fearful exchanges of those who know they do not have long.

There are warnings from recent history of what happens when places are deserted, employment opportunities disappear and businesses leave. During the 1980s and 1990s Britain's coal industry collapsed, driven by cheap imports and a political decision to break the might of the once-feared National Union of Mineworkers. More than 250,000 jobs vanished and in some parts of the country, such as South Wales and North Nottinghamshire, entire villages lost their livelihoods.

The social problems resulting from the demise of the coal industry have been catalogued and trawled over countless times. They include the loss of opportunities, high levels of drug abuse, disaffection and low educational attainment, collapsing house prices, crime and antisocial behaviour – the litany of despair that accompanies the loss of a place's purpose. The Coalfields Regeneration Review Board, reporting in 2010, found a 'multiplier effect' of deprivation: around Barnsley, for example, some 20,000 mining jobs were lost, and it was estimated at least two more jobs went for every one in the coal industry. Specialist suppliers such as engineers were hit first by pit closures, followed by local shops and businesses as once well-paid families struggled to make ends meet.

But the costs of economic decline within communities run far deeper than statistics about jobs and income. In the pit villages of North Nottinghamshire, heroin abuse, especially among young men, became widespread. The county's assistant chief constable said that to feed a £15,000-a-year drug habit, the average user would need to steal goods worth £70,000. The costs of those thefts were overwhelmingly borne by already hard-hit local shopkeepers, businesses and residents.

The problem became so severe that in 2002 the local MP, John Mann, decided to hold his own inquiry, taking evidence from more than 100 drug users. 'People growing up in the coalfields lack the sense of identity afforded to their parents and grandparents who were part of a stable and prosperous mining industry,' he reported.

> The strongest substance used in these communities was beer, and stable employment allowed most a good standard of living. In these communities, with their low educational and employment aspirations, there is a need to escape. Heroin is a drug associated with the need to 'get away from it all'.... Heroin addiction is a national problem, but it is particularly acute in the coalfields. Low aspirations and a desire to escape, without having the means or confidence to do so, leads to a life of addiction to a drug that offers a way out. (Mann, 2002, p 3)

The Labour government elected in 1997 promised to rectify what it saw as the injustices of the previous administration's neglect, yet after expanding the coalfields regeneration programme and spending the best part of £1 billion on numerous interventions to reclaim derelict land, provide training and job opportunities and support local projects, the recovery in many former mining communities was fragile. A quarter of a century after the pit closures, the Coalfields Regeneration Trust was still giving out grants to help people and organisations in the areas affected.

There is a warning for our town centres here. Like the pit villages, many are losing their economic raison d'être. A market town with no market is little better off than a mining town with no mine. And when one local store or public service, cafe or meeting place closes, there is one less reason to visit the others. The economics that told

14

policymakers in the UK it was cheaper and therefore better to import coal than to mine it are mirrored in the economics of scale and convenience that have moved shopping out of towns and into malls, and from the physical world into the virtual. But unlike the choices about energy policy, which lay in the hands of the government, the choices about the use and function of town centres and about the nature of retail are fragmented among a host of players, from local planners to multinational corporations, from individual shoppers to property developers and pension funds. In many cases it is already too late to change or reverse their effects.

Losing our town centres will be like losing the coal industry, but the process will be more protracted and the damage more widespread. Those who follow the money will follow it to the places where the tills continue to ring and better-off consumers continue to consume, while less successful places are successively denuded of shops, services, people and hope. Only this time, there will be no future government prepared to invest billions in an attempt to turn the tide.

An agenda for town centres

The harm is already being done. To stop it becoming catastrophic we must discover ways of reviving our towns while they still have life in them. Since we cannot turn them all into theme parks of life as it was lived before the internet and the out-of-town mall, we need to explore what new or rediscovered functions we can find for them. And to do that, we need to appreciate why they matter and broaden our thinking about what they could be.

This book advocates a citizen-centred agenda for town centres, encompassing the local economy, the built environment and community activity. In doing so it seeks to contest received wisdom about what makes a successful high street, and highlight the need for an interconnected critique of policy and practice, reaching beyond traditional disciplines and professions.

The first part of the book examines where we are today. Chapter 2 explores why our town centres are culturally and socially important, and examines the failure of the much-vaunted 'retail-led regeneration' of the last two decades. It goes on to set out the challenges that must be addressed in order to create resilient town centres for the future.

Chapters 3 and 4 look at the workings of the market – both traditional markets and fairs and modern supermarkets and malls – and ask how the changing nature of retail is affecting physical places. In Chapter 5 we examine the resurgence of independent retailing, and question whether shopping locally can be enough to save our town centres.

Part Two of the book looks at what our town centres could be like tomorrow. Chapter 6 explores the 'new economy', and how towns can prosper by reinventing historic links between producing and consuming. Chapter 7 moves beyond the realm of retail, highlighting the vital role of public services and public assets in creating successful places. In Chapter 8 we focus on the public realm, the often-neglected space in between buildings, and show how it can be given new life; and Chapter 9 explores how town and city centres can once again become places where people make their homes.

The last three chapters deal with some of the overarching issues we must address to give our town centres a chance. Chapter 10 tackles the thorny question of land ownership and access to land; Chapter 11 examines how access to finance is shackling our town centre economies and what can be done about it; and Chapter 12 explores how, by drawing on historic ideas of the commons, we can turn 'me towns' into 'we towns'.

So this book is not only about what we are losing, but also about how we can find something better. It is not just about shops and shopping, but about the human needs around which shops and meeting places spring up. It's about the people we are and want to be, the places we live in, and the kind of society we want. And it starts in a street, a shop, a library, or a cafe near us.

2

Thanks for the memories

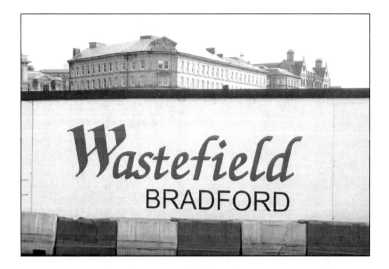

Shortly before the Second World War, the illustrator Eric Ravilious created a series of lithographs of British shops. The medium, with its simple colour schemes and bold treatments of light and shade, was itself evocative of a past that would never return.

There was the baker and confectioner, bright-eyed in the early hours of the morning while it was still dark, the shop lit up and the windows and shelves packed with freshly made crusty loaves, a hand-pulled delivery cart ready for its rounds. There was the West End delicatessen's display of Christmas hams from all parts of England, each cured in its traditional local fashion; the model ship and railway shop where you could order figures of passengers including George Bernard Shaw and Charlie Chaplin; even the submarine engineer for those adventurous souls requiring a diving suit. Each merchant was an expert, not merely a purveyor of goods, but a dispenser of wisdom and advice.

Few high streets these days can boast a naturalist, furrier and plumassier. There was a time when demand was higher: 'When a favourite dog dies, the owners sometimes want to have him stuffed, or his skin made into a rug. They go to a naturalist like Mr Pollard to have this done,' J.M. Richards wrote in the accompanying commentary (p 29). Mr Pollard's staff, it appears, were enthusiasts as well as experts, as we're informed that 'at home Mr Pollard's foreman has got two hundred stuffed mice, each in a different attitude' (Richards, 1938, p 31)

Reviewing the illustrations at the time, the artist John Piper wrote in the magazine *Signature*:

> There is about them the suggestion that you are looking in at a series of gay, old-fashioned parties from the matter-of-fact street in the present. They are records of a passing beauty, but they are full of present-day experience. And they are faithful enough to look like tuck-shops full of sherbet, liquorice and lollipops – which, after all, is one of the chief appeals of the attractive shop. (*Signature*, No. 5, March 1937, page 48)

This sense of loss and wistfulness, not to mention a longing for tuck-shops full of sherbet, has tinted (or tainted) popular perceptions of the high street for the best part of a century. A building that has been a shop for many decades is layered with memories, like the strata of paint on ancient fascia boards that are sometimes revealed when a store is refitted. Delve into library archives or visit a market trader selling historic postcards, and it is the photographs of shopfronts that provide an instant social history, creaking open a window on the way our grandparents and great-grandparents used to live. Unlike the domestic environment, the workplace or even the council chamber, the shop is a thing of the street and the public, its displays and facades a picture of public life.

The store tells a story. And the collections of stores in our high streets spin a longer yarn about the places we live in and how we live there. They project forwards, too, prophesying possible futures for our towns and their communities. The popular concern about the state of the high street is a concern about how these tales will unfold.

As well as being a repository of the past and of loss, the shop and the shopping street exemplify continuity and connection. There's a fascination in knowing that the stores we frequent now were there 50 years before, or in knowing what other functions they might have served. That fascination is amplified when we appreciate the changes, subtle and not so subtle, and realise that they are part of a continuum of interaction and exchange, colour and conversation. The chameleon skins of the shops provide a reassurance that our towns and lives are constantly being refreshed and renewed.

Does any of this matter if we now have more convenient and efficient ways of doing our shopping? If the high street has been dying for as long as we can remember, might it not be time to move on?

A decade or so ago *The Idler Magazine* ran a wildly popular feature called 'Crap towns'. Hundreds of readers flooded its columns with eulogies of British crapness, competing to show how much crappier their town was than everyone else's. Take Wolverhampton, described by reader Michael Thompson: 'Its most attractive feature is an orbital dual carriageway so impossibly difficult to negotiate (unless you're a local) that it actually performs a service to the community by keeping curious outsiders away from this gutter belch of the West Midlands' (*The Idler Magazine*, 2005).

If our towns have ceased to mean anything to us, such an outpouring of vitriol might be hard to understand. Perhaps even behind the bile is a kind of love, a sense of outraged loss of what the place once was or should have been.

This well of sentiment, nostalgic or nihilistic, whispers that moving on is far harder than it looks, and that we often underestimate the losses incurred. Places are signifiers of our histories and identities, individually and collectively. The way we tell the stories of these places helps to frame our own futures. So when places change, those changes are loaded with visceral feelings. What a planner or politician proposes as regeneration is often felt as obliteration. To ignore or dismiss such gut reactions is to dismiss the humanity, in all its exciting and infuriating diversity, that gives each place individuality and character.

To get a sense of this complexity, take a walk along Sandy Row in south Belfast. The pictures here are a far cry from the homely prints of Eric Ravilious. A hop and a jump from the city's bus terminal, this staunchly Loyalist enclave welcomes you with a mural commemorating King Billy – William of Orange – whose forces passed this way en route to the Battle of the Boyne. If that seems slightly intimidating, it's worth remembering that not long ago the same wall was decorated with a sign proclaiming this the territory of the Ulster Freedom Fighters.

Just along the street is a painted tribute to the Northern Irish football association and a welcome to 'Our Wee Country'. Beyond that cheery greeting, there's more football paraphernalia: a mural dedicated to the fallen genius George Best, next to a memorial to Robert Dougan, 'murdered by the enemies' in 1998, the year of the Good Friday Agreement that paved the way to peace in Northern Ireland. There are other vestiges of the paramilitary past: sectarian graffiti and signs warning drug dealers they will be 'put out'. And there is the more respectable side of Loyalism: an Orange Hall, the One Stop Ulster Shop, the Rangers Supporters Club. You belong, or apparently you don't.

But there are ordinary shops, too: takeaways and convenience stores, a shoe shop, a butcher. Outside a cafe a few chairs have been put out on the pavement, and a man in a hat watches passers-by. Paris it isn't, but it's an invitation to join in a place where people live. On most of the shopfronts, though, the steel shutters are down. Some have been down for years. The former Gilpin's furniture store dominates the street, derelict and decaying. This road, once a thriving shopping area with more than 120 stores in Victorian times, looks as if its condition is terminal.

Around Sandy Row is a neighbourhood of modest low-rise houses. For all its pride in the past, this community looks left behind in a city that is struggling to forge a new and shared identity. But appearances don't tell you everything. Slowly, the more threatening remains of 'the Troubles' are being removed. There are hopes of turning the Gilpin's site into a community hub, with space for social enterprises and affordable housing. An outdoor gym has been opened in the local park; Queen's University, just a short walk to the south, is supporting a homework club. Residents have drawn up plans to turn Sandy Row into 'a place to linger, not to leave', supporting independent traders and drawing positively on the history and character of the area to welcome visitors.

Elsewhere, Belfast is trying to create spaces where communities are identified by what they can do together rather than by what separates them. Could Sandy Row join them in becoming a street where all feel invited and at ease? A sign written on a city centre pub offers a way forward, here and for high streets elsewhere: 'A nation that keeps one eye on the past is wise. A nation that keeps two eyes on the past is blind.' Sandy Row's story will have a few twists yet.

Why places are personal

Suspended from Chris Sands' canalside office ceiling is a rusty tricycle. In north London, this might be a playfully surrealist art installation. In Sowerby Bridge, the tale it tells is personal and local.

The tricycle was found in a skip nearby. Someone brought it to Chris, who runs the Totally Locally campaign to support independent shops, because they recognised the name on the frame: Cyril Sands, Chris' grandfather, who, for more than 30 years, ran the West Yorkshire town's bike shop.

On a weekday 50 years ago the pavement outside the shop would be crowded with cycles, the cheap and convenient means of transport for working people. In those days the hills didn't put people off. Cyril ran his shop until the 1970s, and after that it lasted another two decades. The shop is now a deli and the kind of bikes you're most likely to see in the town are those of Sunday trippers, idling along the Rochdale Canal, stopping for a pint by the wharf or preparing to tackle the Calder Valley's challenging inclines.

That tricycle is a clue to a sense of place that's unique to Sowerby Bridge. In every town, there are tales and traces that have not yet been erased by corporate sameness and impersonal branding. But they are becoming harder to find.

But the clues are important. To imagine our high streets as simply a collection of shops, services and meeting places is to miss the magic that happens when people bring places to life, and places give people a stage. The philosopher Martin Heidegger called this *Dasein* – 'being-in-the-world'. Humans live in relation to their environment. That's why Chris Sands' tricycle is much more than just a quirky artwork in a chic warehouse conversion.

The humble shopping street, the urban landscape, the hill or valley, helps to create who we are and how we feel about the world around us. Everyday actions, from popping into the shop to walking the dog, orient us and give us a sense of belonging or alienation. As the geographer Yi-Fu Tuan put it: 'Objects and places are centres of value. They attract or repel in finely shaded degrees. To attend to them even momentarily is to acknowledge their reality and value' (1977, p 18).

The construction of human beings as atomised *homo economicus*, individuals whose choices are determined by a narrow rationality that seeks out the best material deal and whose lives are a succession of cost-benefit calculations, ignores these physical, emotional and even spiritual connections with place and the diverse meanings people assign to these connections. The boards and shareholders who dominate the retail and property industries tend to have a dislocated and decontextualised view of places: they view them as cost centres and markets, which may or may not be viable and profitable. If the location doesn't produce the right returns, the company gets out. Taken to an extreme, as in American cities like Flint and Detroit, whole towns and cities are hollowed out as corporations leave their carrion for others to clean up. A company might view this as a rational way of thinking about places, but it's a rationality achieved by stripping away humanity.

The American landscape architect Lynne Manzo has researched how people value public places as a vital backdrop to their lives, and assign an emotional importance to those places as settings for personal milestones and landmarks. Often when the domestic environment is a scene of trouble or conflict, the public space provides a sanctuary (Manzo, 2005). Public spaces work as echo chambers in which fragments of human lives, hopes and memories resonate, and in doing so they come to life themselves. It's this population of 'ghosts', the friendly and the uncanny, that can give a place its character. As Michel de Certeau observes: 'There is no place that is not haunted by many different spirits hidden there in silence.... Haunted places are the only ones people can live in' (1984, p 108).

The enclosed mall or out-of-town shopping centre may, at a pinch, meet some of our emotional needs. But it does so in a controlled environment where lingering, whiling away time and reinterpreting public space in a personal way are discouraged. The self-service checkout is no friend of romance, and there are few ghosts in the Apple store.

In our struggling town centres, the economic and human understandings of place collide. Our sentimental attachment might be to the town, but the material benefits of most of our spending now flow to the mall and the supermarket. And where city leaders and property developers have tried to weave their own new stories for town and city centres, they have often done so by spending millions of pounds on so-called 'retail-led regeneration' – a blunt instrument that generates more questions than it resolves.

The failure of retail-led regeneration

If you stroll down the hill from Liverpool's Lime Street station towards the city centre and the historic waterfront, you'll find it hard to avoid Liverpool One. This is retail-led regeneration in all its splendour. Spread over 42 acres of prime real estate, it is a brightly lit, glass-fronted apogee of cash-till urbanism, with 165 shops, 500 apartments, two hotels, 25 restaurants, 30,000 square feet of offices and a 14-screen cinema. This billion-pound shopping nirvana was designed to bring new life to a city that had fallen on hard times, and its combination of big retail convenience and city centre setting has brought the crowds flooding in.

The Royal Institute of British Architects (RIBA) swooned over the project, completed in October 2008. As the judges of the regional awards declared:

> The Liverpool One Masterplan has single-handedly reversed the fortunes of the city by bringing a new social and economic vibrancy.... The result is a vibrant and economically successful retail, leisure and mixed-use quarter – an entirely revitalised city centre that now connects properly with the Docks. (Bayley, 2010, p 86)

Entire libraries of technical expertise have gone into making Liverpool One the antithesis of the big-box retail park. Historic street patterns are respected, there are variations of scale and style, and there is open space for weary shoppers in the form of Chavasse Park at the western end of the development. It may all be privately owned and controlled, and as author Anna Minton has pointed out, 'these places are not inspired by the culture of where they are but by the idea that the economy will prosper if they meet the economic needs of the region' (2009, p 36). But that doesn't bother the punters at the big stores.

Liverpool One is, on the face of it, an icon of how a city can retell its tale through retail. It seeks to demonstrate that you can keep one eye on the past while both are firmly focused on the bottom line. It's a story that is celebrated by city planners as distinctively Liverpudlian, yet it is chock full of the ubiquitous names you'll find in every major shopping centre, from John Lewis to Fat Face. The entire development is owned and managed by Grosvenor, the property company owned by the anything-but-Scouse Duke of Westminster. In an extended panegyric, *The Observer* architecture correspondent Stephen Bayley described the development as 'seemingly evolved' and designed to 'provide a controlled level of diversity' (Bayley, 2010, p 91). All human life is there, as long as it can be boxed and gift-wrapped, and subject to the store's usual returns policy.

There's no doubt that Liverpool One contains the ingredients of a successful shopping centre. It has variety of design, it has the stores people like to use, it is easy to walk through, it's clean and modern, and there are plenty of leisure facilities for those whose shopping stamina has been drained. People complain about the cost of parking, but they do in cities everywhere. All the evidence is that Liverpool One brings in visitors from a very wide catchment area to spend a great deal of money.

And there's the rub. The story of place that Liverpool One tells can't be disentangled from the stories of the surrounding places that are less glitzy and far more gloomy: Kirkby, Huyton, Birkenhead and Bootle. Merseyside is a place of contrasts, contested identities and rough edges, none of which have a place in the manicured environment of Liverpool One. What Liverpool One embosoms, it takes from the surrounding area. Nearby Bootle and Runcorn have been named as two of the 'worst-performing' centres in North West England (Briggs, 2013). The wealth is not additional, because people are not better off. Liverpool One is a billion-pound wealth redistribution scheme, with the redistribution heading in the wrong direction.

There's no doubt that Liverpool One has brought shopping back to Liverpool. According to Grosvenor, the city had slumped from third in England's retail pecking order in the 1970s to 17th by 1995;

after the opening of Liverpool One it bounced back to fifth and brought an extra 43,000 shoppers into the city (Grosvenor, nd). But as Grosvenor itself points out, this has been achieved by drawing in more people from the surrounding areas of the Wirral, Chester and Southport. Grosvenor and its supporters within Liverpool have no interest in measuring the effect of removing this spending from the surrounding areas.

Well, one might argue, that's market forces: if the surrounding areas want to compete, they, too, need to invest in the shops and leisure facilities customers want. But who'll invest in a town like Wigan, just 22 miles from Liverpool city centre, with two indoor shopping centres (one already on its last legs) and a market that has seen better days? What's more, the concentration of beggar-my-neighbour redevelopment at Liverpool One has been underpinned by public money: in addition to the £1 billion invested by Grosvenor, half of which is debt, more than £600 million of public funding was pumped into the wider city centre in the first years of the new millennium. Grosvenor can legitimately claim to have received not a penny of grant, but Liverpool's civic leaders can counter that it was public funding and support that laid the foundations for Grosvenor's investment.

Projects like Liverpool One don't create wealth so much as concentrate it. Those trumpeting the city's transformation may feel a legitimate pride in the development, but there are statistics they are less willing to shout about. Out of 64 UK cities, Liverpool ranked 55th for population growth in 2013; it was 59th for the number of businesses per head of population; 58th in terms of jobseekers claiming benefits; and 63rd for its employment rate (Centre for Cities, 2014). Liverpool One may have brought shoppers into the city, but it has not brought prosperity.

If Liverpool has less to celebrate than at first appears, pity those who missed the boat entirely. Across the Pennines in Bradford, many would give their right arm for a shopping centre like Liverpool One, or like Trinity Leeds a few miles down the road ('a stunning opportunity for leading brands to perform on an international stage', according to developers Land Securities).

Bradford wanted to leap on the bandwagon of retail-led regeneration too. You have to admire its planners and politicians for insisting something should be done to restore the city's fortunes after the decline of the textile industry in the 1960s and 1970s. You might be less admiring of the mixed results.

In 2003 the city council brought in Will Alsop to prepare a masterplan. He was the architect famous for the Stirling Prize-winning Peckham Library in South London and for promising to reinvent Barnsley in Yorkshire as a Tuscan hill town, so expectations were high. The premise was that an enhanced public realm would attract investment: offices, retail, leisure. You speculate to accumulate. Alsop's designs were speculation in spades.

But speculation can backfire. Halfway through the grand plan, the property market collapsed and developer Westfield, which was to run the flagship Broadway shopping development, focused its energies on more lucrative sites in London. One night guerrilla artists set to work, and Westfield was renamed Wastefield. For most Bradfordians, though, it was simply The Hole, and a hole it remained for more than half a decade.

Liverpool beat the credit crunch of 2008; Bradford didn't. But there's more to it than timing. Liverpool has a potential catchment of 4.7 million people; Bradford's is far smaller, even though its population is growing rapidly, and it is shared with Leeds, its heftier and more aggressive neighbour.

The story since 2008 has been mixed. Bradford's City Park, with its lake, fountains and events space outside the City Hall, opened in 2012 and provides a grand stage for locals and visitors alike, hosting jamborees like the World Curry Festival. Broadway became a temporary urban garden while Westfield dithered over the scale and timing of its promised investment. Work only recommenced in early 2014. New Victoria Place, the office complex that was to take the place of the much-loved Bradford Odeon on the western side of the city centre, was dumped. Meanwhile there is little sign of the much-touted demand for premium office space in the city centre: the main new office development in recent years, Southgate, went to Provident Financial, the high-interest loans company which was already based in Bradford and simply moved down the hill.

The story of retail-led regeneration is one of concentration, polarisation and anonymisation. Developers like Land Securities want their shopping centres to be world-class: for that, read 'could be anywhere'. Their marketing describes 'a growing mix of restaurant, cafe and leisure destinations ... in Trinity Leeds that will seamlessly join day with night, ushering into the city a new era of world-class entertainment and culture'. Substitute Trinity Leeds for Gunwharf Quays in Portsmouth, Cabot Circus in Bristol or Buchanan Galleries in Glasgow, and scarcely a word of the spiel will need to change.

For the winners the prizes are self-evident. But the notion that every town and city can prosper in competition with neighbours pursuing the self-same strategy of debt-fuelled development and the accumulation of bigger and brighter retail space defies credulity: there will always be losers, and some will lose spectacularly. But nobody imagines that it will be them. Town after town swallowed the bait of retail-led regeneration in the early 2000s, with its smooth-talking consultants and computer-generated images of happy, shiny people strolling along sunlit shopping boulevards.

In 2009 one of the few independent studies of the phenomenon exposed the knowledge gap at the heart of these efforts to reinvigorate town centres. In their comprehensive literature review, Anne Findlay and Leigh Sparks emphasised that despite many years of activity under the banner of retail-led regeneration, there was little comparable evidence of effectiveness, and no study showing how schemes were working over a sustained period. 'Assessment of policy effectiveness is partial, piecemeal and subjective,' they concluded. Furthermore, they argued, the term 'regeneration' encompassed such a wide variety of aims and means that it often obscured rather than clarified understanding (Findlay and Sparks, 2009, p 36).

While the developers of the likes of Trinity Leeds and Liverpool One can crow about the number of jobs they have created or investment they have brought in, their statistics fail to measure what has been displaced from elsewhere. As with most development schemes, private or public, there is a constant temptation to over-egg the claimed benefits and to neglect to measure any downsides.

The impact of schemes like Liverpool One needs to be seen in a broader context. In the process of creating a new narrative for one city or town, stories are also written for the places that surround them. These accounts link back to our emotional, social and economic connections with the places where we live and work, the Bradfords and Bootles as much as the Liverpools.

Economists and the property industry seldom try to measure the value of what is displaced. But this displacement – literally, the loss of place – matters. The psychologist Mindi Fullilove calls it 'root shock', borrowing the term from horticulture: when a plant is taken out of the soil where it grew and is transplanted elsewhere, its survival systems can suddenly collapse (Fullilove, 2005).

Professor Fullilove uses this metaphor to describe the effect of urban change on people. Her work examines urban regeneration schemes in the US, the state of North American main streets, and the impact on New York and New Jersey of hurricane Sandy. Whole towns can suffer from a kind of root shock if the industries or facilities that kept them going disappear, and schemes sold to urban leaders and the public as retail-led regeneration can often be part of that process of obliteration rather than an antidote to it.

Narrowly focused debates about how traditional high streets can compete commercially with new retail developments often fail to acknowledge such connections and complexities. We need to widen our horizons, and think instead in terms of how town centres can be creative and resilient enough to face the future.

From risk to resilience and restoration

Is it inevitable that the Bradfords or Bootles should shrivel as new chapters are written for successful cities? At the heart of the dilemma is this question of the value and function of places, and whether new stories can be told in the towns that won't lead the retail pack, and where Grosvenor and Land Securities will never find rich pickings.

The traditional shopping core will shrink in the majority of towns in the UK and beyond, as retailers reduce the number of stores they need to serve their markets and shift a growing proportion of their trade online. For these places regeneration and renewal must find a different route. Paradoxically, their position on the lower rungs of the retail and property development ladders gives them a chance to take a lead in finding new paths to lasting prosperity.

Vague notions of success and economic development and fond fancies of bustling, busy shopping centres in every suburb and market town will no longer do. The challenge is to create places that work, where people are productive and feel at home, where human beings can flourish as citizens and not just as consumers.

To start to outline these possible futures, we need to think in terms of risk, resilience and restoration. We need a hard-headed appreciation of the real risks facing our towns and cities. There needs to be a desire to build resilience, strengthening and supporting the good that remains, and reaffirming the connections and networks that keep places alive. This needs to develop into a quest for restoration, not of the high street as it used to be, but of a civic and cultural consciousness that will become a crucible for new relationships between producer and consumer, citizen and society, individual and community. Only then can we begin to weave the new narratives our town centres need.

Three types of risk are likely to change the future of our town centres. They are economic, environmental and social, and they are all connected.

Economic risks are often posed in terms of the loss of competitiveness or the obsolescence of industries and technology: places flounder because they cannot keep up with change, or because they cannot drive down their costs. And there is truth in this: the loss of manufacturing in many parts of Europe and the US, from the textile industry to engineering, is at least in part because firms failed to invest in innovation or to match the advantages of overseas competitors.

But competition and cost can be perverse drivers of choices. What a customer saves in cash at the point of sale is often lost further down the line. The result of supermarkets' and governments' drive to keep the price of milk low across Europe, for example, has been to make dairy farming unviable: by 2012 farmers in the UK said they were losing four pence per litre of milk produced, or the equivalent of £4,500 a month on a herd of 3,000 cows (BBC News, 2012a). In Brussels, thousands of dairy farmers sprayed the European Parliament and riot police with milk in protest at price regimes they said were forcing small farmers out of business. If an industry that keeps a rural community alive is lost and that community ceases to function as a productive place, is that a reasonable price to pay for a penny or two off the price of milk?

If we want to assess the real state of our economy we need to pay less attention to GDP (gross domestic product) figures that show whether or not we are in or out of a recession, and focus more on our ability to generate wealth intelligently, value it accurately, share it fairly and recycle it effectively. Intelligent wealth production is driven by long-term investment and a willingness to defer rewards. Accurate valuation takes into account the external social and environmental impacts of economic activity, both positive and negative. When wealth is shared fairly there is a transparent relationship between the rewards received by those at the top and those at the bottom; and when it is recycled effectively it sustains a network of relationships and connections among suppliers and customers and is reinvested in local communities.

But the received wisdom of contemporary economics is that this stuff doesn't really matter. If the economy grows, it's assumed, everything else will fall into place. Interviewed on the BBC's long-running radio show 'Desert island discs', former Tesco boss Sir Terry Leahy described the closure of small shops as 'progress': customers were forsaking them for a better offer (BBC Radio 4, 2013). But neither Tesco nor any of its supermarket competitors have to pick up the tab for the consequences of their notion of progress. Just as we all ended up footing the bill for the decisions that closed the coalfields, we will all pay the price of the decline of our towns inflicted in the name of progress.

Look at what happens in a crisis and you'll see that local resilience – the ability to manage and improvise in an emergency – can be deeply undermined by such 'progress'. In autumn 2000, eight days of protests at rises in the price of fuel left supermarket shelves empty and petrol rationed. One hospital in Hull even ran out of stitches to use during operations. A supposedly efficient and cost-effective food distribution system was at the mercy of farmers and lorry drivers who blockaded oil refineries, and with the disappearance of many of the traditional wholesale and retail markets that could have offered local alternatives, there was no emergency back-up (Simms, 2008).

Government ministers in the UK tend to be smug about the resilience of the nation's food systems, pointing out that despite events such as the floods of 2007 and the Icelandic ash cloud of 2010, the supermarket shelves have never been bare since the fuel crisis of 2000. But in an increasingly complex global market, a crisis at one point in the system can have unforeseen consequences. As Tim Benton, a specialist in global food security at the University of Leeds, points out:

> Take a relatively simple food produced in the UK like a
> chocolate KitKat – it contains cocoa from Africa, milk
> products from the UK, whey from New Zealand, palm

oil from Asia, sugar from South America, wheat from Europe. So we simply can't look at the supply chain in terms of the UK alone. Increasingly, perturbations elsewhere in the world will feed back into the availability and price of food in the UK. (ESRC, 2012, p 4)

Britain relies on just eight large refineries to keep its transport moving, while four large supermarket chains control more than three quarters of the nation's grocery market (Kantar Worldpanel, 2013). Even the Competition Commission, an organisation not known for its readiness to challenge business norms, found that supermarkets were using their market dominance in particular locations to increase their profits by up to £125 million a year, and that they preserved their own margins by passing unexpected costs on to their suppliers (Competition Commission, 2008). Five years on, the discovery in 2013 that many 'value' beefburgers offered by supermarket chains contained horse DNA suggests the incessant drive to achieve value is generating its own unforeseen consequences.

The concentration of activity and ownership is spatial as well as economic. Over recent decades the economy of the UK has polarised, with wealth and resources accumulating in London and South East England at the expense of many other parts of the nation. This imbalance amplifies the risks: a shock to London's economy, as occurred during the global financial crisis of 2007-08, affects the whole country, and the reliance on business and financial services to drive the capital's economy makes it more vulnerable than most to global shocks.

If that sounds like an argument for propping up the current financial system at all costs, as happened in 2008, it is worth noting the major economic risks catalogued each year by the World Economic Forum (2014). The four top risks in terms of likelihood in 2014 were income disparity, extreme weather events, unemployment and underemployment, and climate change. All four of these have the greatest impact on the poorer sections of society, whose disposable income has already been reduced by years of recession and austerity. UK domestic energy prices rose by 30 per cent in real terms between 2005 and 2009 (Bolton, 2010); between 2007 and 2012 real food prices rose by 12 per cent (Defra, 2012). More than one fifth of British workers are low paid and the proportion is higher than in comparable economies (Pennycook and Whittaker, 2012). The lower your income, the more likely it is that increases in the cost of basics like food and energy will push you over the edge.

If that all feels a long way away from your local high street, think again. The shopping economy falls into two broad categories: convenience goods, the basics like food and drink, and comparison goods, the big-ticket items like a new washing machine or computer, leisure purchases like books or games, or clothing and fashion. The more expensive the convenience goods, the less there is to spend on comparison items – unless you borrow.

Combine a financial squeeze on ordinary households with the intensification of economic activity in the most prosperous places, and the concentration of retail development in a relatively small number of prime locations, and the result is a hollowing out of the towns, cities and suburbs where most people live. What is given with one hand in gardens of earthly delights such as Liverpool One or Westfield Stratford City is more than taken away with the other. And all the while the future wealth of all of us, wherever we shop, is predicated on the stability of a global financial system under the custodianship of the same people and institutions that brought us so close to the brink in 2007-08.

Climate change on the high street

The second set of risks is environmental. Climate change and resource constraints might feel a world away from the local butcher or baker, but they are intimately connected. When we think of climate change in terms of parts per million of carbon dioxide in the atmosphere or the changes in the spread and depth of Arctic sea ice, it can all sound technical and divorced from the daily grind. But the effects are already starting to be felt, and will affect all of us. When severe floods hit Thailand in November 2011, The World Bank estimated it cost the country's economy more than US$45 billion. As well as the obvious damage to homes, agriculture and manufacturing, it cost the country around six months' worth of tourism revenue – the kind of spending that supports small retailers, bars and restaurants (The World Bank, 2011). Climate change is happening on the high street.

The impact is increasingly obvious in the UK, too. In June 2007 flooding in Yorkshire and in the Severn basin affected 48,000 homes and led to 13 deaths. The government's Environment Agency put the economic cost at £3.2 billion, two thirds of which were direct costs to households and businesses (BBC News, 2010). The devastation was so widespread that the British Red Cross launched an emergency appeal. In cities like Hull, where 7,208 homes and more than 1,300 businesses were inundated, more than 640 families were still having to live in caravans nearly a year afterwards. The city's drainage system had simply been overwhelmed, an independent report found (Coulthard et al, 2007).

Hull's floods were described as a once in 150 years event. But the frequency of floods that are supposed to happen once in a blue moon is increasing. The following year there was widespread flooding in Northern Ireland, with three inches of rain falling in Ballymena in just 12 hours – a once in 90 years event, according to the Met Office, which dubbed the month 'Awful August' (Met Office, nd).

November 2009 was the wettest month across the UK since records began in 1914. At Seathwaite Farm in Cumbria more than 12 inches of rain fell in 24 hours, a British record. The town of Workington was virtually cut off when one bridge collapsed and another was severely damaged. A policeman who had been standing on one of the bridges died. In November 2010 there was flooding in Cornwall, with several towns and villages swamped. In August 2011 floods hit Dorset and Hampshire.

In 2012, after the wettest April in a century and continued rainfall throughout the summer and autumn, a series of floods brought misery to thousands of homes and businesses across the country. Hebden Bridge in Calderdale, West Yorkshire, was flooded three times in three weeks. The government's Committee on Climate Change warned that without extra investment in flood defences, ways would need to be found to manage the social and economic consequences of more frequent flooding. It noted that one in seven properties in the UK were in areas of flood risk, and around one tenth of the nation's critical infrastructure such as power stations and water treatment works sits on floodplains. And each year, 21,000 new homes and business premises are being built in floodplains, one in five of them in areas deemed to be at significant risk (Committee on Climate Change, 2012).

The warnings were ignored. It was only in February 2014, after the wettest winter on record, when the Thames flooded the Home

Counties heartlands of Berkshire and Surrey, the Somerset Levels were under water for more than a month and part of the main railway connection with the West Country was washed into the sea, that Prime Minister David Cameron famously commented that money would be no object in dealing with the crisis.

Flooding is the most pronounced and visible effect of a changing climate in the UK. Its impact on small businesses and under-insured households is far greater than the effect on large corporations that can spread the risk. For a small town like Hebden Bridge, a succession of floods can be the last straw for independent local businesses.

The impacts of extreme weather run far wider than waterlogged shops and homes. The wet weather in 2012 pushed wheat yields in the UK down to levels last seen in the 1980s; potatoes and fruit were also severely affected (BBC News, 2012b). At the same time droughts in the US, Russia, Ukraine, Kazakhstan and Australia affected corn and wheat harvests. The total world grain harvest fell by 75 million tons, or 3 per cent – not a huge figure, but significant at a time when population and consumption are continuing to rise (Brown, 2012). Because grain is used extensively for animal feed, shortages and price rises directly affect the price and availability of meat: the butcher suffers as well as the baker. It does not take much to trigger a food crisis. In 2007-08, with enough grain stocked worldwide to last 62 days, prices rocketed and countries from Mozambique to Yemen experienced food riots.

The dangers of climate change and extreme weather combine with increased demands on resources of food, water and energy to produce a volatile mix. A water supply crisis ranks third in the World Economic Forum's list of risks in terms of severity. As the Forum's *Global risks* report noted in 2013:

> Continued stress on the global economic system is positioned to absorb the attention of leaders for the foreseeable future. Meanwhile, the Earth's environmental system is simultaneously coming under increasing stress. Future simultaneous shocks to both systems could trigger the 'perfect global storm', with potentially insurmountable consequences. (World Economic Forum, 2013)

These are not the words of climate change activists or anti-capitalists, but of those at the heart of the world's mega-corporations and governments. To imagine that these issues are too huge to take into account when thinking about the future of our towns and communities is a recipe for failure and frustration.

Disconnected communities

The third set of risks we face if we are to create resilient and resourceful places concerns our communities, and the loss or erosion of civic and social bonds and connections. And the way we handle these risks, like the economic and environmental threats sketched out above, will profoundly influence the future of our towns.

The problem of social atomisation and disconnection has been well documented, from the geographical separation of families to the diminution of the social bonds created by churches, clubs or trade unions, and the individualisation of entertainment, shopping and even the workplace through remote working and freelance employment. Some of these trends are a consequence of greater choice and flexibility that has allowed people to live happier and more fulfilling lives in many respects. Children are no longer expected to remain in their parents' hometown or to join the family business; neither faith nor politics demand the local rootedness they once did; the internet has enabled everything from watching a film to buying a carpet to be tailored to our convenience.

Human connection, for the first time in human evolution, is becoming something we can switch on and off at will and take as much or as little of as we please. We can be hermits without the hairshirts, gregarious without obligations. This has far-reaching consequences. It becomes easier to withdraw or hide from social situations we find difficult or troubling. Reciprocity becomes a choice rather than a moral duty. Involvement can be a bargain rather than a responsibility.

Political participation in the UK, for example, has slumped over the last half century. Turnout at the 2010 General Election was 65.1 per cent, down from 71.5 per cent in 1997 and 84 per cent in 1950 (*The Guardian*, 2012). The combined membership of all three major political parties by 2012 was less than 450,000 – the equivalent of the population of just one of Britain's medium-sized cities or two London boroughs (Wilks-Heeg et al, 2012). In the 1960s the Conservative Party alone could muster more than two million members; in 2013 it could barely scrape together 134,000 (Conservativehome.com, 2013). Turnout at local elections is consistently low and increasingly dire, while the 2012 direct elections of police and crime commissioners in England clocked a risible 15 per cent turnout.

Religious observance too is on the wane. Figures from the 2011 Census show that the proportion of people identifying themselves as Christians fell from 71.7 to 59.3 per cent over 10 years. While the Muslim population grew from 3 to 4.8 per cent, the proportion saying they had no religion rose from 14.8 to 25.1 per cent (ONS, 2012a). While neither religion nor its absence is a direct indicator of social activity, the fall in religious involvement weakens one of the traditional connectors between people and place. For most of the population the ancient concept of the parish, where you were 'hatched, matched and dispatched' – christened, married and buried – has become an anachronism.

As many of these traditional local connectors disappear, we are also experiencing demographic changes that are connecting people to places in ways they may not be able to choose. As the population ages, a growing proportion of older people are likely to suffer long-term health conditions that may limit their mobility and opportunities to engage in social life outside the home. In 2010 there were three million UK residents over the age of 80; by 2050 there will probably be eight million. Centenarians will be the fastest growing age group (Cracknell, 2010). In 2008 there were 3.2 people of working age for every retired person; by 2033 the ratio is expected to fall to 2.8. More people will need long-term nursing care, and the cost of providing for a growing number of retirees will fall on a smaller proportion of the population. Globally, the number of people suffering dementia is expected to double every 20 years, reaching more than 115 million in 2050 (World Economic Forum, 2013). Many families will find a growing amount of their time is absorbed in caring for elderly relatives, something that may limit their own capacity to be involved in the social and economic life of their communities. And as the population ages, health emergencies are likely to become a greater hazard: number one on the UK government's *National Risk Register of Civil Emergencies* in 2012 was a flu pandemic (Cabinet Office, 2012).

While the economic impacts of an ageing population are well researched, the social impacts are less well known. But there is a growing awareness that the places we live in will need to adapt. The UK government is already talking about the need for 'lifetime neighbourhoods' that enable people to remain in their own homes and communities for as long as possible, but few have yet thought seriously about how we can achieve lifetime town centres and high streets, and what they might look like.

Head, heart and hand

These economic, environmental and social threats are the vital but often overlooked background to any serious discussion of the future of our town centres. Their effects will be deeper and wider than the usual concerns about changing consumer habits or the effects of technological change, important as those are. In a world that is both increasingly connected digitally and more disconnected physically and socially, we can no longer assume that places will function as they once did. We have to be intentional about the futures we want to create.

In the face of concentrated wealth, a diffusion of social activity and a dislocation of human beings from the environment that sustains them, we still have reasons to be hopeful and a plethora of resources at our disposal. And sometimes, as in the clean-ups witnessed after the 2011 riots, people will come together with striking effects to change the story. In Hull, one of the poorest cities in the UK, it was noteworthy how residents not only survived the 2007 floods, but also showed a remarkable generosity and camaraderie. As Professor Tom Coulthard and colleagues observed in their independent report on the crisis: 'This underlying strength needs to be more fully appreciated and better capitalised upon' (Coulthard et al, 2007, p 10).

Hull's experience shows that it is possible not only to face up to the risks that threaten us, but also to build and sustain local resilience, telling new stories of the places we live in and care about, and of our aspirations for them and for ourselves. The resilience we need to build locally shares the same DNA as the resilience required to address global problems such as poverty and climate change. To do so, as the United Nations' (UN) Secretary-General's High-Level Panel on Global Sustainability reported in 2012, demands a change in direction and mindset: 'Sustainable development is not a destination, but a dynamic process of adaptation, learning and action. It is about recognising, understanding and acting on interconnections — above all those between the economy, society and the natural environment. The world is not yet on this path.' (UN Secretary-General's High-Level Panel on Global Sustainability, 2012, p 6).

To start to change the future of our town centres as well as our global environment, we need to keep our eyes open and minds alert. The Scottish writer and activist Alastair McIntosh spoke of this as a reconnecting of 'head, heart and hand' – our thinking, emotions and actions. 'To have community in a sense that expands what it means to be human and to live sustainably on this earth requires very much more than a mere community of interest,' he declared. 'It needs a shared life-affirming vision' (McIntosh, 2008, p 26).

So where, in the everyday streets and spaces where we live our lives, can such a life-affirming vision be found? There is no doubt that people care: across England, well over 300 'town teams' came together to improve their high streets in the wake of the Portas review. But goodwill and passion alone won't be enough. The following chapters examine how our town centres are evolving, and explore how a life-affirming vision can begin to grow in the streets where we stroll, shop and socialise.

3

To market, to market

Burly and crop-headed, Neil Stockwell patrols the perimeter of his fruit and veg stall at the entrance to Queen's Market in Upton Park, East London, like a lovable bull terrier. For 35 years he's exchanged banter with all-comers, from Asian elders to young West Ham United supporters on their way to a match. Every passer-by seems to know him.

Queen's Market is bright, bustling and hugely popular. It's been here for a century, and is everyone's meeting point, drawing white East Enders from behind their well-clipped hedges in Central Park estate, Bengali and Pakistani families from the terraces that stretch in rows like Venetian blinds north to Romford Road, bargain-hunters from every part of Africa and the Caribbean. All can find a stall selling something familiar – and maybe something new to try, whether it's yams or plantain, dhania or jellied eels. "This becomes a way of life, it ain't a job," Neil says:

> 'You look how many hours you're doing, how many hours you're putting into it, you wouldn't do it. Some weeks you can go home and you ain't earned the diesel that goes in the lorry. But it ain't no good having the hump and swearing and hollering because next week the sun might come out, strawberries might be cheap, everyone's buying 'em and you've got a handful of money.
>
> 'It becomes a labour of love, the people you serve every week – it's not just a job. We've served, say, Joan and Dave for 35 years, all of a sudden one of the partners has passed away, so you can be there like a bit of a crutch to help them.' (interview with the author)

For Neil and his fellow traders, and for many of his customers, trade and community go hand in hand. But the mayor of Newham, Sir Robin Wales, has had other ideas for a long time. For much of the last decade the traders have fought plans to halve the size of the market to make room for a new Asda supermarket and luxury flats.

The traders and locals, who feared some of the poorest people in the East End would be priced out, hailed a huge victory when Asda pulled out of the initial deal in 2006. The developers, St Modwen, and Newham Council came back with a revised scheme. Pauline Rowe, a local resident, coordinated the Friends of Queen's Market campaign, arguing that the council's plans would reduce the traditional stalls to a 'market-in-a-mall' surrounded by the same chain stores that dominate every other shopping centre in East London.

On the developers' side of the divide were ranged bright computer-generated images and the PR big guns of Newham Council and St Modwen. The new building would 'enhance Green Street's status as a visitor destination', with 164 new stalls, more than 6,000 square metres of new shops, a 'state-of-the-art' council office and the icing on the cake, a 31-storey 'residential tower' – on the site, ironically, of the now demolished James Sinclair Point, one of the more hulking and disreputable examples of post-war municipal slab architecture.

On the opposing front stood Friends of Queen's Market, with more than 12,000 signatures on a petition against the plans.

Neil Stockwell says:

> 'I've never ever had a political bone in my body. But I knew it was wrong, I knew in my heart I could not let this man do what he wanted to do to this place. It went against everything I've ever believed in, working hard, treating people with respect.
>
> 'We started going to Asda and we would buy £10 of fruit. And we would put it on the floor in a basket and then we would put £10 of our products next to it. Five tomatoes in Asda is about £1.39. You've got 12 here for a pound. We knew that every time we brought their products list up they could not compete with us. Every single day for a month we spent five pounds in Tesco's, five pounds in Morrisons, and we kept the receipt so we could prove that's what we'd done. And because we kept bombarding them and the papers kept coming down and taking photos of us, it was getting out, people started saying hold on, look what you can buy in the market.'

The campaign may have won over the public, but the planners were harder to budge. In May 2009, however, London's mayor, Boris Johnson, and the Greater London Authority (GLA) rejected the St Modwen plans on the grounds that the proposed tower block was unattractive and disproportionately large. The following year St Modwen cut its losses and parted company with Newham Council. But hostilities are suspended, not over.

Newham Council's 'core strategy' still considers Queen's Market suitable for redevelopment, with an implicit invitation to a new partner whenever the returns look attractive enough. 'The decision to terminate the Queen's Market contract with the developers was made because the delivery of the programme had moved substantially forwards,' was the council's cryptic official line (statement on Newham Council's website, www.newham.gov.uk, now removed).

So Neil Stockwell and the Friends of Queen's Market continue to be vocal campaigners for a market that works for local people, not just the council and its developer allies. They argue that it is thriving, and will stay that way if the council looks after it. For the traders and friends of Queen's Market, the fight is not for a site but for its soul.

'Once you're on the stall, you're on stage'

It's a bitterly cold February Friday, but Tony Sinacola doesn't seem to notice. Behind the counter at Chadwick's Original Bury Black Puddings, he's doing brisk business, with a steady stream of takers for the delicacy his family have made since 1865. A couple in their late fifties, their London accents sharp enough to cut through a Lancastrian fog, are on the receiving end of a good-humoured tongue-lashing on account of their southern ignorance.

Bury Market – Bury's World Famous Market, as the advertising has it – is one of the most successful traditional markets in England. Every year up to 1,500 coachloads of visitors descend on this former mill town to sample the wares at nearly 400 stalls. Market traders boast that you can get everything you need, from cradle to grave. There's even a man who'll do your headstone.

Check out the market stalls and you'll find a lot more than black puddings. Burka-clad women are eyeing yards of iridescent fabrics at one end; at the other an elderly white woman stops to tell anyone who cares to listen that she's been coming to the market for years, and the cheese has never been so expensive. Mrs Ogden's tearoom, with its tiny tables and neatly chalked menus, is packed, and there's a patient queue at Filbey's barber shop. At the second-hand bookstall a weather-beaten stallholder sits serenely among the thrillers, glasses perched on his nose, apparently oblivious to passing browsers.

Tony Sinacola says there's one reason why the market works:

> 'People come and they get an experience. It's not just coming for a black pudding. We take the mickey out of them, have a laugh. Nothing insulting – all the years I've never had a complaint. You can have a laugh which you can't do in a supermarket, so people come back.
>
> 'I think that's what makes any market – the people. On average we have about 1,000 customers a day. You can set your clock by the time some come. As they walk up you can get their order ready, you know what they're having. Others, like today, there's coaches from Stoke

on Trent, some have come from the Lake District. They
come and say I've never had black puddings, so straight
away I start shouting, "Black pudding virgin!" There's not
a lot of them in Bury, mind.' (interview with the author)

Tony's family have worked the market since 1949, and won't go
anywhere else. Every week they sell around three-and-a-half tons of
black pudding, and the age-old secret recipe has been supplemented
by new products such as the Black Dog, a black pudding in a hot-
dog roll topped with home-made mustard. Black puddings, Tony
says with pride, have a history as old as Homer's *Iliad*; a similar dish
was a favourite of Rome's legionaries.

Over at the Barbecue Barn, Steve Moloney is a relative newcomer,
having run his own stall for just eight years, but he echoes Tony's
sentiments. "The main difference between us and the supermarkets
is we still give a personal service," he says.

'You've still got contact with the person that's serving
you. You've still got a friendly bit of banter, but the
crux of the matter is you've got to give good value for
money – quality products at the right price for repeat
trade over and over again. As soon as I walk on the stall
I'm on stage. It doesn't matter what's happened at home
the night before. Once you're on the stall you're on stage
and you start performing.' (interview with the author)

In Bury Market, trade is theatre. Andrew Heyes, the market's
manager, knows that this, coupled with good value and friendly
service, is at the root of its success. Bury Market has been going
since 1444, and looks as if it has a few more centuries in it: it earns
a million pounds a year for the local council. Up to nine million
people visit it every year. As a council service it also provides a
platform for community organisations that can offer information
about their activities or direct punters to some of the town's less
well-known attractions, such as the Grade 1 listed parish church or
the Fusilier Museum.

Andrew Heyes is proud of the market's success and the achievements
of his team. But at the other end of town, the new Rock shopping
centre is stretching Bury's retail core, offering a glass-and-concrete

panorama of Marks & Spencer and Superdry, Costa Coffee and River Island. In between, the 1990s Mill Gate shopping centre – itself a replacement for a 1960s precinct – is struggling, every other shop a discount store and dotted with an acne of 'To let' signs. Bury's planners, it would seem, have also swallowed the myth of retail-led regeneration. Mr Heyes admits:

> 'The market isn't as well supported by local people as it could be. There's a lot of competition – supermarkets across the road, two shopping centres. You go into one of these retail centres and it's free parking, you come into town and it's a fiver for the day before you even start shopping. Without the coach business at the moment we'd be really struggling.' (interview with the author)

The market traders need to move with the times, he says – embracing social media, being ready to change their opening hours, working together rather than as individuals. It's far harder to coordinate several hundred traders than for a supermarket to change its offer in response to customers' tastes or circumstances.

There remains a nagging suspicion, too, that successful markets like Bury owe their survival to a kind of cannibalising. The coachloads of pensioners from Liverpool and North Wales are as much an indication of what is being lost in their hometowns as a sign of Bury's unique offer. Visitors are coming partly because their own markets are declining or have disappeared, and as Bury succeeds it may accelerate that process. The service that once supplied the basics of life to people on low incomes in every sizeable town is now becoming a curiosity and a tourist attraction.

The agora: interaction, not just transaction

There is a world of difference between the market, as expressed in Upton Park and Bury, and the market as imagined by multinational corporations. Although the business of buying, selling and exchange goes on in both, the scale, location, accessibility and context is all-important. For a locality to work well, both buyers and sellers must have fair access and their relationships must be equitable.

The traditional street or covered market represents a human scale. The stallholder becomes something altogether different when, like Tesco founder Jack Cohen, he or she moves from the stall to the global marketplace. A market stallholder might employ family and friends; she knows her customers personally because she serves them; she can't expand beyond a handful of locations before losing that human touch. Similarly, the stallholder vies with others selling similar produce, whether it's halal lamb or fruit and vegetables: competition is healthy and often fierce, but not monopolistic. Stallholders cannot hold suppliers to ransom or demand exclusivity, as supermarkets commonly do; neither can they lock their customers into repeat business other than by providing decent quality goods, attentive service, keen prices and a reputation for honesty.

The traditional market is also constrained by geography. It serves the people of a particular location with the goods they like, whether they're plantains or pickles. The constantly changing mix of stallholders and customers ensures variety and novelty. Nobody will mistake the East End banter of Queen's Market in Newham for the foodie haven and eye-watering prices of Borough Market, a few yards from London Bridge Station.

The market, like the high street, is place-bound. It is an expression of the diversity and individuality of people and cultures, while the supermarket works by creating a blancmange of people and cultures. Even the checkout is increasingly operated without the aid of human beings. As Rachel Bowlby put it, shopping has become 'a relationship between the customer and the goods, with nothing and no one mediating between them' (Bowlby, 2000, p 31).

The origins of the market, however, were as concerned with interaction as with transaction. The economist Tim Jackson put his finger on the pulse:

> Consumer goods provide a symbolic language in which we communicate continually with each other, not just about raw stuff, but about what really matters to us: family, friendship, sense of belonging, community, identity, social status, meaning and purpose in life. (Jackson, 2009, pp 50-1)

It is no coincidence that many cities celebrate their traditional markets as attractions for tourists as well as a service for local people. In Australia, Melbourne's Queen Victoria Market, established in 1878, describes itself as the 'heart and soul' of the city, with everything from an art deco dairy produce hall to String Bean Alley, a row of repurposed shipping containers now used as workshops and stalls. South Melbourne Market is as much a place to eat and drink with friends as a place to hunt for bargains. In Germany, visiting Hamburg's Fishmarket is a Sunday morning ritual for many tourists and citizens, even if they're not shopping; in Berlin, there's Die Nolle, a market that takes place in 16 old railway carriages.

Go back to the ancient Greek idea of the agora and you will find a far richer mix than exists in even the more successful contemporary street markets. The agora was a civic space, not just a marketplace. In the agora of Athens there was the courtroom, places of religious worship, the gymnasium, the mint that produced the city's coinage, and the bouleuterion, the council building where people assembled to legislate and discuss public affairs. The agora was used for theatre and performance, meeting and holding court: it was far more than a shopping precinct.

Urbanist and historian Lewis Mumford described the ancient agora as 'above all a place for palaver'. Citizens had many more reasons to get together than simply to clinch a business deal or buy the bread. 'It is in the open place, with its surrounding cafés and restaurants, that spontaneous and face-to-face meetings, conversations, encounters, and flirtations take place, unformalised even when habitual,' he remarked (Mumford, 1961, p 150).

That sense of consciously being in public persists in many places. In Italian towns the ritual of *la passeggiata* is still commonplace, when young people emerge into the evening air to promenade up and down a street or square, usually in the hope of attracting approving glances and more from prospective partners. At weekends entire families take to the streets, as participants, chaperones or simply as people-watchers. The piazza is where you learn to socialise.

The history of markets in Britain is more rough and ready. But here, too, the market was never only about buying and selling. The medieval market hall was also often the moot hall or guildhall, where the town's dignitaries would decide matters of moment and business leaders would settle disputes. Market towns would have special courts, the Court of Piepowders, to hear cases of beating, cheating or pilfering. The Piepowder court at the Stag and Hounds pub in Bristol continued to sit until 1870, and was only legally abolished a century later. The term 'Piepowder' originated from the French *pieds poudres*, or 'dusty feet', as it dispensed summary justice to travelling merchants or customers: 'free trade' always needed a modicum of regulation. The civic and the commercial went hand in hand: some of the earliest royal charters granting permission for markets included judicial rights. In 1110 Henry I gave the Abbey of Ramsey the right to hold a fair at St Ives with the rights of 'sac and soc and infangthef' – trade, justice and punishment of thieves.

Some of these early markets were also labour exchanges. 'Mop fairs' were recruitment centres for agricultural workers, where casual labourers would be taken on for the following year. By holding a mop aloft workers would signal that they were jacks-of-all-trades, with no special skill to offer. In some, such as Stratford-on-Avon, which dates back to the reign of Edward III, a 'runaway mop' would be held a week later to allow employers to fire workers who failed to cut the mustard in their first week. Once hired, workers would receive a token from their new employer that they could then spend among the fair's many stalls and amusements.

Alongside trade and exchange, British markets and fairs were also places of leisure, often in a much wilder form than that of *la passeggiata*. They offered novelty and cultural exchange at a time when few would venture far from their village or hometown, and forms of fun that could escape the usual constraints of church or manor.

The prospect of disorder was often part of the attraction. The fair was where people could let their hair down, have a laugh and push the boundaries. Nottingham's famous Goose Fair was granted a charter by Edward I in 1284 for an event that lasted 12 days – a major draw that would pull in crowds from many miles around and at one time involved the sale of up to 20,000 geese. Sometimes things got out of hand, most famously in the Cheese Riot of 1766.

Thomas Bailey's *Annals of Nottinghamshire*, published in 1852, recounts:

> Twenty-eight to thirty shillings per cwt being demanded
> by the dairymen for their commodity, the people became
> excessively exasperated at this exorbitant charge, (as it

was then considered) and at once commenced a furious attack upon them. The lots of cheese were taken forcible possession of; much was carried away, and much more damaged by being flung about, and rolled down the adjacent streets and passages. The 15th Light Dragoons were sent for by the magistrates, who, with the force at their immediate command, felt themselves utterly unable to restore peace, or protect the persons or property of the farmers from spoliation and violence. One man was killed by a shot from one of the soldiers. The mayor, whilst endeavouring to quell the disturbance, was knocked down by a cheese, hurled at him by one of the mob, and severely stunned. (Nottingham Radical History Group, nd)

The Goose Fair has been relatively quiet since. Not so London's Bartholomew Fair, which, though originally designed as a money-raiser for the monastery of St Bartholomew, soon gained a reputation for activities that were anything but monastic. As well as being the scene of the execution of the Scottish leader William Wallace in 1315, it hosted a multitude of common or garden sins. Prostitutes would hold court in tents labelled 'Soiled Doves'. Ben Jonson's *Bartholomew Fair*, first staged in 1614, played on a Puritan disapproval of fairground frolics that never disappeared. Two centuries later, the Victorians achieved what their predecessors had baulked at, and the City of London authorities closed the fair for good in 1855.

As well as frowning on them as dens of iniquity, commentators also started to question whether there was any more need for fairs. The nature of shopping and leisure was changing forever, they argued. In his 1875 book *The old showmen*, Thomas Frost concluded with a description of Kingston Fair, where 'One forlorn showman ground discordant sounds from a barrel-organ with an air of desperation, and another feebly clashed a pair of cymbals; but these were all the attempts made to attract attention, and they were made in vain.'

Frost signed off with an obituary that bears comparison with the elegies now being written for the high street:

All the large towns now possess music-halls, and many of them have a theatre; the most populous have two or three.... Bristol and Manchester have Zoological Gardens, and Brighton has its interesting Aquarium. The railways connect all the smaller towns, and most of the villages, with the larger ones, in which amusements may be found superior to any ever presented by the old showmen. What need, then, of fairs and shows? The nation has outgrown them, and fairs are as dead as the generations which they have delighted, and the last showman will soon be as great a curiosity as the dodo. (Frost, 1875, Chapter XI)

The obituary, as it turned out, was premature. Many of Britain's traditional fairs are still going strong, and a myriad of new ones have joined their ranks – from circuses and amusements to trade and craft fairs. Even before spring has arrived you can choose between the Bath Cider Festival, beer festivals in Bradford, Liverpool and Wrexham, a marmalade festival in the Lake District, the Rye Scallop festival in Sussex, or the Wakefield Festival of Food, Drink and Rhubarb. You can tickle your taste buds with the Pork Pie Appreciation Society in Ripponden or Booze on the Ouse at St Neots. The raucous scenes of old-fashioned fairs and markets may have vanished, but in many respects their combination of trade and social life is alive and well. But perhaps not well enough.

Markets on the margins

If the traditional market or fair is a barometer of the health of a town, it would seem many towns are already in dire need of medical attention. Markets are being pushed to the margins, physically, economically and socially.

Go to Stockport on the southern fringe of Manchester, where the Victorian market hall is now stranded on a hillside while the main shopping area has moved to Merseyway at the bottom of the valley. While Merseyway can bring more than one million visitors into its 300,000 square feet of retail space in the run-up to Christmas, the market, which dates back to the 15th century, is having to work overtime to entice shoppers back uphill. Its promotions of handmade products and seasonal food and drink are attractive, but this is where people spend their spare change, not where they buy their daily bread.

No visit to Stockport could be complete without experiencing the hustle and bustle of market day, the local council proclaims on its website, but many locals clearly feel otherwise. What used to be the heart of the town now looks more like an appendage. It's the same in Wigan, where the town's centre of gravity has shifted to a new shopping centre, Grand Arcade, leaving the market on the edge, separated from the main retail area by the echoing voids of the ailing Galleries shopping centre.

Often this physical sidelining is exacerbated by town centre redevelopment schemes marketed as 'regeneration'. As the Retail Markets Alliance pointed out in evidence to Parliament in 2009:

> Regeneration of our towns and cities often results in a shifting of the commercial/retail centre, leaving markets isolated. Equally, regeneration can result in dispersal of the market's traditional catchment population. The result is shoppers' 'footfall' being moved away from the traditional retail markets. (House of Commons Communities and Local Government Committee, 2009, Ev97)

Economically, the old-style market has been elbowed out as supermarkets swallow ever-greater slices of consumers' spending. The Payments Council, which monitors how and where the British public spend their money, has calculated that 58 pence in every retail pound went to supermarkets in 2011, up from 46 pence 10 years before. Cash transactions – the typical market or convenience store purchase – fell from 43 per cent to just 30 per cent of retail spending. While there are still more than 2,000 retail markets across the UK, employing around 100,000 people, Tesco alone has more than 3,100 stores and 313,000 employees in the UK. While spending at markets was estimated – very roughly – at between £1.3 billion and £3 billion in 2008, Tesco's UK revenue in 2012-13 was more than £43 billion, and it knew exactly how much was coming through the tills.

Economic marginalisation brings social marginalisation. With the exception of the new generation of specialist markets, the traditional market now tends to be perceived in Britain as a place for cheap goods, frequented by pensioners and poorer people. Where once the market was the great social leveller, it is now often bypassed by the better-off.

This marginalisation matters because a successful market provides far more than a place to pick up a bargain. In 2009 a House of Commons inquiry concluded that the social benefits of markets were as important as their economic functions. They can bring communities together, help promote healthy eating, provide more environmentally sustainable models of retailing than the large supermarkets, offer opportunities for new businesses, and bring life into town centres. Council-run markets generate revenue for local authorities, which can be reinvested in improvements or used to keep public services running. Smaller markets, MPs heard, 'provide intimate public spaces where traders and shoppers know each other and work well for the community' (House of Commons Communities and Local Government Committee, 2009, p 7).

The bargains are important too: the New Economics Foundation (nef) found in 2005 that a basket of food costing £4.74 from market stalls would set a shopper back £7.18 in a supermarket. A survey by the National Market Traders' Federation in 2008 found that fresh produce was, on average, 32 per cent cheaper in markets than in supermarkets. Markets in areas with large minority ethnic populations also provide produce that you generally can't find in supermarkets. If you want North African food in West London, for example, go to Golborne Road market in Ladbroke Grove, not the local Waitrose or Morrisons.

When local markets' role is relegated, the surrounding areas are affected. Where they work well, they benefit nearby retailers. In evidence to MPs, Vale Royal Borough Council in Cheshire reported that a market day was worth an extra £16,000 in takings to the nearby Asda store. Supermarkets will argue that the osmosis works in reverse too, but this is disingenuous. Their strategy is to bring in-store everything that might be found on the high street. At a Tesco Extra you can shop, bank, visit a pharmacist or optician, and deposit your children in a dedicated play area. Any 'linked journeys', as they are described in the trade, are little more than the crumbs from the table.

Personal service, unique products and friendly banter won't save many of our ancient markets. There's limited scope for others to follow in Bury Market's footsteps and reinvent themselves as tourist attractions for people who want a taste of how things used to be.

Even where they work well, old-school markets won't revive town centres on their own. But they provide some important clues that show how towns can rediscover local identity and prosperity.

From popping up to pricing out

In February 2013 the BBC came to Stockport to film its flagship 'Newsnight' current affairs programme, with a special focus on the death of the high street and the apparent failure of government attempts to reinvigorate town centres. The day was a gift to television. Sleet swirled around empty streets, the few passers-by looked cold and miserable, and the vacant shops of the Underbanks, leading up the hill to the market area, provided an ideal backdrop for the reporter's statistics of doom and despair.

A few weeks later the scene could not have been more different. Again, the BBC was in town. This time they were filming the locally born comedian Peter Kay, touring the area in a motorised sofa in aid of the annual Comic Relief extravaganza. He would not have been there if it hadn't been for the Teenage Market, the brainchild of local brothers Joe and Tom Barratt.

Joe was only 19 when he fronted the town's bid for government funds following the Portas review of 2011. His passion for local culture had already been manifest in the Screen Stockport film festival and plans for Seven Miles Out, a music festival building on the town's almost-forgotten heritage of the Strawberry Recording Studios and big names of the 1960s and 1970s such as 10cc and Scaffold.

The Teenage Market creates a space for young people to show off their talents, from cake baking to music making. Tom Barratt says its purpose is 'to give a free platform to young creative talent but just as important, it's to encourage people of all ages to visit and in some cases, rediscover, the amazing architecture and individual charm and character of the Market and Underbanks area of the town' (*Manchester Evening News*, 2013). Far from being a desperate attempt to preserve how things used to be in the face of overwhelming competition, it's a way of repurposing space and facilities in order to let people do what they want to do anyway.

Where the riots inquiry panel found that young people identified themselves by their association with particular brands and products, the Teenage Market has shown how people identify themselves through their own creativity and their shared enjoyment of each other's gifts and abilities. The creativity isn't confined to Stockport: in 2014, a spin-off Teenage Market was launched in Salisbury, and other towns are looking to replicate the idea.

The Teenage Market is a large-scale example of a 'pop-up' business, a phenomenon that has become fashionable as high street shops and facilities have closed. Pop-ups are temporary and often quirky re-uses of commercial or public property, designed to showcase new ideas, give entrepreneurs a chance to test their business models, animate vacant spaces – or just have fun. Often associated with arts and culture, they might host anything from a community cafe to a handmade furniture store, a vintage clothing shop to an impromptu performance space.

In City Arcade, Coventry, a tired row of council-owned shops on the edge of the city centre became a pop-up cultural quarter. Working with the council's property team, Coventry Artspace filled empty units with galleries and space for performing arts. Theatre Absolute occupied a former fish and chip restaurant to use as a miniature 'shopfront theatre'. Mercurial Arts, a dance company, created spaces for workshops, classes, multimedia installations and performances. Both companies used the pop-up spaces to create new productions at a far lower cost than through traditional channels of hiring rehearsal rooms and theatre space. The projects helped attract businesses to the area, sustaining a commercial street that had fallen on hard times.

Dan Thompson, founder of the Empty Shops Network and author of *Pop-up business for dummies*, argues that pop-ups occupy a particular niche in the town centre landscape – 'pop ups do something different, unusual and interesting; they're not about the everyday way of doing things', he says. 'They're ideal if you want to test a new venture. They're perfect if you run a home-based business or sell on the internet and want some extra exposure' (Thompson, 2012, p 1).

Pop-up uses of buildings and public spaces are everywhere. In Moscow, pods were installed in a vacant building to create a 'pop-up hotel'; in China, undeveloped plots were turned into 'augmented reality supermarkets'. The abandoned Friendship Baptist Church in inner-city Washington, DC, became an art installation. On a beach in the south of France architect Matali Crasset introduced a pop-up library, with 350 books to choose from; in Southwark, South London, a pop-up lido brought the beach to the city.

But as Dan Thompson points out, the joy of pop-up is its transience. If a market, a shop unit or a town centre is a canvas on which pop-up artists can express their individuality, someone still needs to consider the future of the place after the pop-ups have popped off.

Frequently that future is one in which property developers move in and cash in, creating 'value' but removing life from the street. In New York, the Antiques Garage on West 25th Street and Sixth Avenue created a vibrant flea market in a derelict space for more than 20 years, but has now closed to make way for one more hotel tower.

The story of Brixton Village in South London is a salutary tale. In 2009 Granville Arcade, six avenues of 1930s stalls and shops in Brixton's indoor market, was on its uppers and slated for demolition by its new owners, London & Associated Properties. Trade was poor. But the market was passionately loved, if not passionately frequented, by local residents. As in Newham, a vociferous local campaign led to the abandonment of the demolition plans.

This is where Space Makers came in. Loosely organised by writer and activist Dougald Hine, Space Makers was a collective of 'activists, architects, artists, thinktankers, squatters and others' – a motley crew of well-meaning people who suddenly, via contacts in Lambeth Council, had an opportunity to make a difference. The market's owners had approached the council to ask whether it could facilitate the creative temporary use of 20 empty shops, and the council handed the baton to Space Makers.

Space Makers negotiated three months' funding from London & Associated Properties, held a public meeting on a bitterly cold November night, and threw out an open invitation for ideas. Within a week 98 proposals had been submitted, from a recycled clothes shop to a 'community shop' run by Transition Town Brixton, the Market Traders' Federation and Friends of Brixton Market.

For Dougald Hine, the creation of what became known as Brixton Village was an object lesson in collaboration. He suggested there was a difference between the 'market' as envisaged by governments and corporations, and the 'marketplace':

> A marketplace ... is a sociable space in which buying and selling take place surrounded by other activities, a place you come to see friends, to hear stories, to argue

about ideas. Crucially, unlike a Starbucks or a department store, it is a space where your welcome is not determined purely by your ability to spend money.

Brixton Village was a real-life marketplace: you saw people stopping for long conversations, arguing, preaching, putting up posters for club nights or public meetings. If we could build on this, make it known as a sociable space, embedded in the place and the people around it, then perhaps we could draw more people to the market, give the businesses a better chance of succeeding, while keeping what made it special, what made it a marketplace and what made it Brixton. (Hine, 2010)

Eight months on, Hine wrote in 2010, the market was thriving. Seven of the projects put forward on that November evening had become long-term tenants, including the community shop and a local food deli. Visitor numbers were rising. Disagreements between the landlord and traders no longer made the front page of the local paper. In August a glowing report in the *New York Times* swooned over the 'playful pop-up shops' and the delicious modern dishes in Ian Riley's bistro, including 'courgette fritters with watercress, peas and ewe cheese' (Wilder, 2010).

Shortly afterwards, the headline on the front page of the *South London Press* told a different story: 'Rent hikes are kick in the teeth,' it yelled. 'Traders face rises of up to 50 per cent.' (*South London Press*, 17 September 2010, p 1). Delighted with the Space Makers-inspired revamp, it seemed, London & Associated Properties had decided to cash in. Traders complained they had received bills backdated to 2007, the date of the change of landlord. Some were as high as £30,000.

The *South London Press* story was a taste of things to come. In 2012, with the market now operated by InShops, a subsidiary of a French company, on behalf of London & Associated, there was another round of controversial rent rises. The Artists Studio Company, which provided 23 low-rent studios above shops in the market, was told its lease would not be renewed. Early in 2013 the *London Evening Standard* asked, 'Is gentrification killing Brixton Market?' (Godwin, 2013).

Today the Brixton Market website advertises Second Avenue in Brixton Village as 'a little slice of Hoxton'. It is done without any sense of irony. Brixton and Hoxton were both once poor areas, rough and ready places where people made do on very little. Brixton was a centre of London's Caribbean population in the 1970s; Hoxton was traditional white working class. Now Brixton's gentrification is promoted as an echo of Hoxton's, and the make-do spirit of both the traditional market traders and initiatives like Space Makers risks being priced out.

Taking a longer view

The pop-up, ephemeral and spontaneous can bring a market to life, creating splashes of colour among everyday greys. But it takes more than that to keep a market alive. Volunteers can burn out, and will lose heart if they feel they are being exploited as a free resource by others whose interest in a locality is framed by their chances of profiting from it.

Other models may help to signpost a longer-term future. A new generation of specialist markets caters to specific tastes and demands, offering an alternative to both the cheap and cheerful stalls of traditional markets and the flakier business models sometimes evident in pop-up stalls.

The farmers' market movement is one example. Often resented by old-style traders as expensive upstarts catering to middle-class tastes, farmers' markets have grown from a niche activity into national and international networks. In the UK the FARMA cooperative brings together independent producers, farmers and market organisers and claims to be the largest organisation of its kind in the world. It offers advice and a quality certification for farmers' markets, and represents the interests of local food producers to government and industry bodies.

The growth of farmers' markets shows a continuing demand for local, seasonal and high quality produce. Between 2004 and 2009 the number of farmers' markets in the UK rose by more than one third, from 450 to 605 (Retail Markets Alliance, 2009). They tick the right boxes for anyone concerned about where their food comes from, the impact on the environment and the benefits for local businesses. At a time when 30 per cent of the UK's vegetable crop is rejected because it fails to meet supermarkets' cosmetic criteria for size and shape, farmers' markets minimise waste: food is sold rather than dumped, transport costs are limited because produce is sold locally, and unnecessary packaging is cut out (IME, 2013).

As well as a growing range of farmers' markets, there are also more than 350 'country markets' in England, Wales and the Channel Islands. For nearly a century these have existed as local cooperatives where farmers can sell surplus produce, and their combined turnover is around £9 million a year. As well as selling food and preserves, they provide an outlet for designers and craftspeople.

But farmers' and country markets are often the icing on more affluent shoppers' cake rather than working people's bread and butter. The conundrum is to bring the best of the traditional, the pop-up and the locally sourced together in a way that combines the spirit of Space Makers with the guts of places like Bury.

Many markets, like Bury, are still run by local councils and bring money into their coffers. On the face of it such a model should work well, bringing together commerce and community, democratic accountability and local enterprise. Markets were once a symbol of civic pride: Leeds City Council constructed a grand entrance for its Kirkgate Market in 1904, a project that ran a then-astronomical £37,000 over budget. These days the council's civic boosterism is more focused on providing an arena for big-ticket entertainment events, and the market is under threat from sparkling new retail developments, including the planned Victoria Gate shopping centre.

In nearby Huddersfield, the town's Queensgate Market was named market hall of the year in 2013 by the National Association of British Market Authorities. It won particular praise for the way start-up businesses have been encouraged, with free space for students and young people to test their ideas and an enterprise fair to inspire and help prospective entrepreneurs.

But for every council that celebrates and invests in its market, there are more that neglect them or view them as an unwelcome distraction from the real business of local government such as collecting the bins or providing social services. Oxford's famous covered market is just one of many that have been threatened with rent increases that traders fear will put them out of business, clearing the way for redevelopment; traders garnered 11,000 signatures on a petition against proposed rent rises. The connection between investing in a market to bring in new customers and the health of the local economy often goes unnoticed at a strategic level. In such circumstances it is no surprise that some communities believe their markets will do better and become more innovative outside council control.

In Todmorden, at the head of the Calder Valley in West Yorkshire, the town's market hall has seen better days. The town has gained an international reputation as the birthplace of a local food movement, galvanised by Incredible Edible Todmorden, which has transformed neglected public spaces into community growing areas with its simple slogan of 'If you eat, you're in' (see Chapter 8). But the market hall, despite healthy local support and a good selection of traders, is in poor physical shape, and the local council has little money for maintenance and investment. There is talk of transferring the hall to a new community-run company.

Similar approaches are being considered in other towns. If the council doesn't have the energy or resources to reinvigorate the market, the argument goes, let local people do so. The Localism Act 2011 in England allows 'assets of community value' to be identified and sold to resident-led organisations. Local authorities can divest themselves of assets that they cannot manage well; community organisations can get on with putting their ideas into practice without the bureaucracy that often accompanies local government.

The realities can be more complex than that. 'Community assets' can quickly turn into liabilities, especially when they are ornate but poorly maintained Victorian buildings. Local enthusiasm does not necessarily imply local capacity.

Nevertheless, there is a common and hopeful thread that runs through the best local markets, whether they are community-led, run by local authorities, organised by producers' cooperatives or stimulated by temporary events and activities. It is the belief that local benefit and commercial activity can go hand in hand, and that there is room for new and more equitable and engaging forms of exchange.

If we are to rehumanise the concept of exchange and create town centres with the richness and variety of the ancient agora, learning from and applying new ideas to our historic markets could be a good way to start. But as the next chapters explain, there are many obstacles to be overcome if we are to reinvent the agora for the 21st century.

4

Lost in the supermarket

In August 2013, a 64-year-old man died after a fist fight over a parking space at an Asda store in Biggleswade, Bedfordshire. It would be hard to dream up a more apt illustration of the misery of modern shopping. All humanity seems to go to the supermarket or the mall, yet it's where humanity often goes missing.

Catherine O'Flynn's first novel, *What was lost*, is set in a shopping centre, Green Oaks. Part of it is called the Market Place. But as she is quick to point out, it's a far cry from the historic market: 'Market Place wasn't a market place. It was the subterranean part of the shopping centre, next to the bus terminals, reserved for the non-prestige, low-end stores...' (2007, p 2).

In *What was lost*, a young girl goes missing. There's an echo of an earlier novel, Ian McEwan's *The child in time*, published 20 years previously. Here the loss occurs in a supermarket, and again a child disappears. A writer of children's books loses his only daughter, and his own identity is shattered and called into question.

In between these two fictional accounts of unbearable loss lies a real one. In another shopping centre, New Strand in Bootle, near Liverpool, two-year-old James Bulger was abducted on 12 February 1993. He was taken away, tortured, beaten and eventually killed on a railway line. The murder was carried out by two 10-year-old boys, Robert Thompson and Jon Venables. Like the horrific child murders of Ian Brady and Myra Hindley a generation before, the events have been lodged in public consciousness as a signifier of evil.

All these events, the real and the fictional, took place in the most everyday of places, locations of almost mind-numbing ordinariness where frightening events are not supposed to happen. On the way to his death, James and his abductors were seen by no fewer than 38 people and challenged by two of them. Nothing happened. The shopping centre's CCTV cameras witnessed the abduction, but could not prevent it. The grainy footage recorded the apparently mundane occurrence of an older boy leading a toddler by the hand, and turned it into an image of dread for future generations.

Abductions shouldn't happen in full view. Riots may happen on the high street, but the shopping centre is supposed to be the ultimate managed environment, never out of the camera's gaze or the reach of security personnel. Climate-controlled, clean and utterly conventional, it is no place for shocks. So it is all the more disturbing when they find their way in.

Since 1993 the Strand shopping centre has won awards for security. But in managing for security, shopping centres have suppressed surprise without abolishing fear. A generation of places-that-are-not-places has relocated the bustle of the marketplace into semi-sealed containers where interaction is moderated, excitement is confined to the 10-screen cinemas and the unpredictable ushered outside. The more the environment is managed to prevent a horror like that of James Bulger, the more it corrals human exchange into a safe zone where even activities as innocent as taking photographs are pounced on by uniformed security guards.

Here, in a sense, utopia has been achieved, in the creation of places that are, in the original meaning of Thomas More's *Utopia*, 'no place'. Separate from ordinary life and yet sucking life in, in a proliferation of activities that are nothing if not humdrum, a Land of Cockaigne devoid of licence has been created within or on the borders of every metropolis. The Market Place that is no marketplace is no figment of a novelist's imagination. Catherine O'Flynn based it on her own experience of working at the HMV music store at Merry Hill shopping centre in the West Midlands.

Merry Hill: the anodyne agora

Merry Hill is a good place to start an exploration of the new utopias and why we need something better than they offer. Affectionately known by Midlanders as 'Merry Hell', it is the anodyne agora par excellence: so much so that the local council, to circumvent planning rules restricting out-of-town developments, designated it the 'strategic town centre' for the Dudley district in 2008.

As a piece of bureaucratic chutzpah this takes some beating. Instead of berating the forces that stole trade from local high streets, as many councillors have done for decades, Dudley Council simply declared the shopping centre to be the new town centre. And if the town centre is defined by the concentration of shops alone, the logic is overwhelming: Merry Hill has 230 stores, from Argos Extra to Zenn Nails.

What makes Merry Hill a town? As Sicinius put it in Shakespeare's *Coriolanus*, what is a city but the people? Merry Hill is about family: you can buy your mum the perfect treat of a coffee and Krispy Kreme for Mother's Day. If you're a new parent, you can find 'everything you need plus support and advice' at Kiddicare – or you can 'enjoy some special me-time with other mums, dads and carers at our Mummy Mornings'. It's about entertainment, with everything from a visit from Zippo's Circus to Quest, which has the 'craziest indoor golf course you have ever seen'. And it's all about community, as as former owner Westfield explained, shortly before selling its share in 2014 to property group Intu: 'We are an active member of the local community and take pride in contributing to many local organisations. Our support for local communities is varied and includes working with our sponsored football club Dudley Town FC and our nominated charity Help Harry Help Others'.

Does this make Merry Hill a town centre? To be fair to Dudley Council, there's more to Merry Hill than Westfield, even if there wouldn't be much of Merry Hill without it. The 'strategic town centre' aims to link Merry Hill, the nearby canalside Waterfront office and housing development, and the old Brierley Hill High Street half a mile away. But there is no doubt that Westfield Merry Hill is the hub around which the future will be fashioned.

Merry Hill has had time to mature: it's already almost a quarter of a century old. Built during the 1980s, it was designed to bring new life to a former industrial zone following the closure of the Round Oak Steelworks, which clocked out its last worker in 1982 after more than 120 years of production. Construction began in 1984 and the first tenant, the furniture retailer MFI, began trading in late 1985. In that year the Richardson twins, local property developers, bought the site and the adjoining Merry Hill Farm, a popular green space.

Round Oak Steelworks was described in 1868 as a 'vast Cyclopean workshop, which is a standing monument of the enterprise of capital and the skill of labour united' (The National Archives, nd). Some, remembering Homer's one-eyed giants, might consider Cyclopean an appropriate term for Merry Hill today. The enterprise of capital is there too, even if the skill of labour no longer involves actually making anything. The centre's claims to fame have included Britain's first drive-through McDonald's, an aborted attempt to develop the world's tallest tower, and a £22 million monorail system that was closed after just five years.

Alongside Merry Hill – but developed separately on the steelworks site – is the Waterfront office complex, housing HM Revenue & Customs and a clutch of pubs and restaurants. Completed in the early 1990s to bring new jobs to Dudley, it was itself a victim of recession, and many of the business occupiers moved out or closed.

In 2006 a consultancy, Regeneris, produced a report that gave Dudley Council the ammunition it needed to designate Merry Hill the new strategic town centre. A strong part of the case was to demonstrate that Dudley – the town rather than the district, four miles up the road from Brierley Hill – was 'not able to perform a strategic role'. Examine other studies and the main reason why this is so becomes apparent: Dudley town centre is faltering because Merry

Hill has taken its trade. Writing in the *Journal of Urban Regeneration and Renewal*, for example, Simon Wainwright commented:

> When Merry Hill Shopping Centre opened, a number of national multiple retailers, including Marks & Spencer, C&A and Littlewoods, closed shops in the surrounding towns and opened in the new shopping centre. Surrounding towns such as Dudley were turned into ghost towns as a consequence, with dramatic falls in both rental and capital values of commercial property. (Wainwright, 2012, p 127)

An article in *Planning* magazine quotes Ian Brough, Director of External Affairs for the Richardson brothers, who has a refreshing Black Country brusqueness: 'Why would we go to Dudley town centre when we could get a bigger, quicker, return on our investment elsewhere?' (Townsend, 2011).

And thereby hangs a tale. Far from being the sad but inevitable Darwinian outcome of red-blooded free-marketeering, the decline of Dudley town centre and the inexorable rise of Merry Hill were the direct consequence of public subsidy and intervention. The organisations charged with looking after the interests of local citizens were active participants in the displacement of business from local centres, and oiled the machine with public funds.

'The incentives offered, in particular the removal of planning restrictions, were hugely appealing,' Ian Brough told *Planning*. Indeed they were. Merry Hill was one of the UK's first Enterprise Zones, designated by the government of Margaret Thatcher in 1981. The thinking of the time was that by freeing up the market, removing taxes and red tape, business would flourish. Retailers flocked to Merry Hill to take advantage of relief from local property taxes. Marks & Spencer, one of the last big stores to move, closed its shops in Dudley and nearby West Bromwich. Those who believe high streets are dying because shoppers are voting with their feet to go out of town often forget that many of the shops moved first, and that public authorities helped them on their way.

A government evaluation of 22 of the first wave of Enterprise Zones estimated that £800 million of public money was spent between 1981 and 1993. More recently, the Centre for Cities estimated that every single job created in the 1980s Enterprise Zones cost the government £26,000 at 2011 prices (Centre for Cities, 2011). A study by The Work Foundation concluded that up to eight of every ten jobs were simply displaced from elsewhere (Sissons and Brown, 2011). Merry Hill may be a success on its own terms, but that doesn't mean it has made Dudley more prosperous; indeed, in 2011 local business leaders were lobbying for the creation of yet another Enterprise Zone offering a new round of tax breaks to stimulate interest in the ailing Waterfront, the very site that the original Dudley Enterprise Zone was intended to revive. In March 2013 nearly 2,500 people were competing for just 22 jobs at a new furniture store in Merry Hill (*Express & Star*, 2013).

Curiously, Dudley Metropolitan Borough Council continues to market Dudley town centre as 'the big heart of the Black Country', gushing over its 11th-century castle, historic marketplace, zoo and heritage museum, while simultaneously seeking to channel energy and investment into the part of the borough that looks and feels most like all the other office-retail-entertainment melanges developed around the UK in the last quarter-century. Such is utopia.

Hubs of local communities?

Writing on the reviews website TripAdvisor, a visitor from Stourbridge was clear about the pros and cons of Merry Hill. 'When you go outside, it's car parks only, no fresh air, no green space, no beautiful old buildings,' he wrote. 'If chain-store shopping is all you want you'll enjoy the Merry Hill Centre, but if you want a varied day out, or like small individual retailers, best to go elsewhere.'

Compare that with the more generalised comments of Peter Drummond, President of the British Council of Shopping Centres in 2012. Introducing a report on shopping centres' community involvement, he wrote: 'Shopping centres are the hub of local communities. They provide safe, secure, clean environments for people to shop, dine, meet, relax and be entertained' (BCSC, 2012, p 1).

All of which can be done, he omits to mention, without the need for fresh air, green space or beautiful old buildings. Neither do shopping, dining and entertainment require public services such as libraries, post offices and health centres, local charities, clubs and societies, places of worship, schools, or stages where people can perform rather than be performed to.

This is not to say that shopping centres, or their first cousins, the supermarkets, have no social value. The interaction between people, place and profit is complex. We can't simply turn the clock back to a more innocent age, if there ever was one. But the Faustian nature of the pact of contemporary consumption needs to be better understood.

Meadowhall is another mega-mall built on the site of a former steelworks, this time in Sheffield. Like Merry Hill, it has a local nickname: Meadowhell is the preferred moniker. Like Merry Hill, it stands accused of hastening the decline of Sheffield city centre and nearby Rotherham town centre. And like Merry Hill, for all the ire directed at it, it's a big commercial success, so much so that the Norwegian government's pension fund has snapped up a 50 per cent stake.

Look at Meadowhall, or any of the other similar malls dotted around the UK, from the perspective of a shopper and you'll see why. If what you love is shopping, everything you want is under one roof. You can park without charge, stay as long as you like, and spend as much as you like. If what you hate is shopping, everything you want is under one roof. You can park without charge, stay as long as you must, spend the bare minimum and get the hell out.

Most of us shop, unless we are rich or helpless enough to have someone do it for us. For some of us it is a necessary evil; for others a pleasure to anticipate and relish. And for many, much of the time, it is simply something we do. Anything that makes it easier, cheaper or more pleasurable seems welcome. But there are different ways of cutting the bargain.

Luton is the kind of town where shopping areas tell different stories of place and identity. In the town centre is St George's Square, somewhere that sounds quintessentially English – the kind of square that you might imagine with a parish church, a guildhall and regular performances by morris dancers. In reality it's one of those bits of public realm left over from the days when local authorities had money to spend. It has a patch of green, an abundance of hard surfacing, a fountain where children can play, and around the edge, a Wetherspoon pub and a Costa Coffee.

Watching people use the space is informative. People cross to go into The Mall, the indoor shopping centre that sucks in the town's life behind its blank walls. They sit on the edges to wait for a bus or pass through towards the town hall and pedestrianised shopping area. If St George's Square is intended to bring the town centre to life, there are few signs that it has succeeded.

About a mile northwest is Bury Park. To reach it on foot from the town centre you have to risk life and limb crossing multiple lanes of traffic, or traverse a skeletal concrete bridge high above the inner ring road. Bury Park is a different world. Along Dunstable Road the shops spill out into the street, bright peppers and chillies in boxes on trestle tables, huge bags of onions and the smell of Asian cooking from numerous cafes, reflecting the Kashmiri and Pakistani heritage of many locals. Bury Park is also home to Luton Town Football Club, which attracts a very different group on match days. For the most part, the two rub shoulders amicably enough.

The difference between the middle of Luton and Bury Park is the difference between a shopping centre and a community. The Mall and St George's Square seek to provide something for everyone, but do so by offering a lowest-common-denominator approach. Bury Park is an expression of the life of the people who live there, a place to meet friends and neighbours despite the unpromising environment of a through road and crowded pavements.

In the 1990s a team of researchers tried to get under the skin of the connections between the way people see themselves and where they shop, looking at two centres in North London: Brent Cross, Britain's first retail mall just off the North Circular Road, and Wood Green Shopping City, a purpose-built indoor centre alongside a local high street.

Social class, race and gender played strong roles in how people chose to use the different centres. Wood Green was considered working-class and multicultural; it attracted people who felt they were among their peers, and there was a strong sense of friendship and social equality between shoppers and shop assistants in the centre. Brent Cross, conversely, was seen as upmarket and used by more middle-class shoppers – many of whom would have been the very people targeted by the 'shop locally' campaigns organised by traders in nearby Finchley and Whetstone when Brent Cross opened in 1976 (Miller et al, 1998). The *London Evening Standard* described Brent Cross as the 'housewife's dream' at the time.

The research team challenged a range of assumptions that continue to dominate discussion of shopping centres and supermarkets: that they exclude the poor and vulnerable, that they create privatised spaces mediated by a sense of fear, and that they reduce the citizen to the role of consumer.

It is a viewpoint often expressed more vociferously by retailers themselves, who consistently argue that they are only providing what the market or the individual customer wants. What the Brent Cross and Wood Green researchers failed to consider in any depth was the way shopping centres were changing the surrounding town and suburban centres; neither did they examine the way retailers and developers themselves have steered the market. Since that study in the 1990s, the pace of change has quickened, and the consequences have become much more visible.

Shopping centres may have helped create new identities for some places, but even at their best have offered little more than an android alternative to historic human settlements. Every so often the veil is removed, to reveal how little the shopping-centre-as-community-hub offers. In Dongguan, China, the New South China Mall opened in 2005 with enough space to accommodate 2,530 stores, a palm-tree lined plaza and even a replica Sphinx and Arc de Triomphe. One of its star attractions was a Teletubbies Edutainment Centre, based on the BBC children's TV programme. The mall's managers were delighted to catch 'a trusted brand that very young children respond to and interact with' (New South China Mall, 2006). When it was built it was the biggest mall in the world, but Dongguan's factory workers simply didn't have the income to support it. Their lives are lived elsewhere.

The balloon that can only get bigger

The last century spawned a dazzling array of dystopian literature, theatre and cinema. From 'Blade runner' to 'The matrix', *Brave new world* to Margaret Attwood's *Oryx and Crake*, it seems that whenever writers and artists imagine the future, it is the stuff of nightmares.

A common theme in these dystopian visions is the loss of autonomy and freedom. But the theme isn't confined to the creative imagination.

Andrew Simms, in his 2007 polemic *Tescopoly*, commented that Tesco 'almost certainly holds more files on British citizens than the East German state ever held on its own people' (p 96). No need to use the techniques of the Stasi secret police: just remember to take your Clubcard on every shopping trip. In 2007 some 25 million cards had been issued, of which around 10 million were in active use; two years later there were 16 million active users in the UK and another 12.5 million overseas. In 2012 Tesco neatly offered Clubcard users double points for using the social networking site Facebook to 'like' and buy products, gaining access not only to cardholders' buying habits, but also to information about their families, friends, relationships and interests. 'It's our way of saying thanks for supporting us online,' said Matthew Entwistle, Tesco's marketing director for general merchandise online (Tesco PLC, 2012a).

But knowing about your shopping, your friends and your family isn't enough. In March 2013 Tesco launched Clubcard TV, proclaiming that it was 'the first retailer in the UK to reward its customers with their own online movie and TV service'. In exchange for free access to shows like 'The only way is Essex' and 'The real hustle' and films such as 'The wind in the willows', viewers must watch targeted advertising based on their shopping habits, paid for by companies such as Kellogg's and Danone.

Commenting on the new service, Clubcard TV managing director, Scott Deutrom, wrote:

> By using Clubcard, we can look at what customers buy from us, what things they like, and then make an effort to target adverts that are more relevant to them. Better still, we can target adverts based on what our customers bought yesterday, we can show that we are listening to our customers in 'real' time. (Deutrom, 2013)

'Listening to' and 'eavesdropping on' merge into one in the Clubcard consciousness. The notion of Tesco as totalitarian would have seemed fanciful only a few years ago. In 1987 the company had only 377 stores in the UK, having closed many of its small shops to make way for fewer, larger supermarkets. But behind its bland desire 'to create value for customers to earn their lifetime loyalty', growth is the only option. To maintain their share price and deliver increased returns to investors, Tesco and its ilk must get bigger and move into new markets. There is no such thing as 'enough'; that would be interpreted by the stock market as a reason to sell. The balloon must always get bigger. The concept of 'fiduciary duty' means that the corporation has a responsibility to look after the interests of its investors. This is usually interpreted as making as much money for them as possible.

What does 'not big enough' look like? In 2012-13 Tesco had 3,146 stores, earned £43.6 billion, and made profits of £2.27 billion in the UK. It had 2,131 stores in Asia and 1,507 in Europe, although it had dumped its struggling US Fresh & Easy operation. Tesco Bank pulled in another £1 billion and is expanding into the mortgage market. Every week more than 75 million shopping trips are made to Tesco stores. Tesco is also the world's biggest and most profitable internet grocery retailer, turning over more than £2 billion online (Tesco PLC, 2012b, 2013). When Tesco found its market share slipping, its indications in 2014 that it might have to trim its profit margins (the highest in the industry) were enough to send tremors around the media and the stock market (*The Telegraph*, 2014). That failure to keep pumping the balloon eventually cost chief executive Philip Clarke his job.

While you can't help noticing the physical presence of Tesco in most British towns and cities, it's the combined power of the supermarkets that really makes a difference. Supermarkets can influence planning decisions, both negatively by buying up land and preventing alternative uses, and proactively by buying councils off with 'planning gain' payments for improved roads or parcels of land for housing (Friends of the Earth, 2006; Tescopoly, 2011). They have squeezed out competition by devoting growing proportions of their floorspace and their online presence to non-food goods like clothing and electrical appliances, and are now cornering the market in local convenience stores – a move curiously interpreted by the British government as the revival of the high street (DCLG, 2014). After the collapse into administration in early 2013 of photographic retailer Jessops, music store HMV and film hire company Blockbuster, the supermarket chain Morrisons snapped up a string of empty high street stores to turn them into convenience grocers. Local diversity is rapidly becoming a choice between a Tesco Metro, a Sainsbury's

Local, a Co-op, one of the Netto stores now owned by Asda or one of Morrisons' convenience stores.

Successive reports by the Competition Commission in 2000 and 2008 argued that the UK market generally works in customers' interests because they can choose between one supermarket and another, as if this is all the choice that people want or need. But even the Commission, whose slogan might be 'Never knowingly over-regulating', accepted in 2008 that there were 495 'highly concentrated local markets' where one retailer exercised a near-monopoly in the locality and could inflate its profits as a result. Its remedy, however, was to say there should be more supermarkets, not fewer: where one was dominant, there should be a 'competition test' for new development in order to allow others to join in (Competition Commission, 2008). Tesco fought back, claiming the test could prevent 2,500 jobs being created every year (Hall and Fletcher, 2010).

The Commission also chided supermarkets for their exploitation of suppliers, revisiting the recommendation of a code of practice for grocery retailers from its turn-of-the-millennium inquiry. This had proved so ineffective that the 2008 report sought to beef it up, recommending an ombudsman who could arbitrate in disputes between supermarkets and their suppliers. It was another four years before a parliamentary bill to establish a 'groceries code adjudicator' was finally introduced.

For the most part, the Competition Commission's view could be summarised as 'Hear no evil, see no evil, speak no evil'. In the game of retail monopoly, Tesco was not the inevitable winner, the Commission opined: 'Our assessment is that the basis of Tesco's position is not insurmountable; there is nothing that Tesco does that could not, over time, be challenged by competitors' (Competition Commission, 2008).

The Commission's narrow interpretation of its own role and ability to intervene has been widely interpreted as a self-denying ordinance, turning the relationship between the state and the supermarket industry into a form of shadow-boxing while retailers get on with the real battle for market share.

The consequences have been well documented. Joanna Blythman's *Shopped*, for example, outlines in forensic detail the exploitative relationships between supermarkets and their suppliers, the opaque special offers that are less special than they seem, the squeezing out of fresh food that fails to conform to cosmetic expectations of size and appearance, the promotion of high-profit, low-nutrient ready meals and the deals with developers and local authorities disguised as urban regeneration (Blythman, 2005).

More recently and prosaically, Professor Roger Clarke at Cardiff Business School has listed the abusive relationships between supermarkets and their suppliers that are now beginning to stir the sleeping giant of the European Commission. These include late payments that transfer risk from the retailer to the supplier; retrospective changes in contracts; fees for the privilege of a particular place for products on supermarket shelves, or for being considered for stocking at all; 'special payments' to cover the cost of promotions or store refurbishments; and the threat of removal from supermarkets' approved lists (known as de-listing), which, in a market with few competitors, can be enough to put a supplier out of business. Very few European countries penalise abuses. A notable exception is the Czech Republic, where retailers can be fined up to 10 per cent of net turnover for breaking rules on fair dealing (Clarke, 2010).

For Andrew Simms, 'Tesco's innocent offer of "every little helps" masks an almighty, strategic effort to re-engineer the fabric of our communities and essential services in its own profit-focused interests' (Simms, 2007, p 106). But times move quickly. If there is one store to rule them all and in the darkness bind them, it may not be Tesco at all but a company whose shops you're unlikely ever to see on a street or in a mall.

One store to rule them all

When Andrew Simms wrote *Tescopoly*, the 'space race' was in full swing: supermarkets were buying up edge-of-town and out-of-town sites and battling each other for the right to control prime locations through strategically acquired planning consents. Six years later, Tesco and Asda were both announcing that the space race was over. In its 2013 annual report, Tesco described how it had 'called an end to the big store space race'.

Suddenly the companies that seemed to want all the space they could possibly get were realising they had too much of it – or at least, too much in certain places. Leigh Sparks, Professor of Retail Studies at the University of Stirling's Institute for Retail Studies, explains:

"Most of the big grocers added non-food and they have realised that they don't need that much space to do non-food. They misread the signals and on top of that you've got the grocery online now. So there's just too much space" (interview with author).

But the supermarkets are not retrenching – far from it. Around Britain, there are now supermarkets that are packed with produce but that shoppers can never visit. The only evidence most of us will ever see of their existence is the cheery face of the van driver who drops off the groceries we've ordered online. These 'dark stores' are patrolled by pickers who work round-the-clock shifts to take your orders from the shelves and pack them ready for delivery.

Tesco, the market leader here as elsewhere, has a string of dark stores in warehouses near London's M25 orbital motorway, in Enfield, Croydon, Aylesford and Greenford. Asda has similar stores in Leeds and Enfield. Waitrose has a former carpet warehouse in Acton, just off London's North Circular (Wood, 2012).

If shopping malls and supermarkets were the destroyers of high streets since the 1980s, replacing historic streetscapes with placeless containers, their role in turning place into no-place is rapidly being usurped by online shopping. Tesco's online business is growing at 10 per cent a year, slightly below the growth of internet shopping overall, reinforced by a 'bricks and clicks' strategy that aligns internet purchasing with a range of options for delivery, including a 'click and collect' service. By the end of 2013 just under 12 per cent of all UK retailing (apart from fuel sales) was online, a long way ahead of countries such as Spain and Italy (ONS, 2014).

For Paul Kelly, Director of External Affairs at Asda, the giant hypermarket is starting to become redundant. "Your out of town store now is your website, with an even greater range," he said. "An Extra might have 45,000 or 50,000 skews [product lines] – online you can have 700,000 skews" (interview with author).

Online shopping is changing the face of the British high street even faster than the growth of supermarkets and the rise of out-of-town shopping centres. In 2007 Andrew Simms was able to write about Blockbuster as 'yet another example of winner-take-all clone retailing', bemoaning its rapid rise to more than 9,000 stores internationally and 700 in the UK in less than 20 years. In January 2013 it failed, losing 528 shops and 4,000 staff in two separate administrations in the space of a year, following in the footsteps of its original US parent, which filed for bankruptcy in 2010.

Blockbuster's lead administrator, Lee Manning of Deloitte, somewhat disingenuously blamed local councils for pushing up property taxes and parking charges. 'Sadly, the high street is not worth the effort any more,' he told *The Telegraph* (Ebrahimi, 2013). The reality was that Blockbuster, like its contemporaneous retail flops Jessops and HMV, had been outflanked by internet retailing and digital technology. In Blockbuster's case, the films that once came in brick-shaped VHS cassettes are now no longer a physical product at all. You can download or rent them from Apple's iTunes or companies like Netflix or LOVEFiLM without shifting your backside from the sofa. While some will miss the personal service and expert knowledge that might have been available at a photographic store like Jessops, few will shed a tear over losing the experience of picking up and returning a DVD at Blockbuster.

The loss of Britain's bookshops arouses stronger passions. The number of independent bookstores belonging to the Booksellers Association fell from 1,535 in 2005 to 1,028 in 2012. Britain's biggest general bookstore, Waterstone's, was dumped by its previous owners HMV after losing £20.6 million in 2011. Its new owners hailed a 'turnaround' when it reduced its operating losses to £12.2 million in 2013 – but both the number of stores and the value of books sold continued to shrink (Campbell, 2013).

Again, a shift from physical to digital shopping is behind the trends. The bookshop, the first example of self-service shopping where customers could browse at their leisure before taking their purchases to the checkout, was one of the simplest formats to take online. Instead of being limited by the size of the store, an online store could carry publishers' entire catalogues, giving readers an unprecedented choice. Browsers can find out what other readers think of the books they're interested in, discover additional information about authors, and compare titles with similar material in the same genre or subject area.

Then came e-readers. The idea of electronic books has been around for decades, but it was only with the launch of the Sony Reader in 2006, rapidly followed by the Amazon Kindle a year later, that they became popular. The physical product had become digital. In 2010

Amazon reported it was selling 140 e-books for every 100 hardcover books, and by 2011 its e-book sales had overtaken its paperback sales.

Old-style physical shops cannot compete head-to-head with the digital world. Some products no longer require a place to be stored and sold, other than a climate-controlled shed full of data servers; and products that cannot be digitised can be purchased at home and either delivered or picked up from a secure storage locker. The space needed to shift a given amount of stock is much less, and need not be anywhere near the purchaser.

There's technological change, but there's also arm-twisting. Conservative Party activist and political publisher Iain Dale summed up independent publishers' opinion of Amazon, declaring, 'They do give smaller publishers like us a choice. Never let it be said they don't. And the choice is sell your books to us at 60% discount, or we won't take any of them at all' (*The Bookseller*, 2013). Frances and Keith Smith, booksellers with shops in the historic towns of Kenilworth and Warwick, demanded an end to the 'Amazon Swindle' – the online retailer's failure to pay a penny of corporation tax in the UK despite turning over more than £3 billion of revenue.

How did the Smiths fight back? By going online, with a petition that attracted more than 170,000 signatures on the website Change.org. It wasn't the only Amazon-related campaign. On Change.org you could find petitions calling on Amazon to stop exploiting third-party sellers; to stop encouraging shoppers to collect price information from independent stores and then shop at Amazon instead; to stop treating its warehouse workers 'like machines'; and to stop discriminating against gay and lesbian books.

What riles people like the Smiths is neither the idea that Amazon should offer a competing service, nor its innovation in bringing e-books to a mass market: it is the concern that Amazon has achieved a position of market dominance and is now using its power to gobble up or elbow out the competition. It mirrors Andrew Simms' critique of Tesco, but on a global scale.

Amazon sees things rather differently. Its annual reports are awash with heartwarming stories of the liberating power of Amazon in general, and Kindle Direct Publishing (KDP) in particular. Robert Bidinotto, author of the best-selling Kindle thriller *Hunter*, is typical:

Past age 60 and in the midst of the recession, my wife and I found our income options severely limited. KDP was my one shot at a lifelong dream – our only chance at financial salvation. Within months of publishing, KDP has completely changed our lives, enabling this aging nonfiction writer to launch a brand-new career as a best-selling novelist.... As I've happily discovered, there is zero downside risk – and the potential is virtually unlimited. (Amazon.com, 2012)

For chief executive officer Jeff Bezos, Amazon has brought diversity, opportunity and value to a stuffy and arthritic market:

The most radical and transformative of inventions are often those that empower others to unleash their creativity – to pursue their dreams. That's a big part of what's going on with Amazon Web Services, Fulfillment by Amazon, and Kindle Direct Publishing … we are creating powerful self-service platforms that allow thousands of people to boldly experiment and accomplish things that would otherwise be impossible or impractical. (Amazon.com, 2012)

Like Tesco, Amazon does not and cannot have a concept of enough. Its corporate mission could be summed up as 'Everything, everyone, everywhere': 'We seek to be Earth's most customer-centric company for four primary customer sets: consumers, sellers, enterprises, and content creators.' Whatever risks it faces, false modesty isn't one of them. In the fourth quarter of 2012, with the global economy in the doldrums, it posted an eye-watering 22 per cent increase in sales, with takings of $21.27 billion. You can listen to your Amazon Cloud Services music on your new Ford in the US, or buy apps and games on your Kindle Fire with Amazon's very own currency. You can buy Amazon groceries from Amazon Fresh, and grab discount vouchers from Amazon Local.

And then there's Mechanical Turk. Just as Amazon has become the market-maker for books, it wants to be the market-maker for work. Mechanical Turk is a fine example of the trend towards a 'precariat': a growing body of insecure workers, so termed by academics because they are always teetering on the edge of survival. Anyone with access to a computer and the internet can offer their services for a wide range of jobs, most paying well below the minimum wage.

Mechanical Turk, although currently only available in the US, has excited technology-watchers who like the idea that crowd-sourcing can become crowd-working. Instead of hiring employees or negotiating tiresome freelance contracts, anyone who wants a job done that can be done on a computer can simply go to the market and instantly pick from a host of willing or desperate workers.

Mechanical Turk is a tiny niche of the global labour market, but is already being used by some big players, including the US Army Research Lab. So it is worth watching. And Amazon as a corporation is worth watching, given that it aspires to be the world's number one intermediary between buyers and sellers.

Amazon's third-party 'marketplace' sellers already exist under a form of feudalism, where their access to market can be granted or withdrawn at Amazon's directive, their customer lists are not their own and their reputation is mediated through Amazon's own rating system. While Amazon trumpets the way it has opened up global markets to niche and micro businesses, it has had no qualms about turning the screw on them, hiking its 'trader fees' by up to 70 per cent in some cases (Bowers, 2013). Where there is only one viable route to market, the gatekeepers have always found it tempting to increase their tolls.

Amazon tends to be coy about expressing its mission in terms of global domination. For a summary of its power we need to turn to the French technology company faberNovel, which has kept a close eye on what is now the number one retailer in the US. Like the supermarkets, Amazon's model is to pile it high and sell it cheap: its retail model is low prices, convenience and an extensive selection of products. Digital technology allows it to beat the supermarkets at their own game, cutting out investment in physical infrastructure, avoiding property taxes, and moving its international operations wherever taxes are lowest. Like Tesco, it has grabbed market share and then used its dominant position to dictate terms; but what took Tesco the best part of a century in the UK grocery market, Amazon has achieved in just a decade of online retailing in the US. When Amazon moved into the music business, it became the largest online seller of recordings in just 120 days (Distinguin, 2013).

Amazon has also made customer service social rather than bilateral. If you want to know whether a product is any good, you can read customer reviews: Amazon's willingness to publish negative reviews builds trust and confidence that the positive ones will be genuine. As Jeff Bezos has said, if you make customers unhappy on the internet, they can each tell 6,000 friends. Reputation is everything. But having established the reputation, the relationship becomes hard to break. And just to be on the safe side, Amazon has bought the book recommendation website Goodreads.

Amazon's Kindle makes parting harder still. You don't buy a book on Kindle: you are licensed to read it. And once you have a Kindle, you're locked into Amazon's ecosystem; the Kindle Fire tablet computer is sold at a loss because the company makes its money on recurring sales of digital content that can be supplied for a tiny fraction of the revenue received from sales. And with KDP, the author may receive greater rewards as a percentage of royalties, but also takes all the risk.

While the eulogies of its supporters and the ire of its opponents might suggest otherwise, Amazon is essentially amoral. It is a corporation on a mission to grow, like all corporations. But as it grows it is changing the places we live in, probably permanently. Like a marriage vow, the deal is for better or for worse and in sickness and health; unlike a marriage vow it comes with no concomitant commitment to love and to cherish.

The effects on physical places – our town centres and suburban shopping streets – have yet to fully unfold. But as Stéphane Distinguin of faberNovel comments, 'by combining same-day delivery and delivery lockers, Amazon is steadily chipping away at reasons to walk into a store at all' (2013).

Leigh Sparks doesn't believe the store is finished as a physical presence in our towns, but he agrees it is diminishing:

> 'If you look at retail and particularly big retail, then they are remarkably data rich and they use that data to do both tactical decision making and strategic decision making, and are very good at it. The net effect of that is that there is an intensification of space use and an intensification of supply chain delivery, which means that the amount

of space that's required by retail has changed.' (interview with the author)

It isn't just the amount of space needed that's changing, but also the location and nature of those spaces. House of Fraser has experimented with a store in Aberdeen that consists of nothing but a cafe, internet terminals and virtual changing rooms. In Singapore there's a Seven Eleven convenience store in an alcove under an escalator. In South Korea, travellers at Seolleung underground station can simply scan pictures of products with their smartphones at the world's first 'virtual supermarket' and get them delivered to their homes (Strother, 2011). The new world threatens, but it also opens up possibilities. The pace, however, is being set by those who already dominate the retail landscape. Seolleung virtual supermarket is run by Homeplus, a Korean discount retailer wholly owned by Tesco.

"We're going to see whole swathes of towns where the multiple retailer presence will be a click and collect type operation or an Amazon locker based system," Professor Sparks predicts. "Some of the functional stuff, the food stuff and the coffee stuff, sits in there. But the rest of the space, the fashion space and the rest, really isn't going to be there."

A bigger share of a smaller pie

The shopping centre, the supermarket and the internet giant: each in its way is stripping trade out of town centres and away from local businesses. In a rich economy where work is plentiful and credit is easy, the impact may be masked because there is more money in the system: the independent or specialist town centre trader may survive on a smaller share of a larger pie. But since 2008 most British citizens have neither been well-off nor well-served by lenders. Wages have fallen at one of the fastest rates in Europe and have only recently begun to recover, and many of those in work are struggling with debt and insecurity. The pie has shrunk, but the share taken out of town, online and into the supermarkets has grown.

Writing in 2012, Bill Grimsey, former chief executive of the DIY chain Wickes, posed the question of who killed the high street. His answer came in the form of a bullet-pointed list:

- Greed by retailers to be bigger and better
- Greed by property developers who put down more retail space than was ever required
- Greed from private equity players, who extracted value out of store chains without improving the proposition
- Greed by individuals (some of whom have become rich beyond their wildest dreams) who have in some cases pressurised companies to a point of collapse in their quest for financial success
- Greed from the consumer to get more and more for less and less. (Grimsey, 2012)

Bill Grimsey used to be director of customer services at Tesco and chief executive of frozen food store Iceland, as well as head of Wickes, so if anyone knows whether the major retailers have a concept of 'enough', he should.

Pointing the finger is easy. Pointing the way forward is more taxing, which may be why many commentators devote most of their energy to describing the problem. But it's worth pausing to take on board Bill Grimsey's analysis, because he uses language that would never sully the mouths of Jeff Bezos or Philip Clarke. A corporate world in which more is always better is one that has unavoidable consequences.

It would be naïve to assume that the likes of Tesco and Amazon, faced with popular angst or anger about the decline of town centres, will change either their worldviews or the fundamentals of their business model. Indeed their approach is not only to dominate their own core markets, but to colonise the alternatives too. Sick of supermarket produce and want to go organic instead? If you live in London you could get your own veg box delivered by the homely-sounding Soil and Seed. It just happens to be a Tesco service (see www.soilandseed.co.uk/faqs).

Fancy a coffee? Harris + Hoole is 'all about good coffee and happy people'. Its rapid expansion across South East England just happens to be backed by Tesco. As Harris + Hoole's website says, 'few people know the high street better than Tesco'. Want a meal out? There's a chain of restaurants called Giraffe. Tesco has bought that too. Or how about getting away from it all with a spot of gardening? Dobbies, a chain of 32 garden centres operating across Scotland, England and

Northern Ireland, declares on its website that 'It's nice to know that in this busy, modern world of "virtual companies" there are also real companies with real history, run by people who really care. Dobbies has been offering expert advice to horticulturalists since 1865'. Not declared on its website is that it was snapped up by Tesco for £36 million in 2008.

Just as Liverpool One has cannibalised trade from Liverpool's suburbs and satellites, so the rise of out-of-town shopping, supermarket power and internet retail have swallowed much of the trade that once sustained town centres. In June 2012 Sebastian James, newly appointed head of electrical retailers Dixons, was one of a succession of retail leaders to announce the death of the high street. 'The high street will no longer so much be for players like us, it'll be for restaurants and leisure,' he told *The Telegraph*. 'I really hope they can be fun buzzy places, but they might not be where people go to shop' (Wallop, 2012). Investors in shopping, it seems, can't be expected to be investors in good places too.

A stirring in utopia

Every now and again there are indications that the big beasts are less than comfortable with the world they've created. Asda is starting to look at how some of the excess space it has built can be turned over to community uses. Tesco is dipping its toes in the water too. At Asda, Paul Kelly insists this is not just a response to a property problem, but a shift in corporate emphasis, recognising that the company has a responsibility to the communities it serves.

Store managers were given an initial target of 7,500 community uses in nine months; they achieved just under 24,000. In Watford a group of beekeepers used their store as a meeting place; in South Wales a Citizen's Advice Bureau set up an office. This is just the start, he argues:

> 'I think genuinely five years down the line you will see some of our stores being real community centres. I think that will be dedicated, permanent space that isn't meeting rooms and training rooms, offering a range of services that local people want and need, working with third parties. I think you might see us incubating new

businesses and new social enterprises.'(interview with the author)

The initiative raises as many questions as it answers. Will it simply displace community activity from existing town centre locations and shift it into a commercial environment? Might it undermine community organisations that depend on hiring out their own premises to fund their services? Will the initial enthusiasm last? It's a sign, however, that on the edges of our retail utopias, something may be stirring.

There are other signs, too. In Brierley Hill High Street more than a quarter of shops are empty and plans to link the traditional town centre with nearby Merry Hill are on hold. At first glance, Brierley Hill seems on its last legs. One survey found 68 per cent of local people disliked their high street. People interviewed on the street in 2011 described it as dull, boring, "a dirty, scruffy place". Too many kebab shops, too many charity shops, some said. "A lot of the people who come in say I forgot it was here," one shopkeeper commented.

But others said they were proud of its working-class character and its social mix. "They're golden people in Brierley Hill," one elderly woman said. "I wouldn't go nowhere else" (quoted in Brierley Hillness Project, 2011).

Look beyond the shuttered shops and the peeling paint and there's another story. The town has an active civic society, church groups and a revived community forum. A recent arts project celebrated what it termed 'Brierley Hillness' – the sense of place and community that makes Brierley Hill unique. Local people made music, created films and designed a mural; poetry, dance and drama brought people's views of their home town to life. More than 360 people contributed to the project.

Utopia doesn't only mean 'no place'. It's a pun on the classical Greek *ou*, meaning not, and *eu*, meaning good or happy. In the communities around Merry Hill and against the odds, people have unearthed some of the ingredients that can turn a no-place into a happy place. Perhaps even among our 21st-century utopias, what was lost may be rediscovered.

5

Declaring independence

The long main street of Totnes in Devon springs from Old Market, with its fine views across the Dart Valley. Dropping swiftly past Rotherfold, where the bulls used to be penned on market days, it eases the casual visitor past Drift record store, Social Fabric knitting shop, Sacks Wholefoods, The Happy Apple, the colonnaded Butterwalks, and a succession of gift shops, fashion shops, coffee shops and trinket shops.

If you can shun the temptations of the pubs along the way, from the Bay Horse to the Royal Seven Stars Hotel, you'll have time to take in the slate-hung upper storeys that are a particular feature of this town, the market square with its stalls selling cheap tools and expensive knickknacks, the ruddy tower of the parish church of St Mary standing aloof from the main street's greys and pastels, and the imposing arch of East Gate where High Street becomes Fore Street.

You might begin to wonder how this town of just 8,000 people, the size of a large urban overspill estate, can support such a huge variety of independent traders. They include three local butchers, Roly's fudge shop, a toy shop, even one selling harps. Ray Reynolds, preparing his chorizo wraps in Market Square, takes a moment from chargrilling his sausages to boast that Totnes has the best market in Devon, with more than 50 stalls at its regular Good Food Sunday – and this is from a veteran who previously plied his trade at London's prestigious Borough Market.

Travelling through the West Country in 1720, the writer Daniel Defoe was similarly struck by the apparent local prosperity. Fish and other provisions were so cheap, he observed, that the town was a very good place to live for outsiders with large families, and 'many such are said to come into those parts on purpose for saving money, and to live in proportion to their income' (Defoe, 1927, p 225).

Today people are still moving to the town, although it's nowhere near as cheap as it once was. Outsiders, although disdainfully described as 'blow-ins' by locals, have kept Totnes thriving while other Devon towns have fallen on hard times. Even outside the tourist season the town looks buzzing and prosperous. The library, tucked down a narrow passageway at 27a High Street, is full too, with parents helping their children choose picture books and pensioners dozing over newspapers.

There are some clues to why this place is different. The library must be one of the few in the country to have bound volumes of *Ethical Consumer* magazine in its reference section. The high street is dotted with vegetarian cafes and stores selling crystals. There's a preponderance of bookshops. There isn't a Greggs to be seen.

This is Alternative Central, occasionally reaching a state of self-parody. Where else would a jeweller call itself Stoned? Where else would flyposted litter bins carry notices of a forthcoming bookshop opening by environmental guru Satish Kumar?

But while many of the independent traders here are green-tinted, they face the everyday problems of trying to make ends meet in a place where, despite the frequent casual purchases of tourists, two thirds of the £30 million spent by local shoppers on groceries goes though just two supermarkets (Transition Town Totnes, 2013). High Street and Fore Street are dotted with empty shops, like nearly every other main street in Britain. Some shops offer discount vouchers to reward local loyalty; others, like the Arcturus bookshop, simply plead for customers to stay, with notices warning that 'The internet is killing the high street'.

The new Luddites?

New technologies have always been a mixed blessing. In November 1811 mysterious warnings began to appear in Nottingham, signed by a General Ludd or King Ludd. Factory and workshop owners were threatened with painful consequences if they failed to remove new machinery from their premises – equipment that could be operated by unskilled and poorly paid factory hands, putting the talents and jobs of better-paid weavers at risk. Smashed apparatus and burned-out mills were the signs of a Luddite visit; across Nottinghamshire, Yorkshire and Lancashire employers faced the wrath of workers desperate to preserve their livelihoods.

The backlash from the authorities was severe. In Parliament, legislation to outlaw the protests was tabled in the form of the Destruction of Stocking Frames, etc Act 1812. The death penalty was considered an appropriate punishment for breaking a loom, or even for entering a property with the intent to cause damage. In 1813, 15 Luddites were hanged at York for the murder of mill owner William Horsfall, and it was said that more troops were employed against the Luddites in 1812 than were fighting Napoleon.

In recent times the term 'Luddite' has been a popular epithet deployed against anyone deemed to stand in the way of progress and advances in technology. Contemporary usage carries associations of backwardness and stupidity, obstinacy and wrongheadedness. Lord Wolfson, boss of the clothing chain Next, accused 'Luddite' councils of killing the high street by refusing planning permission for large new stores (Ruddick, 2013). Who in their right mind would want to keep things as they were?

At the time of the Luddite uprisings, however, some recognised that the weavers were fighting for survival. The poet Lord Byron made a rare parliamentary appearance to defend the Nottinghamshire workers: 'Nothing but absolute want could have driven a large and once honest and industrious body of the people into the commission of excesses so hazardous to themselves, their families, and the community,' he asserted. 'You may call the people a mob, but do not forget that a mob too often speaks the sentiments of the people' (cited at www.luddites200.org.uk/LordByronspeech.html).

Today many who want to preserve the unique character of our towns are considered 21st-century Luddites standing in the way of development. Nobody is burning down superstores or being transported to Australia, but the risks to local livelihoods and income, and the power of the major retailers and property owners, are real enough. Just occasionally, however, today's 'Luddites' score a small victory for the local and the independent.

One spring night in 2012 two huge posters went up in Totnes. Bearing a remarkable similarity to the publicity for Danny Boyle's film 'Trainspotting', they advertised 'Clonestopping', with the strapline: 'Choose local. Choose independent. Or choose Costa?'

Costa Coffee, Britain's fastest-expanding coffee chain, had targeted a large shop opposite the Old Bakery at the bottom of Fore Street. The landlord was a Bloomsbury-based property company, London & Western Holdings. The previous occupant, Greenlife, had gone bust. The property was designated for general retail use rather than for food and drink, so needed planning permission for Costa to move in. But Totnes already had more than 40 independent cafes, restaurants and coffee shops. What riled locals wasn't the competition – the local market is nothing if not competitive – but the erosion of the town's character and the loss of local opportunities and economic benefits.

Unlike the Luddite protests, the campaign to stop Costa started with celebration rather than sabotage. The town held a coffee festival, making the most of its diverse and independent culture. At the festival and on market days in the months to come the campaigners gathered more than 5,000 signatures opposing the conversion of the Greenlife premises into a cafe. While local people signed the petition and brewed their strategies for independence, the forces ranged against them were formidable. They included a distant landlord, one of Britain's biggest food and drink companies, and their own local authority, South Hams District Council.

The landlord's concern was to maximise the rent. Responding to a letter from local MP Sarah Wollaston, Company Secretary Christine Walters commented:

> It must be borne in mind that as the premises are large
> … the rental level is likely to exceed that affordable by a
> local trader and the premises have attracted interest from
> national traders including Costa. In our experience if a
> major company has earmarked a town in which it wants
> a presence then it will do so eventually. (quoted on 'No
> to Costa' website)

But what London & Western presented as inevitable appeared to be a deliberate decision not to engage with alternative proposals for the premises. Oxfam had wanted to use the space for a mix of retail and events, including its successful 'Oxjam' days where local musicians use its stores as performance venues. Devon Ingram, manager of Oxfam's Totnes branch, said London & Western "made it quite clear to all interested parties that they did not want local business or charities as a tenant, irrespective of the expense, time and commitment already invested." Another local resident's proposal for a cooperatively run store was similarly rebuffed.

Costa had already attracted attention for its cavalier approach to planning rules and aggressive expansion strategy. In Bristol, local MP Stephen Williams complained in a House of Commons debate about Costa's tactic of converting shops to cafes without planning permission, knowing that any process of enforcement would be time-consuming and expensive enough to deter most local authorities: '… when permission is refused by a committee of local councillors, the applicant goes ahead and opens the business because they know that an appeal will take a long time. That is a loophole that Costa has certainly exploited and it needs to be blocked' (*Hansard*, 17 January 2012, col 712).

Bristol isn't the only location on the receiving end of this approach. The 'No to Costa' campaign unearthed details of 17 other towns where the company had opened shops first and asked for planning permission afterwards.

Costa is part of Whitbread PLC, long ago a brewer and now 'the UK's leading hospitality company', running Premier Inn, Costa, and restaurants including Beefeater and Brewers Fayre. Its vision, which reads like a pastiche of corporate Newspeak, is to 'grow legendary brands by building a strong customer heartbeat and innovating to stay ahead'. It illustrates this with a diagram of a blue arrow with a red heart in the middle. On one side of the heart is 'winning teams'; in the middle is 'customer heartbeat'; and at the arrow's tip is 'profitable growth'. There is no doubt it knows about the latter, with revenues of £2.29 billion in 2013-14 and profits up 16.5 per cent to £411.8 million (Whitbread PLC, 2014).

Costa Coffee has more than 1,400 stores across the UK and 40 per cent of the nation's branded coffee shops. Whitbread's chief executive, Andy Harrison, reckons many towns could support three or four Costas. 'Most people won't walk more than 100 yards to get a coffee,' he told one newspaper. 'In large towns we could have a Costa at both ends of the high street, one in a retail park and one at the station and they could all do well' (Neate, 2011). In Purley, Surrey – a suburb of Croydon and not a large town by any stretch of the imagination – there is a Costa shop in Brighton Road, as well as concessions in a local pub, a Tesco supermarket and two petrol stations, all within half a mile of each other. Costa has a seat at the top table when it comes to government policy on high streets, too: Jason Cotta, the company's UK Retail Managing Director, is a leading light in the government's Future High Streets Forum (Quinn, 2014).

The 'No to Costa' campaign saw Costa's expansion in a less rosy light. Local shops tend to use local suppliers: signwriters, joiners, electricians, solicitors. National chains package up their contracts to maximise economies of scale, cutting out the local trader, they said.

> Unlike our small traders, Costa Coffee have a centralised facility producing and distributing their food products from Northamptonshire. They will have block contracts with cleaning and maintenance companies. So, while Costa would like to trumpet local jobs and contributions to our community, the only individuals who will truly benefit from their undeniably impressive growth are Whitbread shareholders of whom Costa is a wholly owned subsidiary. ('No to Costa' campaign, 2012)

The third force lined up against the campaigners was their own district council. While the council presented itself as an impartial decision maker, its interpretation of planning rules clashed with its members' role as local elected representatives. This was less a case of opposition to local residents as one of fear of company power: officers felt they did not have the technical grounds to refuse Costa, and that if they did so, Costa would probably win on appeal, a costly process for the local authority. The council picked the easier option – much to the displeasure of residents who packed the council chamber for the decision on 1 August 2012.

Michelle Denton, a former political strategist who became a driving force of 'No to Costa', said she was "dismayed by the way the council rolled over". She feared that the arrival of Costa would herald spiralling rents and a grim future for the town's independent retailers; London & Western were understood to have agreed a rent with Costa of £18,000 a year more than Greenlife had paid.

What happened next was unprecedented. Far from giving up, the protesters sought – and got – a meeting with Costa Managing Director Chris Rogers, facilitated by Dr Wollaston. Mr Rogers dressed down for the occasion, turning up in a fleece and jeans; the Costa campaigners, determined to look business-like, wore their smartest outfits. After hearing local concerns, Mr Rogers promised to go away and 'reflect'; and having done so, pulled out, saying the company "recognised the strength of feeling in Totnes against national brands".

Michelle Denton recalls:

> 'I walked out of the meeting with Chris Rogers thinking that's it, he didn't get it – we've come to the end of the road. Then ten days later Sarah Wollaston got the call. To have a Tory MP who walked beside us the whole way and worked with us was absolutely critical.' (interview with the author)

Writing in *The Guardian*, Totnes resident and Transition Network founder Rob Hopkins said the town had rescued the idea of choice from a narrow concept of being able to pick between competing brands:

> Surely it should be our choice if we want a high street resilient to predatory markets and remote corporations? It is the reweaving of local food webs, community-owned enterprises, a culture of entrepreneurship focused around community resilience that, in the long term,

truly offers choice, rather than the no-holds-barred dash for economic growth at all costs that is currently being forced upon us. (Hopkins, 2012)

Whether the anti-Costa campaign has given Totnes a foundation for the future is questionable. Different groups – including the town's Chamber of Commerce, the Town Council and Transition Town Totnes – all have different ambitions. There is a lot of work to be done to turn these into a shared vision. There is also some underlying resentment against incomers who are buying into the town's alternative culture or its historic character at a time when many locals cannot afford homes there.

Michelle Denton – an American herself – argues that the incomers may be the town's best hope, bringing new skills and ideas. This part of Devon has certainly had its share of radicals and visionaries, with Schumacher College and Dartington Hall nearby flying the flag for sustainability and environmental awareness, as well as the more recent Transition Network. Transition Town Totnes has joined forces with the Town Council, Totnes Development Trust and others to launch a 'local economic blueprint' (see Chapter 7). It may be that despite the local tensions, something is growing in the rich red soil here that can challenge the firepower of the retail and property industries.

The independence fighters

Far from being the knee-jerk opposition to progress of 21st-century Luddites, the campaigns to save local shops and stop the advance of 'clone' brands reflect a pride in local entrepreneurship and creativity and a sense of place that no national or multinational company has yet been able to superimpose on its target markets.

As the Totnes campaigners pointed out, there is far more to an independent trader than the person who serves you across the counter or the name on the shopfront. With their networks of local suppliers and the fine-grained relationships with neighbours that encompass both competition and collaboration, independent traders are part of the social as well as the physical and economic infrastructure of a high street.

In many towns, they are the ones who have kept places alive when chain stores have collapsed under the burden of their debts.

For some independents, running a shop has been a lifetime dream; others moved into retail by accident or through desperation, having lost jobs in industry or the public sector.

As the recession ground on after 2009, a wave of new independent retailers arrived on British high streets. But they faced challenges of access to finance, high rents, and business taxes that remained pegged to pre-recession property values. Figures from the British Independent Retailers Association reveal the fragile nature of independent retailing as well as wide geographical disparities. In the second half of 2012 a total of 7,743 independent outlets shut, while 7,704 opened. Many enterprises are marginal and short-lived. Today a new shop is more likely to be a barber or a nail salon than a florist or bookshop; 213 new hairdressers opened in 2012, while 32 independent bookshops, 45 florists and 178 clothes shops pulled down the shutters (BIRA, 2013).

In the West End area of Morecambe, Lancashire, nine out of ten shops are still independent; Lincoln's Eastgate and Glastonbury are close behind. Compare that with Telford, where nearly three quarters of outlets are chain stores, or Solihull and Runcorn, where just 29 per cent are independent. In many towns, the independents are leading the charge against the 'clone town' syndrome, celebrating local distinctiveness or seeking to carve out a niche that attracts visitors.

Ludlow in Shropshire has badged itself as a centre of 'slow food', a movement that began in Italy in 1986 as a reaction against the stress, unsociability and poor quality associated with fast food culture, epitomised by plans to open a McDonald's near Rome's famous Spanish Steps. A medieval town centred on an 11th-century castle, Ludlow has 450 listed buildings, and a three-day food festival that has been running for two decades and features a 'sausage trail' where connoisseurs of the British banger can do blind tastings. It's also the home of the Shropshire Prune Damson, giving the damson devotee everything from mulled damson wine to damson cheese, pickles and puddings.

Slow food celebrates what's 'good, clean and fair' and seeks to reconnect people with the producers and processes that bring food to the table. It applauds the local and distinctive. Five UK towns are now part of the international Cittaslow movement, which seeks to create the infrastructure needed for a successful slow food culture. Aylsham and Diss in Norfolk, Berwick-upon-Tweed, Mold in North

Wales and Perth in Scotland are all Cittaslow towns, signing up to a daunting list of 55 separate goals, ranging from well-maintained public green spaces and a register of local producers and products to easily accessible public toilets and provision of multilingual signposting and visitor information.

Cittaslow is local loyalty systematised and structured to a degree some might find intimidating. At the other end of the scale are 'just do it' approaches, such as the shops that offer their own loyalty discounts and spontaneous resident-led campaigns. In between is a plethora of home-grown initiatives with a common theme of supporting independent traders and preserving local character.

In Frome, Somerset, the 'Keep Frome Local' campaign group started in response to development plans that threatened to foist a large supermarket on a town that prided itself on its individual distinctiveness. An 'Independence Day' event celebrated local talent and debated the power and influence of supermarket chains. In Sherborne, Dorset, the former 'Blue Peter' children's show presenter Valerie Singleton joined a crowd of placard-bearing demonstrators protesting against plans for a 28,000 square foot Tesco. Ten thousand people signed a petition against the proposals.

In Northumberland and Gateshead, residents objected to Tesco's plans to convert two pubs – the Victoria and Albert in Seaton Delaval and the Honeysuckle Arms in Gateshead – into Tesco Express convenience stores. One Gateshead trader, Shami Ghafoor, told the local paper there was no need for another Tesco as there were six supermarkets within a two-mile radius. The council's planning director explained that the authority couldn't consider the impact on existing businesses when deciding whether or not to approve the change (Davies, 2012).

Alongside the many campaigns that arise when plans for another giant superstore are revealed, there are also dozens of positive celebrations of local life. In Wells-next-the-sea in Norfolk, Wells Maltings Trust coordinated a three-day pirate festival, highlighting the town's history and providing entertainment at the same time. More than 5,000 people visited Wells, taking part in a pirate market, ghost walks, theatre performances and a treasure trail.

In Wantage, Oxfordshire, the Wantage Means Business forum brought together residents, the Town Council and businesses to look at ways of reviving the town centre, from a loyalty card for independent retailers to a series of Sunday events and free short-term car parking. The proportion of empty shops halved from one fifth in 2008 to one tenth in 2012 (Action for Market Towns, nd, a). In Wilmslow, Cheshire, an artisan market once a month provides an opportunity for artists and traders to display locally made products, offering an attraction that nearby out-of-town shopping centres can't match. The market provides a platform for the town's charities and voluntary organisations, musicians and performers, and nearly tripled in size in just over a year. The Wilmslow branch of Barclays Bank now opens on a Saturday as a result, and the number of vacant shops has fallen (Action for Market Towns, nd, b). In Penrith, Cumbria, a local lottery raises funds for community organisations and events that have been hit by cuts in council funding.

The buzz of activity in the UK is mirrored on the other side of the Atlantic, where campaigns to support local businesses have achieved a national profile in the US through the Business Alliance for Local Living Economies (BALLE). BALLE advocates 'thinking local' rather than just shopping locally, encouraging supporters to see themselves as stewards of their hometowns rather than simply as shoppers.

Among the more successful campaigns supported by BALLE is 'Shift Your Shopping', backed by more than 160 organisations across the US and Canada. 'Shift Your Shopping' focuses on the holiday period between Thanksgiving and New Year (November 1 to December 31), encouraging people to buy gifts and to celebrate the holidays in ways that support local businesses. It cites surveys suggesting that areas with such campaigns saw revenues rise by 7.2 per cent in 2011, compared with an increase of 2.6 per cent in other localities (ILSR, 2012).

When the fight fails

Nearly 300 miles from the coffee republic of Totnes, another high street slopes uphill. Few visit Yorkshire Street in Rochdale for its independent shops, although a handful of them struggle on. This is the street where even McDonald's pulled out after 28 years of fries and happy meals. The Cash Store, Cheque Centre, H&T Pawnbrokers, Albemarle Bond, Cash Converters, Simply Cash and Cash Generator tell the story of a town where the little that people have is handed over to help families survive from one week to the next.

A profusion of charity shops illustrates a local economy where frugal living isn't a lifestyle choice but a necessity. You can buy your furniture and electrical appliances from one of the two British Heart Foundation shops; for more day-to-day needs such as clothes or little extras there's Barnardo's, the YMCA Shop, Cancer Research UK, Scope, Mind, or the Rochdale and District branch of the RSPCA. In an environment like this, getting any retailer to stay at all is a challenge. Finding a future for independent traders can be even more daunting.

Paul Turner-Mitchell is one of Rochdale's most outspoken businesspeople, writing columns in the specialist press and keeping central and local government in the spotlight in a drive to expose their failure to stand up for independent retailers. In 2007 he and his wife Kelly set up their 25 Ten boutique in the town centre, specialising in young fashion – and a year later the bottom began to fall out of his business. He recalls:

'Young girls at that time were being thrown credit at them left right and centre as soon as they turned 18. They were coming in and regularly spending £100 a week on a dress. It's not my job as a retailer to say that's morally wrong, you satisfy demand and the demand was there at the time, and the banks effectively created that demand, by so much credit being available to such young people. And obviously in terms of young fashion in particular, those lines of credit for the very young just dried up overnight. So from going to spend £100 every week or probably upwards on a dress, they had to change the way in which they spent their money ... that is a big, big difference when that is your key market.

'And in 2009, early 2010, we had this realisation that we were on a secondary location, a relatively small floorspace, 650 square foot, and that secondary locations were no longer getting the passing trade they used to. So a building came up on quite a prime location on the high street, the landlord had invested quite a considerable amount of money into it, and we thought the economic conditions were right to take advantage of it. We did a partnership with the local council to sublet the first floor to provide a cafe and four start-up incubator hubs. The hope was they would bring their products to market, test them on a prime location at a low affordable rent, and hopefully if they could make it pay they could fly the nest, so to speak, and take up an empty shop in the town centre.' (interview with the author)

On the face of it, this was a creative solution both for Paul Turner-Mitchell's business and for Yorkshire Street. An independent retailer was getting a prime site; new uses were being created within an unused building; there were opportunities to give new businesses a flying start. Making it happen was a nightmare. It took well over a year for the cafe to open and even longer to fill the incubator units. By contrast, once the lease had been agreed, 25 Ten took three weeks to move in.

As councils have lost government funding they have grown more risk-averse, Paul Turner-Mitchell believes – and Rochdale has lost more than most, with the deepest cuts per head of population in Greater Manchester. The result has been to intensify the problems:

'The wheels of local and central government turn so slowly, yet the wheels of private business turn so quickly that you can have a business fail in the space of a bad trading week. I think local authorities just don't get private business, they just don't understand it.'

While the council was working on bigger long-term plans (see Chapter 7), Rochdale town centre was deteriorating. In the end, he, too, decided to take his business elsewhere. Rochdale has little left to offer, he said.

'There aren't many places to get something to eat. So the hospitality offer's poor. The leisure offer's poor. There's nothing for families. The retail offer's depleting all the time. You've got to have a reason for people to go into towns. If there's nothing there you're not going to go, are you? And all I see is more decline, more depletion.'

In July 2013 Mr Turner-Mitchell moved his shop to Littleborough, an enclave of affluence up the road towards the Pennines. His partner, Kelly, told *Rochdale Online*: 'Small villages seem to be the best places for independent businesses these days. There just wasn't anything left in Rochdale town centre' (Westlake, 2013).

The struggle to keep an independent heart in a town can often feel like a David and Goliath battle without the happy ending. Campaigns burst into life, burn brightly for a few months, and then sputter and die in the face of the seemingly inevitable. Along the Suffolk coast the towns of Aldeburgh and Southwold, and Saxmundham a few miles inland, have all had to admit defeat in their efforts to stop Tesco's expansion.

In many places, too, anything can seem better than more boarded-up shops or pawnbrokers. A Costa or Tesco might feel like a lifeline on a dying high street, even if their effect is to draw what little local trade there is away from independent stores. The battle can seem unequal and not worth fighting.

There are times, too, when attempts to create a distinctive local identity can themselves feel alien and out of place. In June 2003 Blaenavon, a former coal and steel town in the South Wales Valleys nicknamed 'plywood city' after the demise of its industries, unveiled itself as an unlikely 'book town'. What entrepreneur Richard Booth had achieved in leafy Hay on Wye, his acolyte James Hanna believed could be done in a town scarred by poverty and unemployment.

Big ideas weren't new to Blaenavon. Thirty years ago the Big Pit became the national coal museum of Wales, part of a Unesco World Heritage Site nominated because of its industrial history. Around 160,000 visitors a year descend the Big Pit's shaft to explore its tunnels and learn about the life of a coal miner, but few give the town more than a passing glance. Buildings have been given a facelift using regeneration funds and Broad Street, the main thoroughfare, has been restored as a Victorian-style shopping street. A council leaflet in 2009 tellingly quoted local greengrocer Janet George: 'It's lovely to see the town now – it looks beautiful, it's really uplifting. All we need is the trade.'

Booktown was an attempt to bring the trade back. Ten bookshops opened in Blaenavon in 2003 as entrepreneurs rode a wave of media interest. But by March 2006 it was a different story, with only two remaining, and James Hanna had vanished. Today only Browning

Books, a children's bookshop, remains; Broadleaf Books, the other store still open in 2006, has moved to more prosperous Abergavenny.

In Blaenavon you can buy a terraced house for less than £50,000. One fifth of the working-age population of the wider Torfaen area have no educational qualifications and unemployment is higher than the Welsh average. James Hanna was last heard of back in his native US, where he was given a 60-year prison sentence for child pornography offences.

Blaenavon needs more than a bold and bookish experiment to bring life back to Broad Street. Like many other towns, its future depends on rebuilding the web of local commercial, social and civic relationships that make a place viable.

From failing better to moving mountains

Dan Thompson, founder of the Empty Shops Network, likes to quote the playwright Samuel Beckett: 'No matter. Try again. Fail again. Fail better.' Experiments do fail. It's the attempt that matters.

One of Thompson's many projects was Retail Ready People, a training programme led by the youth volunteering charity vInspired and the Retail Trust charity. Young volunteers were given the chance to work in teams learning the skills needed to open a successful pop-up shop, from design and marketing to display and customer service. In Brighton, artists produced screen-printed t-shirts and bags at a pop-up shop called Make-Away; in Enfield, North London, volunteers kitted out a shell unit on a new retail development and used it to sell handmade products.

The scheme then expanded to Leeds and Rochdale, taking on a new wave of 30 volunteers keen to learn business skills. Some of them may emerge as the independent entrepreneurs of the future, lauded by politicians as paragons of an enterprise culture, after learning their trade on a pop-up photographic studio in Rochdale or a 'social space' for creative artists in Leeds. Many will move on to other things, but will have imbibed essential skills of teamwork, communication and confidence. Most will probably look at their towns in a different light as a result of their training.

Britain today is full of experiments to celebrate and support the local and independent. In Chatsworth Road, Hackney, traders and residents got together to form an association to promote a long suburban shopping street as 'a vibrant high street, a safe and enjoyable public space, and a community hub.'

They started with a Sunday market in the summer of 2011. They went on to conduct in-depth surveys with local people, including traders and community representatives, to find out what kind of place they wanted. They are now seeking to create a neighbourhood plan for the area, setting a standard for its use and development rather than reacting – as many campaigns do, usually too late in the day – to the encroachment of national businesses or property developers. Their vision is of a street that is sociable, diverse, accessible, independent and sustainable, one that by definition cannot be delivered by the big players in retail and property.

Chatsworth Road has been described as 'the front line of gentrification' in London's ever-shifting territorial struggles between the haves and have-nots. But the association's aspiration is to be inclusive, 'a place where people of all ages, incomes and creeds live and work side by side, where we are exposed to different cultures, tastes and beliefs to our own but still feel at home' (Chatsworth Road Traders and Residents Association, nd).

A few miles away in Crouch End, there's another experiment to support independent traders. Clare Richmond, a marketing consultant, was distressed by the number of empty shops in her North London high street when she returned from working in the US in 2007. With two colleagues she developed a 'brand identity' for the town, bringing retailers and community organisations together under a common banner and creating an online guide to local shops, events and services. Clare says the approach is to see the town centre 'like an interesting department store, under which all businesses and local organisations can individually operate but which presents one easy access point to customers' (The Crouch End Project, see www. thecrouchendproject.co.uk).

Across Britain, and internationally, towns are experimenting. Some of the experiments, like the Crouch End Project, seek to take the big retailers on at their own game, presenting the high street almost as a kind of open-air mall with a distinct corporate identity. Others prefer quirkier, more anarchic approaches. What is striking is the sheer volume of activity, and the way it continues to tap into a rich vein of local pride and creativity.

As the experiments continue some important themes are emerging. One is the power of a simple idea, an idea like 'Totally Locally', for example.

Totally Locally is "more than a shop local campaign", says founder Chris Sands. "It's about working together to lift your whole town." Since 2009 Chris and his colleague Nigel Goddard, aided by a host of friends and supporters, have been preaching the Totally Locally gospel. The simple idea is that every adult should spend £5 in a nearby independent shop rather than online or at a supermarket. If every adult in Calderdale, West Yorkshire, did so, it would pump an extra £41 million into the local economy, Chris reckons.

Wherever Totally Locally goes, the £5 message is the line that sells it to traders and residents. It's supported by a set of pre-designed marketing materials than any town can adopt. The materials are distinctive and eye-catching, and they're free for any town to use as long as they respect copyright. Teams of volunteers from Christchurch in Dorset to Lanark in Scotland are spreading the Totally Locally love. It's not just a UK phenomenon. There's a Totally Locally campaign in Eudunda, a small town in South Australia, and one in Waiheke Island in Auckland, New Zealand.

What Chris Sands has noticed is what economists call the local multiplier: money spent locally supports local jobs and businesses. One of the sparks that started it was a holiday on the Greek island of Kalymnos.

'There was no supermarket and we stayed there for two weeks. We came back and had to pick up some cat food, I think it was. I walked into Asda and for the first time in my life I had a panic attack. The loudness, the brashness. And I said to my wife, we need to find another way to shop here. Two weeks later we discovered Todmorden market and we started using that and really enjoyed it.

'If you did a like for like test quality wise, Todmorden was way cheaper. Then we started to get to know people. I always remember there was a butcher, Paul Stansfield, and we'd been away and said to him, you can't get goat, can you, because we can't get goat anywhere. He said just a minute, and he picked the phone up and said, Mary, when are you killing those goats for me? It was that connection. Rather than going and picking something up and throwing it in the trolley – it was that connection, you're connecting through one other person.'(interview with the author)

The Totally Locally message is all about helping others renew and sustain those connections. The idea of spending £5 locally just caught people's imagination, Chris said.

'It was almost like, it's that easy to shop locally and to support where I live, and I can do that. And we got loads of people saying I've decided to buy my sandwiches before I get on the train rather than when I get off the train. It's just little things like that. And that was the simplicity of it. But what happened from there was it started to change people's thinking.'

Far from mounting a campaign to boycott supermarkets or shopping centres, Chris Sands argues that they can work together – but there needs to be choice and diversity. Spending money locally helps to make sure that the choice is always there and that change can happen through positive actions. One of the most popular ideas is the 'Fiverfest', a day or weekend when everyone makes a point of supporting local traders. People understand that they can do simple things that make a difference.

At the root of Totally Locally is a belief that building relationships and trust is at the heart of improving places. You do business together because you live together. Commerce and community become yin and yang. As Chris Sands put it: "I do believe that if you can get the right set of people together with the right attitude you can just move mountains. It doesn't take money, it just takes a shift of attitude."

From independence to interdependence

Building local relationships and celebrating local character go hand in hand. In the heart of Perthshire, Scotland, Aberfeldy is becoming one of Scotland's first Fairtrade towns, emphasising better ways of doing business, both globally and locally. The town, supported by the Scottish Government, has raised money to restore the art deco

Birks Cinema, which now offers full digital facilities including live streaming from the Met Opera and Bolshoi Ballet. Too far from large centres of population to be of much interest to national retailers, the town is creating a culture of independent commerce, from fashion stores to a converted water mill hosting a bookshop and coffee shop.

Malcolm Fraser, the architect who chaired the Scottish Government's town centres review in 2012-13, reels off a list of towns that give him reasons to be cheerful:

> 'Callender has some very entrepreneurial people offering people going up to the Highlands some great cooking and locally sourced this and that.... North Berwick's just a nice place to live, the high street's great, it's bustling with all sorts of local stuff. Peebles is far enough away from Edinburgh for it to feel that it still centres an agricultural community, and that will always be important. Then there are other places that have worked hard like West Kilbride and its craft town, community groups around Govanhill, what people are doing with energy at Fintry, they've got a windmill and are using the money that comes off that well.' (interview with the author)

At the other end of Britain, the mayor of Bristol, George Ferguson, cites similar reasons for optimism. He compares his city's independent entrepreneurs with the merchant adventurers of the past:

> 'I see it happening all over the place, maybe simply coming out of an economic situation where they can't find the job they want, and a desire to change their lifestyle.... You take Mark's Bakery [in Bedminster] – a wonderful example of a guy who was in the computer industry, whose wife gave him a baking course for his birthday, and he fell so much in love with the craft of baking that he decided to throw in his computing career and start a bakery. He's now started a cafe in what was an old garage, and I come across lots of little stories like that around the city. It will be individual adventurers like that who really give me hope that the high street will

become more interesting again, and it will be the thing that will define Bristol too, more than any investment from national companies can do.' (interview with the author)

Not everywhere works like Aberfeldy or Bedminster, Crouch End or Todmorden. But they are all sufficiently different and distinctive to show the advantages of doing business on a human scale. What is striking is that while large firms tend to focus on their corporate policies and branding, and view their customers as a segmented mass of data, it is the smaller and independent traders who often have a wider view of place and society. They operate in networks rather than bilateral dealings, because they have to: their success depends on a web of relationships, commercial and social, with those around them. Things happen because they can tap into those relationships at the right place and time; and frustration builds when relationships are replaced with people who hide behind the fortifications of organisational culture and policies, whether it's the local council, the landlord or the large retailer.

A network where large numbers of members are interlinked is one where knowledge, information and calls to action travel rapidly. Bottlenecks occur when individuals or organisations act as 'gatekeepers' of information between one set of members and another. An effective network – a town or community – works through influence rather than control (Mackie, 2011).

Back in Totnes, Frances Northrop pithily sums up the power of networks. As someone who cut her teeth working in bookies' shops in Manchester and now works for Transition Town Totnes, she's seen both sides of the high street. "There are two ways of giving people hope," she says. "The false hope of the lottery and betting shops and gambling or the hope of getting people together" (interview with the author).

Getting people together can involve setting up a cooking class on a housing estate or a coffee festival in the market, campaigning and celebrating. But it also includes bringing conflicts and differences to the surface and working through them. Nobody expected Costa to climb down in Totnes, and Frances is convinced nothing would have changed without the meeting between Chris Rogers and local campaigners. "Once you get people face to face things happen," she insists.

For independent retailers, civic activists and experimenters today, the real issue is not simply to preserve a few remnants of what's distinctive and local in the face of the relentless expansion of commercial behemoths. It is to move from independence to interdependence, recreating the kind of community, commercial, cultural and civic networks that not only bring a place to life, but also keep it alive, creating what Frances Northrop calls the 'magic' of human interaction.

Independent traders won't save the high street. Nor will hosts of people spending £5 or £10 at a time, although it will certainly help. But if we can activate the networks they are part of, the impossible can become possible. The rest of this book explores how this can start to happen. It examines how business can be done better, how revitalised public services can turn high streets into places of possibility, how creative uses of in-between spaces can bring new life into our towns, and how town centres can once again become good places to live in. It explains why all of this requires a new look at property ownership, access to finance, and a philosophy of common interest and shared value.

Part Two

Tomorrow

6

Raise a glass to the new economy

Sitting in the stripped-out hollow of an old-fashioned department store in Ripon, Anthony Blackburn was at his wits' end. Philip Hall, the store he had taken over in the North Yorkshire town seven years earlier, had failed after 62 years of trading, with debts of more than £400,000.

> 'You think about its former glory in the sixties and seventies, and I was sat there in the shell of a building thinking, it's failed, what can I do? We had made 13 people redundant. In a local community that's a big story as well, so every time you walk onto the high

street someone's looking at you thinking, "That's the guy whose business has failed."

'It put my marriage under a lot of pressure, not least because I'd invested quite a lot of personal money. We ended up having to sell our house, so we were in a very, very low position. You do consider whether or not you can carry on because you feel you've let so many people down.' (interview with the author)

The story of those dark days of mid-2012 will be familiar to many retailers whose businesses have gone belly-up in recent years. It is one that will be repeated, too, as others collapse under the weight of historic debts and business models that no longer work.

But this was the beginning of Anthony Blackburn's journey, not the end. New stories are emerging of business models that are linking creators and consumers, and online and face-to-face businesses, in innovative and collaborative ways. From local brewers to artisan cheese makers, from car sharing to renting out spare rooms to travellers, these new forms of enterprise are spreading below the radar and pointing towards a society where shared value matters as much as individual gain.

Anthony's story began in a desperate place. The traditional department store, selling clothing, household goods and gifts, was no longer wanted. He had no cash, and hardly any options.

'The business was going into liquidation and at that stage I didn't really know what I was going to do. The banks had basically said they were going to try and get their charge on the property to sell my property. The only asset I had left was a business which was worth nothing. I thought to myself I cannot, I cannot let the banks get the property, I've got to try and keep hold of it. But what I had to try and do was demonstrate that we could repay the outstanding debt to the bank through using this property to generate income.

'I sat there one day and thought, right, if I was a retailer starting out now, what would be my first step onto the high street? What would happen if I looked at this big space, 5,000 square foot, and broke it down into small spaces and offered them up on flexible terms to local businesses? And I just put a little A4 poster in the window with my telephone number on, and people started to ring me.'

Instead of trying to recoup his losses by letting the building to a single tenant, he opened it up to a host of local producers. There was no shortage of them: craftspeople, artists, food makers, fashion designers, a woman who wanted to open a vintage tea salon, even a man selling carnivorous plants. They were people who wouldn't fit within a traditional market and who couldn't afford to kit out a shop of their own. Many were running small online enterprises from their homes, making a few extra pounds rather than a living. Others were selling at craft fairs and jewellery parties. Some had ideas but nowhere to try them out. None could have borne the cost of trading in a traditional high street shop.

Anthony Blackburn started interviewing prospective tenants to decide who could go into his new 'Handpicked Hall'. The deal was that they would commit to a certain number of days a week and pay only for the space they needed: no big cash deposits, no long-term commitment and no pages of small print detailing endless service charges and penalty clauses. Suddenly 20 businesses had a route to market that did not exist before. Handpicked Hall opened in October 2012, and within weeks the building was four fifths full. When it opened only a quarter of the traders were there every day. Now three quarters of them are, and Handpicked Hall brings in three times as much in rental payments from individual traders as it would have done had the building been let as a whole.

Connections are at the heart of what makes Handpicked Hall work, Anthony says.

> 'It's being able to have that one-to-one contact, up close and personal, with customers. That's our experience – I don't care what people say, people like to touch and feel and find out a little bit about the person behind the product. And that's the beauty of Handpicked Hall, because you've got every person in the business talking passionately about what they do, and they encourage people to find out more about what they do.'

Within six months Anthony had gone into partnership with a property company, buying a former Co-op store in Skipton and turning it into a second branch. By summer 2013 he was opening a third Handpicked Hall in the Grand Arcade in the centre of Leeds. Unlike chain stores, each one is different, showcasing the work of creative entrepreneurs within the locality. The fact that few if any of them could have run a business on a typical high street speaks volumes about the way genuine value has been squeezed out of our towns through landowners', corporations' and local authorities' obsession with maximising financial returns.

The next stage for the Skipton store is to combine retail space with workshop and learning areas, where craftspeople can make their products and others can learn creative skills. Anthony imagines wood turners, potters, artists, jewellers, rag ruggers, and chocolatiers, with small manufacturing spaces on the upper floors and selling to the public on the ground floor, aided and amplified through social media. It's a bit like a 21st-century adaptation of Birmingham's Jewellery Quarter or the 'little mesters' workshops of 19th-century Sheffield.

There's talk of pulling in 'business angel' investors who are looking for new products to bring to market. "We could be getting three or four hundred brand new products from entrepreneurs, starting in Handpicked Hall and then becoming global products, and that to me is quite exciting," Anthony enthuses. Suddenly there's a model that brings together investment, property, making and selling – all in a local high street.

That may be some way off. In the meantime there are individual stories that spur Anthony Blackburn on.

> 'I look at one lady in particular, she'd done 31 years as a night manager in a care home. She started with me with her own little jewellery business, just two days a week on her days off. She's now gone full time in Ripon, given up that job, the mortgage is paid off on the house and she's become a full time trader in Ripon. She's so much in love with life again.'

Swimming against the tide

In a sparsely furnished upstairs room at Sheffield's University Arms, a dozen or so people, mostly men of a certain age, have gathered to hear nuggets of wisdom from the acknowledged guru of British beer. Roger Protz is the author of the annual *Good Beer Guide* and a founding father of Camra, the Campaign for Real Ale. Waistcoated and grizzled, he wears his expertise lightly.

The event is part beer tasting, part celebration of an astonishingly diverse and lively industry of small-scale craft beer producers. First up on the night is a beer called Bengal Tiger, a traditional India Pale Ale from the Concertina Band Club in Mexborough, the last working men's club in England still to have its own brewery. Next is Cavendish, a 'golden ale' from Welbeck Abbey, near Worksop in Nottinghamshire. It's followed by Pale Rider from Kelham Island Brewery in Sheffield. Roger Protz describes how Dave Wickett, who founded the brewery at the Fat Cat pub, did so against a backdrop of the closure of six large breweries in the city, victims of the decline of the steel industry and the loss of the clubs and pubs where workers would down their pints at the end of a shift. In the post-industrial wasteland of 1980s Sheffield, opening a brewery was an act of faith. Dave Wickett used to say he ran the biggest commercial brewery in the city. That was because all the others had shut.

We move on to Abbeydale's Absolution; Jaipur, brewed by Thornbridge Brewery in Derbyshire; and Gorlovka, a rich chocolaty stout from the Acorn Brewery in Barnsley, named after the town's twin city in the Ukraine. Not one of these breweries was in business 20 years ago. Abbeydale opened in 1996, Acorn in 2003, and Thornbridge in 2005. In 2012 a total of 158 new micro-breweries opened in the UK. There are now 651 small breweries across the country, supporting more than 5,000 jobs. For every job in brewing, according to Brewers of Europe, another 21 jobs are kept going: one in agriculture, one in distribution, one in retail and 18 in pubs (Ernst & Young, 2011). Across Britain you can now find more than 3,200 kinds of real ale, with another 5,000 'seasonal beers' such as winter ales – enough to challenge even Roger Protz's imbibing capacity.

'This urge to brew is an urge to be local,' says the Society of Independent Brewers:

It may be a pub, creating the most local point of
difference in its portfolio; it may be a standalone business,
seeking to build a local reputation by supplying within
a manageable radius; it may nurture dreams of growing
that reputation beyond tight boundaries while letting
no-one doubt its local roots. What it most definitely
is, is a reflection of a spirit of enterprise that is now a
memory for much of British manufacturing but lives on
in our very own local beer. (SIBA, 2013, p 7)

Sheffield is a prime example. The city that once mass-produced steel
fuelled its workers with mass-produced beer from Wards, Bass or
Whitbread. The big breweries' works are now home to civil servants'
offices and young professionals' apartments, but there are half a dozen
new breweries titillating topers' tastebuds, from Bradfield on the edge
of the Peak District to Abbeydale in the south of the city, Kelham
Island Brewery near the centre of town, and the Sheffield Brewery
Company in the factory that used to produce Blanco polish, the
scourge of Army squaddies in years gone by.

The resurgence of Britain's independent brewers points towards
the potential resurgence of our high streets. Small-scale brewing links
production, consumption and place in a way that used to happen
everywhere but has now become a rarity. More than that, it celebrates
craft and skill: you don't have to be an aficionado to appreciate the
difference between a pint of Harvey's Mild in Lewes, East Sussex, or
Titanic Brewery's Anchor in Stoke-on-Trent, and the bog-standard
glass of Guinness or Carling you'll find in any bar around the world.

It's traditional to think of pubs as places of consumption. The
growth of micro-brewing has shown us that pubs can be places of
production too.

The Ivy House in Nunhead, South London, is the kind of pub
that helps to give a place its character. Thirty-five years ago, then
known as the Newlands Tavern, it was at the heart of the capital's
emerging punk movement, featuring bands such as Joe Strummer's
101ers, Ian Dury's Kilburn and the High Roads, and singers like
Elvis Costello. Graham Parker, one of the musicians who played
there, recalls turning up to rehearse with a new backing band who
helped themselves to beer through the afternoon while setting up
for the night's gig: 'We worked in a back room when the pub was

closed after lunch, and the creaking, wooden stage of that venerable London venue, just a few feet away, started to look like something that would soon be within my reach, an idea hard to imagine mere months before' (Parker, 2009).

That's a description of creative production. Today the Ivy House is one of a growing wave of pubs that are owned or being taken over by local communities. In 2013 it became the first pub in London to be listed as a 'community asset' under the Localism Act, giving locals a breathing space to raise funds to take it over and stop it being converted into flats. The pub's users are becoming the pub's owners.

Pubs around the UK are closing at the rate of around 16 a week, according to Camra. Many are owned by large pub chains and are being sold for housing or turned into convenience stores by the big supermarkets. But alongside this wave of closures, there is growing interest in preserving pubs as neighbourhood hubs.

It takes a huge effort to re-open a pub as a community resource, and it only happens where people not only value their local pub, but are prepared to put time and money into taking it over. Nevertheless, there are already more than a dozen community-owned pubs in England and Wales, from the Old Crown in the tiny Lake District village of Hesket Newmarket to the Star Inn in Salford, the first of the new wave of cooperatively owned pubs to open in an urban neighbourhood. The Bell Inn in Bath raised £778,000 to become a cooperatively owned pub by selling shares to local people.

Witnessing the proliferation of small and independent brewers and the resurgence of pubs like the Ivy House, one might imagine Britain is surfing the wave of a beer renaissance. The reality is that two things are happening at once. On the one hand, the relentless concentration of economic activity continues apace, with pub companies and brewers squeezing the last drops of profit from pubs while supermarkets turn hostelries into convenience stores and undermine those that remain by selling cheap beer and wine. On the other hand, a proliferation of craft brewers and the revival of pubs that provide important community venues is helping to build a new economy that values craftsmanship and cooperation.

In the context of the 'old economy' of concentrated ownership, standardised products and places that look increasingly alike, these new producers and consumers may be swimming against the tide. But against all the odds, they are making headway. It's time to raise a glass to the new economy, because it's the best hope for our high streets.

The creative spirit of cheese

"How can you govern a country which has two hundred and forty-six varieties of cheese?" the French President Charles de Gaulle famously remarked. For presidents of nations or corporations, diversity is frustrating. It looks like the opposite of simplicity and efficiency. Difference, it seems, is ungovernable, but that's not because it lacks governance: the consistency and quality of a Reblochon or Cantal cheese is not the result of a free-for-all, but of a pact between producers and consumers to value provenance and artisanship above cheapness and standardisation.

British cheese, like British beer, is emerging from the shadows as buyers seek products that are well made and locally produced. Often they only exist at all because people are prepared to fight for their livelihoods and authentic local products.

Real Yorkshire Wensleydale is made at Hawes, in the heart of the Yorkshire Dales. But it was very nearly made in Lancashire, a slap in the face for Yorkshire folk and foodies alike. There's nothing wrong with Lancashire cheese, but Wensleydale it isn't. Real Wensleydale draws its particular blend of sharpness and sweetness from the grasses that grow on the limestone hillsides above the River Ure. The creamery at Hawes sources all its milk from farms within the valley, ensuring the cheese keeps its unique flavour, giving suppliers a guaranteed market and building its trade on a series of strong local relationships rather than simply on price competitiveness.

But it wasn't always that way. Wensleydale cheese has been farm-produced for well over 850 years, but only manufactured on a commercial scale since 1897. In 1935 local businessman Kit Calvert, with the help of nearby farmers, raised enough money to save the dairy from closure after the 1930s Depression, building the business up before selling it in 1966 to the Milk Marketing Board.

In 1992 Dairy Crest, which had taken over the creamery, decided it was no longer economic and closed it down, with the loss of 59 jobs. That may not compare in scale with the actions of global food giant Kraft in taking over chocolate manufacturer Cadbury in 2010, but there's a similarity of approach – a view that business owes little to the places that create it and enable it to flourish, and that agility and efficiency count for much more than a social contract between an employer and the host community.

The Wensleydale Creamery was reopened after four former managers and a local businessman completed a management buy-out. It had to begin again on a small scale, taking on 11 former workers. Now there are more than 200 staff, and the creamery is helping to boost the economy of a vulnerable area. It is doing so in a place and through an approach that breaks the rules of easy transport connections, access to services and cheap production.

Like Britain's small, locally distinctive breweries, the Wensleydale Creamery shows how grounded, responsible businesses can help to refashion a locality's economy and revive its pride. Many of the new cheese makers are tiny, artisan operations, from Pextenement in Todmorden to Ticklemore Dairy in Totnes. Some, like the Wensleydale Creamery, have become significant employers in their areas. All are doing their bit to preserve a joyous ungovernability in the face of a dispiriting homogenisation of places and products.

This reconnection of production with consumption, at a time when the major supermarkets continue to centralise distribution and offer uniform products and services nationwide, is a sign of an emerging new economy. It isn't just a matter of local crafts, beer and cheese: the rapid rise of farmers' markets in the last decade underlines the growing interest in indigenous food. There are now more than 20 farmers' markets in London alone. After the horsemeat scandal of early 2013, there was a notable increase in the proportion of people wanting locally sourced fare. A survey by pollsters Mintel found that 74 per cent of the public wanted retailers to support British farmers and growers, up from 68 per cent the previous December, while the proportion citing local origin as the most important issue when buying food rose from 17 to 21 per cent (FARMA, 2013).

Whether what is being produced is a physical product or a cultural artefact, there is a burgeoning of creativity that is starting to reinvigorate many high streets. The advent of 3D printing allows small-scale, highly localised manufacturing to be done in homes and studios; the University of Exeter even produced its own Easter eggs from a 3D printer. Much of this activity is temporary, taking over empty spaces and reimagining them in ways that can sow the seeds of change.

Sometimes the temporary sticks. Jelly, an arts charity in Reading, started in 1993 in a disused shop that was scheduled for demolition. Twenty years on it's still going strong, moving into vacant buildings as opportunities arise, and has become an integral part of the town's culture. Producers, punters and places are coming together, and as they do so, local identity is flickering back to life.

Peer-to-peer business

Sitting over your locally brewed ale with a hunk of artisan cheese, you might find some of the new lingo of economic activity a bit baffling. A clutch of phrases has entered the lexicon: collaborative consumption, the peer-to-peer economy, the sharing economy, the circular economy. Are these just buzzwords or the beginning of something new?

While the immediate driving forces might be issues of quality and local identity, global factors are also driving the trends towards sharing and collaboration. The world's biggest businesses are waking up to the fact that resources will become more constrained as the world's population rises, and a mushrooming middle class demands the type of lifestyle that has hitherto been enjoyed mainly in Western Europe and North America.

A typical citizen in a developed nation will buy 800kg of food and drink a year and 20kg of new clothes and shoes, along with 120kg of packaging. A 'linear' model of consumption, where raw materials are extracted, manufactured products are created and then they are dumped when they're no longer required, cannot meet the growing demand for consumer goods. Around 80 per cent of these materials currently end up in landfill, incinerators or wastewater. But the UK will run out of landfill space by 2018 at current rates, while Beijing only has four more years of landfill space left. And landfill itself creates greenhouse gases that increase the impact of climate change (Ellen MacArthur Foundation, 2013). Yet, as the Institution of Mechanical Engineers has found, supermarket buying practices mean that around one third of British vegetable crops are wasted for purely cosmetic reasons (IME, 2013).

So ways need to be found to reduce resource consumption at the beginning of the process, extend product life in the middle, and re-use every possible element at the end. Simple processes such as recycling spent brewers' grain as animal feed rather than sending it to landfill can create employment and extend the life of a natural resource. Food waste can be used to put nutrients back in the soil through anaerobic digestion. Unwanted clothes can be customised and re-used as 'vintage' wear, given to charity shops or made into new products.

Paul Polman, chief executive officer of Unilever, is just one of the business leaders who is publicly acknowledging the new reality of constrained resources:

> It is evident that an economy that extracts resources at increasing rates without consideration for the environment in which it operates, without consideration for our natural planetary boundaries, cannot continue indefinitely. In a world of soon to be 9 billion consumers who are actively buying manufactured goods, this approach will hamper companies and undermine economies. We need a new way of doing business.
> (quoted in Ellen MacArthur Foundation, 2013, p 1)

These new ways of doing business will happen either because companies and consumers choose to change, or because change overtakes them, forcing up prices to unaffordable levels. They will have an impact on our high streets because the goods that tend to be sold there – the stuff the trade describes as 'fast-moving consumer goods' – account for 35 per cent of the materials used in our economy and three quarters of all municipal waste.

The idea that it is always possible to produce more in order to satisfy expanding demand is being tested to destruction. Despite the genetic modification of seeds, the increasing grain yields seen over the second half of the 20th century have slowed to well below the increase in the world's population. World grain reserves have fallen by one third in the last decade. Water shortages are causing rising tensions between agricultural producers who need water to grow their crops, and city leaders who are demanding increased supplies to service water-intensive urban lifestyles (Brown, 2012).

So the 'circular economy', where products are designed for re-use and recycling, is not just a fad but also an environmental imperative. On the high street it could make a difference to the products we see in our stores, but it could also support new forms of production that seek to reduce transport and manufacturing costs and highlight the value of direct links between producers and users.

If the circular economy is being driven by pressures on global resources, the 'sharing' or 'peer-to-peer' economy is being fuelled much closer to home. Falling real-terms incomes and job insecurity are forcing individuals and households to examine how to make their money go further. People are waking up to the realisation that the dream of ownership is not all it seems: it can be a hugely expensive way of getting the benefit of a product. Access is what matters.

The average car, for example, sits idle for between 20 and 23 hours a day. For the privilege of having it available you'll pay several thousand pounds in capital or borrowing; several hundred a year in insurance; maintenance costs; taxes; and the cost of depreciation. That's a costly status symbol.

So car rental services like Zipcar in the US and City Car Club in the UK are starting to take off. In Ulm, Germany, and many other European and US cities, you can hire a car through Car2Go, pick it up at a pre-arranged point and leave it at your destination for another user, all for less than €50 a day. It's the motoring equivalent of the smart cycle hire schemes that are now familiar in cities like London and Paris. They work because everyone benefits: the user gets access to the car or bike, while the streets are less congested with parked vehicles. At the same time people are more likely to make sustainable transport choices, taking a 10-minute walk or bike ride instead of hopping into the car whenever they need to go anywhere.

This kind of transaction is what is known as collaborative consumption: people working together to gain greater individual benefits from a resource. Hot-desking and shared workspaces are another example, with an explosion of 'hubs' where freelancers, sole traders or travelling businesspeople can simply turn up with their laptop and find a desk, Wi-Fi and as much coffee as they can handle.

Alongside the shared use of assets provided by third parties, such as cars or workspaces, are peer-to-peer arrangements, where individuals trade with each other, facilitated through an online service that usually takes a transaction fee. The peer-to-peer economy is becoming big business. Airbnb, an alternative to hotel stays in which people hire out their spare rooms to travellers, was valued in April 2014 at more than US$10 billion and had succeeded in raising a total of US$826 million in equity. In just five years it spread to nearly 200 countries with more than 600,000 properties listed.

eBay is probably the world's biggest example of the commercial peer-to-peer economy, linking millions of individual sellers with buyers who bid for their unwanted items. Unsurprisingly, eBay has also spawned a host of micro-businesses or 'power sellers' who use its online platform as a way of removing the need for physical premises, lowering their production and distribution costs.

A study commissioned in 2010 by *Shareable*, an online magazine, found that 78 per cent of people surveyed had already used peer-to-peer sharing services, and two thirds would share possessions such as cars and bikes if they could make money from it. People who shared information online through social media tended to be more willing to share physical goods; it appeared that the distrust of strangers was lower among those who used online services regularly. While saving or making money was a strong motivator, people also wanted to share because they felt it would benefit the environment and society (Latitude, nd).

A leader in *The Economist* gushed over a world in which everything is a money-making opportunity, facilitated by the power of the internet. Before the internet, it pointed out, you could rent a parking space or a power tool, but it was usually more trouble than it was worth. Now that has all changed: '… technology has reduced transaction costs, making sharing assets cheaper and easier than ever – and therefore possible on a much larger scale. The big change is the availability of more data about people and things, which allows physical assets to be disaggregated and consumed as services' (*The Economist*, 2013).

But the peer-to-peer economy isn't just about making money or crunching data. It also facilitates re-use of unwanted household goods and encourages local connections. Services like Freecycle and Freegle create online spaces where individuals can list surplus items within a given area, from cots to garden tools, or ask for items they need. Freegle also lists community activities, encouraging volunteering and enriching the web of local relationships. A 'thank you' from a stranger can be better for your quality of life and mental wellbeing than a few extra pounds in your pocket.

People-centred economic development

Collaborative consumption and the peer-to-peer economy open up new possibilities for trade and commerce, but they also open the door to what has been called the 'civic economy'. This is where the social, public and private overlap with a clear aim of creating and sustaining the public good, driven by community values and digital technologies (Nesta et al, 2011).

If that sounds a little abstruse, some concrete examples might help. The Arcola Theatre in Dalston, East London, an area where more than 100 different languages are spoken, combines community performance projects with a service promoting environmental sustainability. In 2008 the theatre produced its first show powered entirely by hydrogen fuel cells and LED lamps, cutting its energy consumption by 60 per cent compared with previous performances. Fab Lab Manchester, owned by The Manufacturing Institute, encourages new enterprises and inventions by giving residents and students access to equipment such as 3D printers and a computerised embroidery machine. More than 3,000 individuals, school groups and small businesses have used Fab Lab to experiment and test their ideas. In Copenhagen, the Baisikeli workshop salvages dumped bicycles, repairs them and rents them to tourists in order to provide low-cost bikes in Tanzania.

The Museum of East Anglian Life (MEAL) in Stowmarket, Suffolk, is another example. Once a traditional local history museum, it is now a flourishing social enterprise that hosts community events, a beer festival and a Gypsy arts festival. Since 2007 it has also been running training and therapeutic care services for disabled people, ex-offenders and the long-term unemployed. More than 40 people have found jobs and 150 have been trained through MEAL's work. Director Tony Butler says museums don't exist just to display curiosities or make money, but to make the places they inhabit better. Even in hard financial times, he argues, 'there are small scale interventions which civil society organisations make every day, which make their communities a better place' (Butler, 2013).

Another way of describing the civic economy is to say it's more than the sum of its parts. It's where private enterprises, charities and voluntary groups, public agencies or individuals work in a way that maximises social benefit without demanding a payback. In a context of austerity, it's an approach that values openness, generosity and a willingness to experiment. Social networks and trust count for as much as assets and finance, and a culture of testing and learning is more highly valued than strategy and management.

The civic economy works by creating 'positive externalities', benefits to all that are not appropriated by the individuals or organisations that help to provide them. Just as a skilled workforce is a positive externality that results from parents' personal desire to educate their children well, or a cleaner atmosphere is sustained when your neighbour decides to plant a tree, the civic economy seeks to create spillover effects that do good beyond institutional or corporate boundaries.

At its heart the civic economy is people-centred. The UN Research Institute for Social Development has coined the term 'social solidarity economy', bringing together the 'social economy' of charities, voluntary groups and community organisations and the 'solidarity economy' of cooperatives, mutually owned businesses, the public sector and locally owned or family-run private firms. It's an economy in which ordinary people play an active role in shaping their economic lives – 'an ethical and values-based approach to economic development ... that prioritises the welfare of people and planet over profits and blind growth' (Kawano, 2013).

Notions of the civic economy or social solidarity economy may seem esoteric, but essentially they are recasting ideas that are ancient and are attracting new interest as philosophers, economists and politicians seek to square prosperity with sustainability and equality with self-realisation. Ideas of the commons and of public goods – the assets and products, tangible and intangible, that we all share and benefit from – are enjoying a resurgence as awareness grows that neither the state nor the private market have successfully protected and nurtured our landscapes, water resources, forests, air and food sources, and community life. But little attention has been paid so far to the 'commons' of our towns and cities, and the shared value created for all when everyone plays their part in creating prosperous places. How to create, preserve and increase this shared value is the theme of the rest of this book. To begin that exploration and to understand how the new economy is building on ideas that already have deep roots, we need to rewind more than a century-and-a-half and return to Rochdale.

'Why not go to our own shop?'

It's a Saturday night in Rochdale, in the heyday of Victorian industry. The town is surfing the wave of a textile boom. Solid stone-built cotton mills and rickety cottages for their workers are spreading across the hillsides. The town centre is heaving. But the throngs aren't spilling out of pubs and bars, the worse for wear after spending their week's wages from the factories. The place to be, it seems, is the local Co-op in the enticingly named Toad Lane.

George Holyoake, chronicler of the world's first successful cooperative shop, writes that 'cheerful customers literally crowd Toad Lane at night, swarming like bees to every counter'. The scene he paints is a far cry from the grim northern mill towns depicted by L.S. Lowry.

> Buyer and seller meet as friends; there is no overreaching on one side, and no suspicion on the other; and Toad Lane on Saturday night, while as gay as the Lowther Arcade in London, is ten times more moral. These crowds of humble working men who never knew before when they put good food in their mouths, whose every dinner was adulterated, whose shoes let in the water a month too soon, whose waistcoats shone with devil's dust, and whose wives wore calico that would not wash, now buy in the markets like millionaires, and, as far as pureness of food goes, live like lords. (Holyoake, 1907, p 41)

The industrial districts of England had no sight like the Rochdale Co-operative Store on a Saturday night, Holyoake enthused. And while we might allow him the licence of the era's penchant for effulgent description, it would be a mistake to underestimate the difference the Rochdale Society of Equitable Pioneers made in one of the more miserable engine rooms of the Victorian empire.

The rationale for the Co-op was expressed simply enough several decades earlier by William King, founder of *The Co-operator*: 'We must all go to a shop every day to buy food and necessaries – why then should we not go to our own shop?'

It sounds easy. By taking charge of your own shopping you can get quality produce at a fair price, and share in the profits too. But as King and many others who tried to set up cooperative shops in the early years of the 19th century found, putting the idea into practice was much harder. Other traders resented competition, bringing to mind Adam Smith's axiom that 'merchants of the same trade seldom meet together, even for merriment or diversion, but the conversation ends in a conspiracy against the public, or in some contrivance to raise prices.' Low-paid workers were suspicious or cynical. Holyoake himself recounted the endless petty disputes, arguments about rules and regulations, and commercial misjudgements that bedevilled many of these early experiments.

The main achievement of the Toad Lane shop in its first years was to survive. Its beginnings were not auspicious. After spending years collecting subscriptions of twopence a week, the Pioneers had cobbled together £28 – enough to rent a shopfront in 1844 and to sell a very modest selection of basics from a counter formed of a plank of wood laid across two barrels.

The initial response to this fledgling enterprise was ridicule. One local trader boasted that he could turn up with a wheelbarrow and carry the entire stock away. But within three months it had expanded its range, adding more upmarket goods such as tea and tobacco. The shop developed a reputation for selling unadulterated produce – in stark contrast to some of its competitors – and pioneered the dividend system, where customers received a share of the profits.

In 1846 the store opened a butcher's counter, and the following year it began selling fabric and clothing. Later it started its own shoemaking business, with three workers and an apprentice. In 1849 the savings bank in Rochdale went bust, and residents turned to the Pioneers, who offered interest on members' capital – becoming, almost by accident, one of the first cooperative banks. By the 1860s Rochdale was hosting visitors from as far away as Germany and Russia who wanted to know how a successful cooperative could work.

In his *Principles of political economy*, John Stuart Mill put its success down to 'carefulness and honesty'. Holyoake, with characteristic hyperbole, declared that 'human nature must be different in Rochdale': 'They have acted upon Sir Robert Peel's memorable advice; they have "taken their own affairs into their own hands"; and what is more to the purpose, they have kept them in their own hands.'

The Co-op on the corner might now be the public face of the cooperative economy on Britain's high streets, but its roots go deeper and its branches extend much wider. Today, despite the widespread decline of cooperatives in the second half of the 20th century and the much publicised troubles of the UK's Co-operative Bank, which infected the entire Co-operative Group in 2014, there are more than 6,000 cooperative businesses in the UK, a tally that grew by more than a quarter between 2008 and 2012 as traditional businesses felt the brunt of recession and austerity. Between them cooperatives in the UK turn over £37 billion and are owned by 15.1 million members who share in their success (Co-operatives UK, 2014). Worldwide, three times as many people are members of cooperatives as there are shareholders in corporations.

Outside the UK, cooperatives have shown a remarkable resilience in the face of economic crisis. In Bologna, Italy, one in ten residents works in cooperative businesses and six out of ten are members of at least one. In Spain, the Mondragon network of cooperatives in the Basque country forms the nation's seventh largest business, employing more than 83,000 people in industrial, financial, distribution and knowledge enterprises, with annual sales of nearly €14 billion.

The Mondragon Corporation has its own technical and managerial education system, invests 40 per cent of profits in research and development, gives 10 per cent of its profits to local charitable and social causes, and uses the rest to ensure all its workers have a generous pension. When one part of the business is struggling, other parts can offer workers alternative employment. The result is that levels of inequality in the area where Mondragon operates are among the lowest in Europe. As Michael Lewis and Pat Conaty observe, 'Mondragon has demonstrated that it is possible to develop highly participative companies rooted in solidarity, with a strong social dimension, and still achieve outstanding business excellence' (Lewis and Conaty, 2012, p 251).

Doing business for the common good is an alternative to state control as well as corporate dominance. In China, the reforms of industry and agriculture after the death of Mao Zedong were driven at first not by privatisation but by 'village enterprises' that raised funds through local levies. They generated profits and reinvested them in wages and local benefits. 'They had few of the usual instruments of corporate control: no shareholder controls and no threat of takeover,' wrote the economist John McMillan. 'To our accustomed ways of thinking, these firms simply should not have worked. Yet they functioned efficiently' (McMillan, 2002).

The fact that 'accustomed ways of thinking' have failed to encompass the notion of doing business for the common good speaks volumes in itself. Cooperative businesses and mutual associations have often been regarded either with suspicion and hostility – both Nazi Germany and Communist Russia suppressed them – or with dewy-eyed naivety as a solution to all economic ills. But as Mondragon has demonstrated, if you can successfully run businesses for the benefit of the wider community the rewards can be enormous.

Running a business well for mutual benefit, as the Rochdale Pioneers found, can be harder than running an ordinary firm for private gain. Before you can build Utopia you have to build a business; and cooperatives can be as susceptible to business blunders as any traditional firm. The UK's Co-operative Bank has staggered from crisis to crisis since its rescue of the Britannia Building Society – another mutual – during the global financial crisis of 2008-09. In May 2013 the Co-operative Group's finance director was forced to resign after the bank posted a £662 million loss; in March 2014 the group chief executive, Euan Sutherland, quit. Losses for 2013 totalled £2.5 billion, forcing the group into a fire-sale of its farms and pharmacies. Some of the losses were due to the need to compensate customers for the mis-selling of payment protection insurance, a practice that suggests talk of cooperative values had failed to penetrate parts of the organisation.

We won't rescue our high streets simply by sprinkling cooperatives around like magic dust. There are good and bad cooperatives just as there are good and bad independent shops, but when a mutual business works well, you can begin to see why George Holyoake became so effusive. The ideas behind the new economy have deep foundations.

Build it and they will come?

Walk up Rochdale's Yorkshire Street today and you'll come to a shopping centre called the Wheatsheaf. Opened in 1990, it's a gloomy place, like many indoor shopping centres in hard-hit towns. The Wheatsheaf moniker is particularly ironic, being the symbol of the cooperative movement. Alone, each ear of wheat falls over. Together they stand upright. This Wheatsheaf fell down long ago. The centre was taken into administration in 2010, ending up on the books of the Bank of Ireland, itself the recipient of a government bail-out.

Rochdale Council has big plans for the area. Opposite the Wheatsheaf is another indoor centre, Rochdale Exchange. Yet the council believes the town needs a third shopping centre, with proposals for a £100 million project known as Town Centre East designed to create a 300,000 square foot retail and leisure area, with an 80-bedroom hotel, cinema, car park, an 80,000 square foot department store and even more shops. The developer for the much-delayed scheme, where work began in spring 2014, is Genr8, a joint venture between property company Chelsfield and John Early, former executive chair of Amec.

If council officers spent more time in Yorkshire Street, they'd understand that the main reason why Rochdale is suffering is that people are short of money, not short of places to spend it. Simon Danczuk, the town's MP (and owner of a local deli), is blunt in his view of the new development and its prospects.

> 'I think the proposals aren't deliverable. They've put all their eggs in one basket. I think they're making a big mistake. I speak to people at a national level who are involved in building shopping centres, and they basically say that it's a non-starter. And yet the council have poured loads of taxpayers' money into it, in terms of demolition of the old municipal building, in terms of demolition of the old bus station. This is a real gamble for a town like this.
>
> 'I said at the time, it's all on the record, you'll have no interest, nobody will bid because of the recession. I take a keen interest in regeneration and it weren't difficult to read that. And they ended up drawing up a shortlist of one company, Genr8, that hasn't got a pot to piss in if you'll pardon the phrase. They have no cash.
>
> 'We've got the Wheatsheaf shopping centre, two thirds empty or something, they could have reconfigured that, they could have reconfigured the Rochdale Exchange shopping centre where the market is and brought the

market out. That would have easily created the space at a fraction of the cost.' (interview with the author)

This faith in the coming boom would be touching if it were not so potentially disastrous. The 'build it and they will come' approach to retail has long ago been superseded in all but the prime locations, yet Rochdale appears stuck in the thinking of the 1990s. Its town fathers might be better advised to return to Toad Lane, where the original Pioneers' shop has been converted into a museum, to pick up some ideas about the philosophy required.

A new kind of local economy

Today's retailers and property developers are in the business of maximising returns. The Rochdale Pioneers, too, sought to maximise returns, but had a different idea of the returns they were looking for: better and cheaper goods for local people, with profits reinvested in the community. The thriving high streets and town centres of the 21st century will be those that rediscover how to maximise returns to their communities.

The department store John Lewis is often held up as a fine example of a business that achieves social as well as economic value. For customers it promises the kind of quality products one would expect to find in respectable middle-class homes, backed by the value-for-money pledge of being 'never knowingly undersold'. Unlike its competitors, however, John Lewis – and its supermarket sister, Waitrose – is owned by its employees.

John Lewis was originally a private limited company, but when its founder died in 1928, John Spedan Lewis, who inherited the business, inspired by the 'guild socialism' of the thinker Arthur Penty, set up a trust to own its assets for the benefit of the workforce. He sold the business to the trust for £1 million, securing both his own future and that of the company – a contrast with many of today's entrepreneurs whose exit strategy is to sell to the highest bidder and enlarge their personal fortune.

In 1929 John Lewis had 1,500 staff who shared in the company's profits. Today there are more than 90,000, and in 2014 each received a bonus worth 15 per cent of their salary – the equivalent of eight weeks' pay (BBC News, 2014). Michael Lewis and Pat Conaty describe the three pillars of the John Lewis model as 'share the gains, share the knowledge, and share the power' – provide fair wages and a share in profits, be transparent about business performance and listen to workers' views, and give staff a say in the way the business is run through a representative 'partnership council' (Lewis and Conaty, 2012, pp 280–1).

The John Lewis vision goes beyond staff welfare, encompassing an aspiration to be 'a force for good' in the communities it serves. This includes encouraging customers to nominate charitable causes; seconding managers and providing voluntary help for community organisations and activities; and giving financial support to charities, including an annual donation of £100,000 to the British Red Cross disaster relief fund. It has also made space in its stores available free of charge to voluntary groups, using its premises to help organisations that can't afford to rent town centre meeting rooms.

John Lewis brings together some of the most important elements we should look for in a business that maximises returns to local communities. It pays its staff a fair wage, putting money into local economies; it gives them a say in how the organisation is run; it donates a share of its profits to charitable causes; and it is looking at ways of using its physical assets for community benefit.

In other respects, however, it still has far to go. Its chair, Charlie Mayfield, is paid 60 times more than non-managerial staff at the company (Wallop, 2012), and the firm is ambivalent about its commitment to town centres rather than out-of-town shopping malls. In Northern Ireland it has lobbied hard for an extension to the out-of-town Sprucefield Centre, refusing to consider Belfast city centre as a location. And for many smaller towns across the UK, a John Lewis store is out of the question: like most big name retailers, the firm is shifting its focus towards online shopping and 'click and collect' services combining online browsing with collection at existing stores. John Lewis won't revive our high streets, but its principles and corporate structure are a model others could follow.

At a local level, businesses can maximise returns to the community by re-linking consumers with local producers. Local micro-breweries or independent producers such as the Wensleydale Creamery help to build social supply chains that make the most of a town or region's assets, keeping the benefits of trade flowing within the locality.

In 2013 Transition Town Totnes published a 'local economic blueprint' for the town, worked up in partnership with the town's Chamber of Commerce, the Town Council, Totnes Development Trust and three local colleges. Similar studies were done for Herefordshire and Brixton in South London: the circumstances are very different, but the challenges and opportunities have much in common.

By supporting local food producers and retailers, investing in renewable energy and improving homes' energy efficiency, the Totnes report concluded that more than £5 million a year could be ploughed into the local economy – without closing any supermarkets or advising people to deny themselves many familiar comforts. These initiatives, they reckoned, could sustain dozens of jobs and provide new business opportunities in the town and surrounding district. More importantly, they would make Totnes less vulnerable to change, building the networks of connections and relationships that help to make a place resilient.

Fiona Ward, who coordinated the project, says the blueprint 'tells the story of a new kind of local economy, one based around people, their wellbeing, and their livelihoods, and which better respects resource limits'. The town's Conservative MP, Sarah Wollaston, says that 'by taking action to promote local enterprise, and finding a healthier balance between local, national and international trade, local economic groups can take their destiny into their own hands'. Local wellbeing crosses political and social divides (Transition Town Totnes, 2013).

The blueprint is not about backwoods isolationism or making do with second-best; it seeks to maximise public benefit by redirecting money that is already being spent. The partners recognise that even a small town like Totnes is part of a global economy. But they believe small changes like supporting local producers and investing in energy efficiency could create new opportunities in a town where decent jobs are hard to come by.

The cost of retrofitting improvements such as insulation and double-glazing to local homes has been estimated at £26 million, work that could provide business opportunities as well as lowering residents' energy bills. More than 500 households have already taken part in the town's Transition Streets initiative, which encourages families to use energy more wisely and invest in energy-saving home improvements, saving £580 a year on average.

One of the biggest future challenges for Totnes and similar towns is the rising cost of social care as the population ages and public services continue to shrink. Community-based services could reduce costs and create jobs and opportunities at the same time. A 'neighbourhood health watch' pilot project is already exploring how people can look after each other better at street level, doing small tasks such as picking up the shopping for neighbours convalescing from illness or hospital treatment. A network of trusted local service providers could offer reliable and good value professional care or do the vital practical jobs that enable people to stay in their own homes for longer.

These are all simple ideas that could support local businesses, rebuild prosperity and improve people's quality of life. Most importantly, they will help to weave the webs of social connections and cooperative working that align community benefits with business success.

As Anthony Blackburn has realised, it is the human connection that makes the difference and that creates value that cannot be measured within a company's profit and loss account:

> 'If Handpicked Hall was to fail tomorrow, I've actually given so many people a chance and I think that's wonderful. People often think, oh, he's expanding his business and making loads of money, but it's not about that. These things fall into place, but the starting point is giving great people a chance.'

7

An unexpected buzz in the library

At the dead of night on 29 May 2012 a posse of council workers, heavily supported by police and security staff, descended on a North West London suburb. Their mission? To remove books from a library.

Out went the biographies, histories, reference books and travel guides. Out went the children's fiction. Out went the novels and poetry. Out, too, went the furniture, the murals installed in the 1930s, and the brass plaque marking the opening of Kensal Rise Library by Mark Twain in 1900.

Local people and literary celebrities, alerted to the council's move at 2.30 in the morning, could only splutter their outrage. Maggie Gee, Vice-President of the Royal Society of Literature and a local resident, accused the council of philistinism. So did the biographer Sir Michael Holroyd. The playwright Michael Frayn compared the raid with the totalitarian regimes of the mid-20th century: 'So the library is now an unlibrary, in the way that people became unpersons in the darkest days of the Soviet Union. I hope they took the titles of the books off as well' (Jones and Flood, 2012).

This bizarre episode of municipal counter-insurgency was an unlikely milestone in Brent Council's 'libraries transformation project'. Transformation, in this instance, meant closing six neighbourhood libraries on the grounds that it would enable the authority to keep the remainder of its service open. Kensal Rise, one of the six earmarked for closure, had been the focus of the most vociferous protests, with residents pitching tables and chairs on the pavement outside its doors to prevent council officers removing its books. Authors including Philip Pullman, Zadie Smith and Alan Bennett joined a sustained chorus of eloquent disapproval.

It certainly wasn't the kind of transformation Mark Twain, who gained much of his learning in a public library, would have had in mind when he opened the Public Reading Room among a clutch of bewhiskered dignitaries a century earlier. Neither would it have been imagined by the Fellows of All Souls College, Oxford, who gifted the land to the municipality as long as it would be used as a free library; nor by the steel magnate Andrew Carnegie, another benefactor of Britain's libraries, who donated £3,000 to extend the Kensal Rise building in 1904.

There are serious questions to be addressed about the future role of libraries in a digital age, and how best they can serve the needs of today's population. Visiting Kensal Rise Library in January 2011, Maggie Gee described a few of the ways it was serving local people before its closure. Parents and childminders were dropping in with children on the way home from school. Teenagers were getting to grips with homework. Elderly people were reading newspapers or magazines. The building hosted computer classes for beginners and a weekly knitting and crochet class, as well as a reading group. A special needs teacher at the nearby Manor School described the library as an 'irreplaceable resource' for children with learning difficulties.

Put another way, a library is a social hub. A parliamentary report found three quarters of all children and two in five adults use libraries in the UK (House of Commons Culture, Media and Sports

Committee, 2012). A library in or near a high street is a social hub that helps keep the street alive. It provides a reason to go out and an opportunity to meet others. But for many libraries the writing is on the wall. Opening hours are being cut, staff are being retired or laid off, and councils are looking at new – meaning cheaper – ways of providing library services. The Chartered Institute of Library and Information Professionals estimates that 3,300 library jobs were lost between 2010 and 2012, and one in five councils are looking to merge libraries with other services such as housing offices or leisure centres (CILIP, 2013).

A welcoming, functioning town centre provides a wide range of services and meeting places, attracting people from all walks of life and income groups. There are the activities directly provided by public bodies, such as libraries and health centres, register offices, tourist information centres, bus and railway stations. There are schools and adult education centres, post offices, courts and police stations. Then there are activities provided by voluntary organisations and charities, from workspaces and meeting rooms to services for people with disabilities, drop-in centres and lunch clubs. There are places of worship, theatres and arts centres. There are services provided by private businesses too, such as local newspapers, that serve a civic as well as a commercial function. None of these are predominantly about retail, yet they all lay the foundations of a sense of place.

Look at old pictures or descriptions of British high streets and you'll see this social infrastructure to the fore, complementing and underpinning the street's commercial functions. Today they're often relics, to be found on the names and inscriptions of buildings. In Sheffield's Division Street the former municipal waterworks and fire station are now pubs. In Cardiff city centre there's a bar called The Old Library. In Shrewsbury the Old Market Hall is a cinema and cafe. In St Ives, Cornwall, there's a bed and breakfast hotel called The Old Vicarage; in Redmire in the Yorkshire Dales there's a B&B called The Old Town Hall; and in St Andrew's in Scotland there's one called The Old Station. In Kingswinford, near Dudley, there's The Old Courthouse, another restaurant.

In many cases these changes are the natural result of the growth and expansion of towns, or the creative repurposing of buildings that have outlived their original use. But a high street where the main memory of civic functions lies in the names of pubs and restaurants is one that has let go of its anchoring institutions in exchange for activities whose vulnerability is exposed by the first frosts of recession.

The rise and fall of the civic

The relentless conversion of civic facilities into commercial premises can be read as a hallmark of late 20th- and early 21st-century values and priorities. A century-and-a-half earlier, there was more concern about the absence of civic infrastructure and the squalid conditions resulting from municipal and social neglect. To see where we might go, it can be useful to revisit the past.

Birmingham in the second half of the 19th century was in dire need of change. One local councillor, William White, described parts of the city centre where 'little else is to be seen but bowing roofs, tottering chimneys, tumbledown and often disused shops, heaps of bricks, broken windows and coarse, rough pavements, damp and sloppy'. He continued: 'It is not easy to describe or imagine the dreary desolation which acre after acre of the very heart of the town presents to anyone who will take the trouble to visit it' (quoted in Power and Houghton, 2007, p 32).

In the first years of its corporate existence, Birmingham Council's only vision was to keep costs down – a priority echoed by many of today's local government leaders. In the 1850s the city was run by newspaper proprietor Joseph Allday, whose group was known as the Economists. One of Allday's first actions was to dismiss the borough engineer and replace him with his assistant, on half the salary. Allday cut spending on the roads by 50 per cent and moved council meetings to a local pub, the Woodman Tavern.

But in three years of relentless activity in the 1870s, a new mayor, Joseph Chamberlain, turned a backward, short-sighted and insular council into a paragon of municipal virtue. He had visited Paris and seen the broad boulevards constructed by Georges-Eugene Hausmann, and was appalled at the councillors' lack of ambition. He allied himself with the 'civic gospel' preached by nonconformist clergy, who argued that the moral condition of the poor was inextricably linked with their material wellbeing. Improve the conditions, Chamberlain argued, and the people will be more content, healthier and harder working.

After becoming mayor in 1873 Chamberlain's first priority was the city's gas supply. The city bought out the two local gas firms, Birmingham Gas and Light Company and the Staffordshire Gas Light Company. The purchase raised the city's debt from £500,000 to £2.5 million – but within five years the price of gas had been slashed twice, a success described by the *Birmingham Mail* as a 'fairy tale'. Local businessmen were delighted at this municipal magic.

In 1875 the city bought up the Birmingham Waterworks Company. Chamberlain appointed a medical officer of health and set up a drainage board. The object here was not just to improve the city's infrastructure and raise funds through a municipal monopoly; it was what commentators were starting to call gas-and-water socialism – civic action as a route to social reform.

As Chamberlain remarked: 'A private company must needs look to profits, whereas a Corporation, having public funds at its command, would be able to improve the quality of the water, and give an abundant supply, irrespective of commercial return.'(quoted in Hunt, 2004, p 340). Landlords were obliged to connect their properties to the town water supply – there was no opting out of Chamberlain's civic project. Streets were paved and lit, six public parks were opened and public transport was introduced. And in typical Victorian fashion, there was an imposing town hall, or Council House, to go with it.

Chamberlain's last big project was his most ambitious. He had seen Paris: now he would reinvent the French capital in the heart of Birmingham. Ninety acres of slums would give way to the new Corporation Street – or, as its detractors soon named it, *la rue Chamberlain*. The Birmingham Improvement Act 1876 allowed the council to buy up property worth £1.3 million; and, in a move mimicked by city planners many times since, the city would showcase regeneration through shopping. Chamberlain wanted his new city centre to be 'the retail shop of the whole of the midland counties of England' (quoted in Hunt, 2004, p 351).

Chamberlain's vision corresponded in many respects to the concept of the 'agora' outlined earlier in Chapter 3: a multifunctional place that brings a community together for social, civic, recreational and economic purposes, and where there is a common cause between social betterment, civic provision and commercial success. Chamberlain understood that a successful city needed a determined and enterprising council, and that addressing ignorance, deprivation and squalor could not be left to market forces.

Today the UK still enjoys a multilayered legacy of more than a century of municipal and social nurturing. Our town centres are dotted with buildings that reflect this investment, from town halls to theatres, meeting rooms to post offices. The difference now is that many of these facilities are facing the axe as central and local government and their associated agencies, taking their cue more from Allday than Chamberlain, seek to slash their costs and the range of services they provide. High streets that face a retail crisis are also facing a civic and social crisis.

In late 2011 and early 2012 local government officers in England began referring in hushed tones to a document that became known as the 'Barnet graph of doom'. Prepared by an official at the London Borough of Barnet, it suggested that without radical change, within 20 years virtually all the council's budget would need to be spent either on social care for vulnerable adults or on children's services, leaving only a few crumbs for everything from bin collection to enforcement of trading standards, planning to environmental health. Far from being civic visionaries, councils would be reduced to stretching out an ineffective safety net for increasingly vulnerable people.

A detailed analysis by the Local Government Association (LGA) painted a grim picture of the future for local government finance in England. Pointing out that councils were 'cut earlier and harder than the rest of the public sector' in the austerity programme imposed in 2010, and allowing for the use of reserves and income from increased fees and charges, the association warned of a funding gap of £16.5 billion per year by 2019-20 – or 29 per cent less money coming in than going out. The only way forward had to be a 'genuinely free conversation between councils and local residents about how much tax they want to pay and what services they want to receive in return' (LGA, 2012, p 2).

But it is taxing to have such a conversation in the context of short-term pressures, demands from central government, and immediate requirements for savings from councillors and auditors. The tough calls for local councils will get tougher. The respected Institute for Fiscal Studies has warned that the UK faces at least two more 'austerity elections', while separately pointing out that wages have fallen further even than during the 1930s Depression (Allen, 2013; Watt and Inman, 2013). The Keynesian concept of counter-cyclical investment by the public sector to see the private sector through hard times has been defenestrated: instead, the only solution on offer seems to be more and harder cuts.

Local services, like local shops, are in constant flux. New ideas are trialled and tested, some more successfully than others. Technology and needs are shifting. If public services, like some kinds of shop, were closing to be replaced by others that are more effective or appropriate, there would be little cause for concern. But that isn't happening. Nor are voluntary or charitable organisations stepping into the gaps: the National Council for Voluntary Organisations reckons non-profit bodies in England will lose at least £1.7 billion of funding from 2010-11 to 2017-18. Charities, too, are looking at the buildings they occupy and the space they use, and asking how they can make ends meet (NCVO, 2013).

Pop into your high street post office and you'll observe a similar dynamic at work. A century ago the post office was a civic institution, often occupying a grand building in a prime location. Today it's more likely to look like a glorified convenience store, rammed to the rafters with greetings cards, confectionary, magazines and anything else that looks as if it might keep an ailing core business afloat. The Post Office describes this process as 'transformation'. In reality, it's more of a desperate struggle to keep the majority of its 11,800 branches open as long as possible. In seeking to avoid the Scylla of diminishing government funding, the Post Office has crashed into the Charybdis of cut-throat retail competition. This increasingly puts it head-to-head with the supermarket chains that are gobbling up a growing share of the convenience store market. It is becoming ever harder for sub-postmasters, who run local branches as franchised businesses, to keep their heads above water. Their average pay fell by 9 per cent between 2009 and 2012, while the cost of overheads rose by 21 per cent (House of Commons Business, Innovation and Skills Committee, 2013). You could use a lot of words to describe that trajectory, but sustainable isn't one of them.

In the dog-eat-dog world of local newspapers, the retreat from town centres has become a stampede. The days when a market town would host two rival papers have long gone; today the local reporter, if there is one, is as likely to work from home on a freelance contract as in a high street office. In November 2011 Cannock Chase, a town of 60,000 people in Staffordshire, lost its local newspaper and editor Mike Lockley, who had just celebrated 25 years at the helm of the *Chase Post*. Now its affairs are covered by whoever happens to be on duty at the Wolverhampton *Express & Star* 10 miles away. In 2010 the *Long Eaton Advertiser*, which had served the Derbyshire town for more than a century, rolled off the presses for the last time. At the time of its demise there were still 5,200 people prepared to pay for a copy, but the paper's owner, Trinity Mirror, said it could not find a buyer for the title. It put its decision to shut up shop down to a combination of difficult trading conditions and a 'strategic review' of its portfolio (Christopher, 2010).

Between 2005 and 2011 at least 242 local papers closed across the UK, while just 70 new titles were launched (Ponsford, 2010). Many towns have no dedicated newspaper at all, while a large proportion of those that remain are threadbare imitations of their former selves, with little notion of any civic role as journals of record. The days when the local newspaper editor was a force to be reckoned with are long gone. At the same time the local magistrates' courts, where junior reporters would cut their teeth on drug offences and Saturday night punch-ups, are vanishing: 93, from Barry to Bishop Auckland, were culled in December 2010, along with 49 county courts. A town where little is done and even fewer people talk about it is one that has lost its soul.

For many services faced with tighter budgets and expensive premises, joining forces with others seems an attractive option. So libraries are looking to relocate into council offices or leisure centres; post offices are contemplating how they could become 'one-stop shops' for local government; churches are opening community cafes; health centres are planning on-site gyms.

A wealth of creative and innovative thinking is emerging about how public and civic services can be reimagined, co-located, and delivered more effectively. But the corresponding reality is seldom acknowledged: every co-location and shared service, and each mash-up of civic and commercial functions, leaves physical spaces redundant. That's where the cost savings occur, but it's also where the risk of blight is greatest. Whether through neglect or through rethinking, the inevitable conclusion is that less space is needed.

Emptied, stretched, dismembered

Head to Stirling, scene of William 'Braveheart' Wallace's stand against the English in 1297, and you'll find evidence both of the collaborative spirit needed to revive our towns, and the fragmented and fractured interests that have helped to suck the life out of them. For a town that hosts one of Scotland's most popular tourist attractions, Stirling Castle, the traditional shopping strip of King Street is jaw-droppingly empty.

Trudging up King Street, it's not surprising there are few people about. Past the charity shops and coffee shops at the bottom of town, bypassing the Thistles shopping centre, there's the One Stop Mini Mart (now shut), an Indian restaurant (now shut) and another vacant shop decorated with a graphic advertising the delights of Stirling. There are more of those further up the hill in Baker Street, before you get to Nicky Tam's Bar and Bothy with its resident ghost, the landlord cheerily looking forward to the last week of the month when everyone gets paid. In the tastefully decorated Stirling Arcade, tastefully empty shop units bear witness to the town's failure to persuade passers-by to part with their money, and property owners' failure to imagine viable alternative uses for their premises.

This town has been emptied, stretched, and dismembered. The university is on a purpose-built out-of-town campus, the cinema is out on a retail park, the high school has been rebuilt on a brand new edge-of-town site. Teachers, filmgoers and students have no reason to visit the town centre. Only the hotels, it seems, have kept faith, clustering around the castle at the top of the crag in a kind of hospitality hill fort.

Stirling is a good place to visit to investigate what's happening to our high streets. The university hosts the respected Institute for Retail Studies, where Professor Leigh Sparks is all too aware of how a series of disconnected decisions have helped to kill town centres, shifting activities and services into anonymous edgelands:

'The football ground was walkable from the town centre so people came in, not in huge numbers given that it's Stirling Albion, but they came in. Now it is five miles away on a ring road. The leisure centre that was in the town centre with a swimming pool is now five miles away at the ring road at the football ground. The irony that we're in a university that is four miles away from the town centre doesn't escape me. The school that you will pass on the bus as you go into town was in the town centre. We have taken everything we could possibly take out of the town centre. Why would I go there? Why would anyone go there?' (interview with the author)

In the smallest of ways, some people are trying to turn the tide. Towards the bottom of town, in one of a series of temporary locations, is the Made in Stirling shop, with its window displays of craftwork and handmade jewellery. In this shop you can choose from the creations of more than two dozen artists and makers, from screen-printed t-shirts to felt hats and 'upcycled' costume jewellery. Felt maker Lynn Ramsbottom, who comes in two days a week to manage the shop, is clear that this isn't simply a craft store. "We're not just a shop, we're a community of artists," she stresses. Everyone whose work is on sale comes in at least once a week, and many find they sell far more when they're able to explain to customers how their creations are made and the stories behind them.

Made in Stirling is one of the more long-lived outcomes of Startup Street, a two-year project by Stirling City Council and a team of partners, galvanised into action by town centre manager Andy Kennedy. The idea was to "take all the good stuff that already exists in Stirling and connect it together in a new way" to address issues of dead space and high levels of local unemployment. For town centres that have lost their way, interventions like Startup Street are just the beginning of a long-term process. Rethinking the use and function of a high street and repopulating it with new enterprises, projects and services takes time. Few organisations or public bodies, it seems, are prepared to invest consistently in catalysing such initiatives. Whether Startup Street makes a long-term difference remains to be seen: the risk is that it will fall into the trap that catches many regeneration projects, where action is dictated by the availability of short-term funding rather than a lasting vision.

Initiatives like Startup Street, whether temporary or long term, are special not because of the return on financial investment they deliver, but because they create places of potential. But for that reason they tend to be vulnerable: possibilities don't pay the rent. Someone has to choose to make such openness available and to facilitate the conversations that occur. It's energy consuming and can feel like an unaffordable luxury in tough times.

In tough times, however, towns need places of possibility far more than when all is going well. Rows of empty shops or pawnbrokers tell their own story: old models have failed. The response starts with a place to meet and to begin a conversation, and with people who are prepared to create that space without demanding an immediate payback.

Beyond economic value

Imaginative or desperate, a growing range of people are recognising the importance of a civic and community presence in the high street, after many decades of unquestioning faith in salvation by shopping. The Portas review of 2011 acknowledged that 'town centres are a civic space, not a private one', although it had little to say about the role of public services (Portas, 2011). Two years later, the independent Grimsey review envisaged 'multi-purpose community hubs' at the heart of the future high street, although it, too, left much of the what and the how to the imagination (Grimsey, 2013).

The role of civic and community infrastructure has also been to the fore in the Scottish Government's review of town centres. The review's chair, Malcolm Fraser, harks back to the Scottish pioneer of urban planning, Patrick Geddes, for inspiration: Geddes' three pillars of 'folk, work and place' offer a convenient shorthand embracing the vital functions and characteristics of a town. Of the six themes of the review, one covers community uses for empty or under-used buildings, while another focuses on the importance of public services.

The key, Malcom Fraser believes, is to understand the wider consequences of decisions and how they affect the place as a whole:

'At the moment we might care for a town, and all the councillors care for a town, and then some decision is made for some bizarre reason to close down everything and move it out into a "community campus". What's a community campus? Some distressed developer's site out of town. What do we do for the town? Oh well, we'll compensate by repainting the park benches. And that's an actual example from a lovely Scots town. So what's happened there? Well the decision has been made on the very narrowest economic grounds. How can that decision be made better?' (interview with the author)

'Place-based reviews' of key decisions could help to ensure that wider issues are taken into account when deciding to relocate a service or to provide it in a different way, he says. Such reviews would draw in expert advisers who understand the built environment and the local economy, as well as people who use the services affected. They cement into the decision-making process an understanding that the ripples of individual choices by local service providers spread far and wide.

This Geddesian understanding of folk, work and place may be taken as read in some academic and policy circles, but the cognitive dissonance between intellectual debate and real-world decisions can be extreme. Nevertheless, there are shafts of light in the gloom, even at government level.

The Sustainable Communities Act, passed with cross-party support in 2007, provides local authorities in England with an important tool that can be used to improve residents' quality of life and support local producers and traders. It allows functions to be transferred from one public body to another where that might be in the public interest, or to change rate relief to support small businesses. Importantly, it allows the public to put forward their own ideas for improving their towns and neighbourhoods. In Hackney, East London, mayor Jules Pipe has proposed using the Sustainable Communities Act as a mechanism to create special planning rules for betting shops and payday loan companies to limit their expansion in the borough's high streets. In August 2014 the Scottish Government made its own move, announcing a consultation on proposals to restrict the proliferation of payday lenders and betting shops.

The Public Services (Social Value) Act 2012 is another piece of legislation that encourages a wider consideration of public benefits. It requires public bodies in England to consider how they can improve the economic, social, and environmental wellbeing of their areas through the services they procure. At the heart of the legislation – and the wider debate about social value – is a belief that the worth of an activity or service should be measured not just on financial grounds, but on the wider benefits it brings to society.

The legislation's broad-brush approach to 'economic, social and environmental wellbeing' enables commissioners of services to consider a very wide range of factors when purchasing a service, from the employment of vulnerable people to the environmental impact of a contractor's supply chains. As the trade organisation Social Enterprise UK put it: 'If £1 is spent on the delivery of services, can that same £1 be used to also produce a wider benefit to the community?'

The Localism Act 2011 is another law that, in principle at least, offers communities new rights to improve their town centres and high streets. The 'right to bid' allows community organisations to put in an offer for valued land or buildings when they are put up for sale, such as the Ivy House pub in Nunhead (see Chapter 6). The 'right to build' enables communities to build affordable homes or facilities such as play areas without going through standard planning processes. The 'right to challenge' allows them to pitch to run local services if they think they can make them better or more cost-effective; and neighbourhood planning is intended to give communities more say over developments in their area. In the context of widespread cuts to publicly run services these rights offer very limited safeguards, but for some they will enable local assets and facilities to be created or preserved for the common good.

Even the Treasury, often cited as the ultimate barrier to intelligent decision making in the UK, recognises the importance of non-financial considerations when planning services or investments. Annex 2 of its *Green Book*, updated in 2011, makes it clear that policymakers should value 'non-market impacts' of policies or projects. 'The full value of goods such as health, educational success, family and community stability, and environmental assets cannot simply be inferred from market prices, but we should not neglect such important social impacts in policy making,' it comments (HM Treasury, 2011).

Towards an information commons

Even as services and facilities in our high streets are closed or threatened, there are signs of change. Many of these signs are individual projects, isolated sparks rather than a blaze of innovation.

Few, if any, towns have yet learned to join these projects up in a strategic way and consider how the rethinking of each service can benefit the whole community. But there are clues that can be followed if we want to create new civic high streets from the current crisis.

In the small market town of Wooler, high in the Cheviot Hills of Northumberland, visitors can find one of those signs. A few years ago both the library and the tourist information centre, which serves a rural area of 250 square miles and a population of 6,000, were under threat of closure. Northumberland Council was looking for savings, and the fortunes of a distant town with a small population were not prominent on its agenda.

Wooler was fortunate in having an established community trust, Glendale Gateway, that was prepared to fight to keep services open and work up constructive alternatives to the council's proposals. Instead of closing or scaling back the library and tourist centre, the trust suggested moving them both to a community hub, the Cheviot Centre, which had been converted from the town's former workhouse in 1999. First the tourist information centre was moved to the Cheviot Centre's ground floor, allowing extended opening hours and creating opportunities to sell tourism-related merchandise, increasing the centre's income by 70 per cent in the first year. Next, the Cheviot Centre was extended to accommodate the library: the revamped library saw a 20 per cent increase in lending, while membership more than doubled. The final phase of the project was to transfer the old library building to the trust, to be converted into affordable housing. The new library is run on behalf of the county council at a reduced cost, the service has been improved, and the trust will gain long-term income by providing much-needed homes for local people. This is a practical example of how the Portas and Grimsey reviews' aspirations for community-focused high streets could be made real.

This approach contrasts with the heartfelt but often one-dimensional tactics of 'Save Our Library' campaigns, and the similarly blinkered views of many local authority finance departments. It involves thinking about how the whole place can work, not just isolated bits of it.

The scale of a town like Wooler makes such comprehensive thinking easier than it might be across a city suburb or large town.

Much of the innovation that is starting to emerge elsewhere is necessarily beginning with individual buildings or services, because joining everything up is either too complex or frustrated by the attitudes of individual organisations, service providers or property owners. In such circumstances it can come down to determined or disruptive individuals to make a difference. In Rotterdam, where the city council decided to close 15 out of 21 neighbourhood libraries, residents of one block of flats persuaded their landlord to let them turn an empty apartment into a 'reading room', stocked with shared books. At the same time they took to the local park to invite neighbours to imagine what a community-organised library could look like. The result was Leeszaal Rotterdam West, open five days a week and managed and run entirely by volunteers (see www. leeszaalrotterdamwest.nl).

The idea of libraries run by volunteers can seem attractive. But as Britain's National Federation of Women's Institutes found in the course of its 'Love Your Libraries' campaign in 2011, volunteers can end up being used as 'sticking plasters', left without support and expected to do the duties previously covered by trained professionals. Far from opening the doors to a brave new world of community-centred provision, this piecemeal shuffling off was threatening the library service as a whole and undermining the role of professional staff (National Federation of Women's Institutes, 2013).

In the 1920s and 1930s local Women's Institutes took matters into their own hands and formed volunteer-run libraries. But the objective then was to pressure councils into providing a new service, not to pick up the tab for one that was being dismantled. Research for Arts Council England found that one in three of England's 151 library authorities now have at least one library managed by volunteers or community organisations. Across England in 2013 there were more than 170 'community libraries', nearly all of which were established since 2011, with at least another 250 in the pipeline. In some cases, such as Grappenhall Library in Warrington and Primrose Hill Library in North London, the library is now completely independent, with no local authority involvement at all. In Warrington, the building is being leased long term from the council at a nominal rent, the 5,500 books are mainly donated by local residents, and there is no longer any integration with the council's library IT system (Arts

Council England, 2013). It is unclear why this should be seen as an improvement.

Grappenhall Library is at one end of the spectrum: like the Rotterdam reading room, it is a library in the sense that it is somewhere where you can borrow and read books, but it is hardly a comprehensive service. At the other end is the concept of the Idea Store pioneered by Tower Hamlets Council in East London, combining the library service with homework clubs, employment advice, adult education, arts and leisure facilities and meeting rooms. Users can access subscription-only magazines free of charge on electronic devices via their Idea Store card, and an 'ask a librarian' service is available 24 hours a day. Tower Hamlets Council has calculated that since it opened its first Idea Store in 2002, the number of active library members has risen by 45 per cent and the number of visitors by 240 per cent, from 621,556 to 2.1 million (see www. ideastore.co.uk). The Idea Stores have come at a cost, however: the council invested £20 million in improving its library service, mostly at a time when funding from central government was much more generous than it is now or is likely to be again.

A different kind of library investment is the University of Sheffield's Information Commons, an 'integrated learning environment' opened in 2007 and designed to be flexible enough to accommodate the next half-century's advances in technology and learning methods. The university is particularly proud of the name:

> We chose to use this name because, like 'library' it's rooted in history. And by re-introducing it to the UK we're signalling the exciting scale and innovation of this new learning environment, with its shared resources providing access to the world's knowledge. (quoted from the University of Sheffield's website, at www.sheffield. ac.uk)

Up to a point. Elsewhere on the university's website you can find out that the idea of the Commons is interpreted rather narrowly: even the university's alumni have to book a visit in advance, and the library has opted out of the South Yorkshire Access to Libraries for Learning scheme, which opens the resources of academic institutions to the wider public. It would be more accurate to describe it as an Information Enclosure.

But the idea of an Information Commons is an excellent one, and could help councils and communities as they rethink their library services. Some academic institutions, such as Massachusetts Institute of Technology (MIT) in Boston, US, are promoting the concept of open access, making the fruits of higher education widely available. Many universities now make lectures accessible as podcasts. Closer links between local authorities and academia could help to create much more integrated library services, with electronic information freely available through shared catalogues. Every town centre library could make stock from municipal and academic institutions publicly available in line with local needs, prioritised so that those requiring materials for study or research aren't disadvantaged. At neighbourhood level a more informal mix of local libraries and community-run 'reading rooms' and learning spaces might operate, drawing on ideas such as the Uni Project in New York, which turns public places into temporary libraries. These local experiments should be connected to the wider library network online and linked with schools and colleges rather than operating in isolation.

The key, as Arts Council England's research points out, is to ask the strategic questions about the purpose and function of libraries, not just what physical premises and staffing levels can be maintained with a diminishing level of funding. What kind of material or facilities should be made available freely to the public and why? Reading material may be freely available on the internet, but one in six people in the UK still struggle with literacy, according to the Literacy Trust (Jama and Dugdale, 2012). So libraries still have an important role, not only in providing reading matter but also in helping people to use and enjoy it. This is why a physical space is important too: a comfortable and welcoming environment and human contact makes learning easier and helps people overcome shyness and embarrassment. But these spaces need to adapt to changing technology, demographics, social habits and ways of learning. They need to work better, rather than simply being preserved for posterity.

Asking strategic questions about purpose, premises and potential can help to create a library service that puts life into high streets and local communities, and provides places of possibility rather than a financial and administrative burden for bureaucrats. As MPs noted in a House of Commons report in 2012: 'Although the current crisis may appear to bode ill for the future of public libraries, it also presents an opportunity for a thorough reassessment of their role and of the way they are organised' (House of Commons Culture, Media and Sport Committee, 2012).

So what might a real Information Commons, preserving the principles of open public access and social benefit, look like? Just as Wooler brought together the library and tourist information service in a community hub, local library networks around the country could link a range of complementary services and facilities. Many already partner with education services, running classes and facilitating research; this could be expanded to host skill-sharing schemes such as Trade Schools, where people teach each other skills such as music or languages, or timebanking, where people exchange their time on the basis that one hour of, say, help with accountancy is worth one hour of help with cleaning or gardening.

For Annemarie Naylor, one of the pioneers of community-run libraries, it's the information rather than the buildings we should consider first. What knowledge and skills exist within a local community and what kind of spaces should draw them together and enable them to be shared? What revenue-earning opportunities might arise from such creative collaborations that could help to sustain the spaces where they occur?

Libraries, like bookshops, cannot escape the fact that information is changing and is increasingly being curated via digital technologies. Ms Naylor argues that libraries should embrace the digital age and use it as an opportunity to create 'digital assets' for local communities, putting the power of knowledge into their hands. In practice, this calls for experimentation and a fair degree of trial and error. The Waiting Room in the St Botolph's area of Colchester is one such pioneer, combining the idea of a library with the concept of a hackspace – a hub for technological tinkering and invention – and a makerspace, a place for the production of physical artefacts. The Waiting Room, converted from a disused space in a bus station, includes a 'give-get' library where all who use it are expected to contribute, drawing from local knowledge (starting with a history archive) and contributing their creative skills and ideas to generate new publications and resources.

This approach to rethinking libraries from the ground up is risky, she admits:

> Only time will tell whether our vision can help others establish 'libraries as the hub of a community, making the most of digital technology and creative media, resilient and sustainable'. We are, for our part, determined to maintain an emphasis upon play, creativity, experimentation and prototyping with a view to exploring the 'art of the possible' when places, spaces and services are shaped by a community. (Naylor, 2013)

More strategically, an Information Commons could bring together the library and post office network, instead of trying to turn post offices into catch-all general retailers. Post offices are already exploring ways of providing local government services at branch counters. In Westminster, for example, residents can pay council tax or apply for parking permits at post offices, while in Ryedale, North Yorkshire, the council made it possible for residents to pay bills at post office counters instead of going to separate council buildings. In Sheffield, young adults leaving council care can get support payments at neighbourhood post offices (BIS et al, 2012). Port Clarence Post Office in Middlesbrough runs a health centre and a cafe.

A partnership between libraries and post offices could use library premises for postal facilities and council services including payments and information, in a setting that allows visitors to relax and browse books or the internet while waiting for service at a counter, and which is flexible enough to adapt to new digital services without a major outlay on new or refurbished buildings. Community-based financial services, such as credit unions, could also operate from libraries, which could provide confidential spaces for financial education or debt counselling.

A recent research report by the Royal Society for the Encouragement of Arts, Manufactures and Commerce (RSA) has argued that post offices should reinvent themselves as 'community enterprise hubs', promoting and servicing local communities of micro-businesses and makers. It argues that post offices are 'first and foremost commercial businesses', and proposes a series of measures that could make them more effective, both as enterprises and as neighbourhood services

(Dellot et al, 2014). A partnership between libraries and postal services, on the other hand, would underline that the local post office has a social as well as a commercial role. As a parliamentary inquiry concluded in 2009, post offices serve as 'an instrument of social cohesion', offering spaces that can be shared by all (House of Commons Business and Enterprise Committee, 2009).

A further step towards a local Information Commons could be to use libraries as a centre for reinventing local media. While local newspapers are struggling, a plethora of 'hyperlocal' websites and community news networks has emerged in recent years. Many of these are individual bloggers and citizen journalists, passionate but often untrained and unresourced, doing their best to provide local information. Few have found it possible to generate meaningful revenue from their activities, and frequently these local blogs vanish after a few years as the volunteers behind them become exhausted or move on. A few, such as Haringey Online in North London and the Culture Vulture blog based in Leeds, have become popular and successful. As a study in 2010 showed, when they work well they provide a dimension to local information that did not exist before, and can enable people to feel more involved in their community and take action to change things – or simply get together to enjoy shared interests with new friends and previously unknown neighbours (Flouch and Harris, 2013).

Libraries won't stop the decline and fragmentation of local media, but they could help new media outlets to grow. Making libraries available to citizen journalists as a physical space where they can meet, conduct interviews, and share information could help to join up the advantages of online and physical communities and make emerging local media more accessible, especially to those struggling to engage with online information. In an era where it is increasingly difficult to extract revenue from news, there is a strong argument for using libraries as a base for free and open sharing of news and intelligence.

This combination of open access and adaptable physical space could give town centre libraries a key role in democratising and localising a rapidly changing media landscape, using the power of digital technologies for the benefit of the locality. By putting high street libraries at the heart of a new Information Commons, our towns could reassert their distinctiveness and individuality and better reflect the communities they serve.

Places of possibility

Cooperation and collaboration, often between unexpected groups
and individuals, is at the heart of such places of possibility, whether
they are public services or voluntary arrangements, whether they are
the result of strategic thinking by local authorities or the inspiration
of passionate individuals.

Across the world new kinds of spaces are being created, from
the Living Room in Rotterdam where local residents have turned
a corner shop into a community space where they can share meals
and look after each other's children, to the Pirate Supply Store in
Los Angeles that combines a pirate costume shop with projects to
help young people improve their writing skills. In Copenhagen the
Laundromat Cafe combines a cheerful venue offering coffee, cake
and free Wi-Fi with a traditional launderette, turning a chore into a
pleasure and potentially a social occasion. In Chelmsford, the Ideas
Hub offers training courses and is developing a shared workspace in
an empty shopping centre unit. These shared spaces might combine
learning and making, as in the network of Fab Labs spreading across
the world from their early roots at MIT in Boston; they might
involve simply sharing a hobby, like the 'stitch'n'bitch' groups that
have spread from Amsterdam to Adelaide.

Joining together to pursue and discover shared interests is nothing
new, whether the backdrop is the agora of ancient Athens or the
mediaeval craft guilds. In 21st-century town centres, however,
there are new opportunities to collaborate in ways that transcend
professional or social boundaries.

Trading Spaces is a concept developed by Tessy Britton, an educator
and community practitioner now working with Architecture 00:/.
The idea is to find ways of bringing together retail enterprise and
social projects that benefit both the retailer and the community,
using the high street as a setting for experimentation and learning.
So a greengrocer's shop could partner with a community growing
project or a fruit harvesting scheme; a hardware shop could work
with teachers to improve DIY skills; or a cycle shop could host repair
workshops where owners can learn to fix their own bikes.

Loaf, a bakery in Birmingham, is a good example of the Trading
Spaces approach. It combines traditional breadmaking with courses
for people who want to learn the art of sourdough, a cookery school,

and an approach to social enterprise that closely links commercial and social objectives. Borrowing from the US concept of 'community-supported agriculture', Loaf asks customers to commit in advance to buying a certain quantity of bread at a set price. This enables Loaf to invest in ingredients and equipment, and provides a reliable guide to the quantities the appropriately named director, Tom Baker, needs to produce from his ovens. Profits are ploughed into food-related projects and campaigns, and there is no wastage: any leftovers are distributed to local charities. Originally run from Tom's home, Loaf now operates from a shop on Stirchley High Street, helping to keep alive a suburban centre.

In Sidcup, on London's southeastern fringe, a project called the Discovery Incubator took over a vacant shop in order to generate more projects like Loaf. With a focus on collaboration, it offered a place where people could drop in and explore what kind of spaces they would like to see on their high street, with examples of projects from around the UK and further afield illustrating some of the possibilities. Visitors were asked what would encourage them to start a new enterprise in the town, and invited to explore ideas rather than fit into a pre-ordained vision of what the high street should look like. Working with Bexley Council and the mayor of London's outer London fund, it was part of a wider scheme called In Store for Sidcup that seeks to re-establish the high street as the heart of the local community.

In Lambeth, South London, the notion of creatively reusing a high street shop has been taken a step further. The Work Shop in West Norwood was a temporary drop-in centre where passers-by could discuss Lambeth's plans to become a 'cooperative council' in which residents worked alongside the professional officers and elected councillors to shape the future of local services.

Reflecting on these projects, Tessy Britton describes the high street as the ideal place for the sort of community initiatives that might previously have been hosted in a run-down neighbourhood centre or a draughty church hall:

> 'People love these ideas. When you paint them a picture of what the high street could be, not just a place to buy stuff, but somewhere where you could make stuff together and do this kind of co-working, all of the social

stuff that's missing, they really like it and I think it really speaks to people. That's the kind of world they'd like to be creating and it has to be easy for them to be involved if they want to be.

'If you imagine community projects in the middle of nowhere, you're wasting all the secondary effects of the activity. So the secondary effects of footfall and life and energy and all those things, if you place that in the high street it just seems appropriate – these spaces used to be like that.' (interview with the author)

The magic of social spaces is that they encourage people to think of physical assets in different ways: to imagine what could be done there instead of assuming that only certain activities are appropriate or allowed. People who are used to thinking of themselves as consumers or shoppers begin to consider their use of the town centre as citizens; shopkeepers and council officers can begin to emerge from their bunkers.

This is a far cry from trying to preserve in aspic a high street of the past, an Eric Ravilious print of a vanishing world of specialist retailers. It allows people to let their imaginations free. But moving from imagination to making projects a reality is labour-intensive and time-consuming. Collaboration is a skill and a set of behaviours that have to be learned, and there are few shortcuts.

Collaborating for the common good

The illustrator Joel Pett penned a famous cartoon for *USA Today* just before the Copenhagen Climate Conference in 2009. It showed a bearded presenter explaining the benefits of environmental action: energy independence, preserved rainforests, green jobs, liveable cities, clean water, healthy children. An outraged member of the audience stands up and asks: 'What if it's a big hoax and we create a better world for nothing?'

A similar cartoon could be drawn to illustrate discussion of the future of town centres. What if economic recovery takes hold, retailers flock to high street premises and landlords are once again able to ratchet up rents? What if we invest in more sociable, equitable, inclusive and attractive places for nothing?

Those who would like to see the public purely as shoppers, to be satisfied with a sparkly new bag or a shiny new shopping centre, will resist the hard work and long-term thinking that cooperation demands. But when you ask people what they want, and progress beyond the shallow approach of standard consultation processes, there is no shortage of interest and enthusiasm. The Work Shop project in West Norwood is instructive: in the course of more than 500 conversations, residents suggested everything from a new cinema to affordable premises for business start-ups, pop-up supper clubs in empty shops, a Christmas family fair, and 'community shops' acting as local social centres (The Work Shop, 2013).

To the proverbial visitor from another planet, the idea of rethinking local services and activities without at the same time considering the vitality of the place where they operate might seem absurd. Time and again, however, cuts are made or services reconfigured with little thought given to the wider context of place and space, let alone the context of time and the likelihood that services will need to keep changing to meet new demands, developments and expectations.

Just as we can imagine a better future for libraries if we consider the other services that might cluster with them and how they might best serve the physical locations where they operate, so, too, we can envisage other public services operating in ways that are more accessible and that make town centres livelier and more useful. High street health centres could be located within or alongside leisure centres or gyms, with doctors prescribing courses of physical activity alongside or instead of medication. On-street clinics could provide healthcare where people work and shop, reducing pressure on the big hospitals' accident and emergency services and complementing the services offered by neighbourhood general practitioners. Town centre premises could be used for health information services and smoking cessation clinics, for antenatal care and routine health checks.

Blaydon Leisure and Primary Care Centre in Newcastle-upon-Tyne, created on the site of a former comprehensive school, illustrates the range of services that can be provided on one site. It has a swimming pool, studios for fitness and dance, and hosts football and athletics clubs; it provides family doctor, physiotherapy and mental health services; and it has Wi-Fi hotspots and charging points for electric cars. While town centres won't always be able to offer the scale and scope available at a large site like Blaydon, redundant shops or office accommodation or former public service buildings could be converted to provide many of these facilities in a high street setting. As healthcare technology develops, too, there may be a growing role for town centre clinics as locations for tele-medicine, linking local practitioners with highly skilled specialists at national centres of excellence.

Bringing health and leisure services together helps to shift the focus from treating sickness to promoting wellbeing. A whole-person approach to health might also draw in those responsible for parks and green spaces, encouraging outdoor activities, preventing or managing obesity, diabetes and heart disease through walking, gardening or 'green gyms'. This, in turn, could contribute to plans to turn empty town centre premises or vacant lots into urban farms and community gardens rather than temporary car parks or boarded-up development sites.

The Faculty of Public Health and Natural England, drawing on extensive research, have concluded that green spaces help to improve mental health and wellbeing, increase rates of physical activity, counter crime and antisocial behaviour, and reduce the health gap between rich and poor – as well as bettering the local quality of life. They argue that local authorities and health professionals should do more, not less, to provide green spaces and enable people to use them. In particular, they recommend 'green prescriptions' as an alternative to medication for mental illness, and support for programmes of health walks and exercise (FPH, 2010). Better cooperation between parks departments, leisure service providers and healthcare practitioners could result in healthier, happier town centres.

In the same way, charities could work together to make more imaginative use of town centre spaces. Many high streets are dominated by strings of charity shops, often selling a familiar mixture of worse-for-wear tweed jackets, not-old-enough-to-be-retro football annuals, slightly bashed furniture and UB40's greatest hits. Much as they rile independent traders who pay full business rates or councillors who would rather see upmarket boutiques, they provide an important service, enabling people on low incomes to obtain goods at affordable prices and raising funds for charitable causes, as well as giving unwanted clutter a new life. But by sharing resources they could provide a more attractive retail setting or create more specialist stores, focusing on books, music or furniture.

They could join forces with local volunteer bureaux or councils for voluntary service to set up town centre information hubs, advertising volunteering opportunities and promoting their causes and campaigns. Sharing resources could be a better way forward than trying to force charities to reinvent themselves as profit-seeking social enterprises in a savagely competitive commercial world.

How such partnerships work out and who is involved in them can't be prescribed from above. Each locality needs people who will look at the space in a high street or town centre as a whole; think holistically about the services, resources and ideas that exist in the local community; and work to bring them together to find new ways of making the most of their assets.

Stourport in Worcestershire is a market town of around 20,000 people. Its civic centre was built in the 1960s and is being vacated by Wyre Forest District Council, which is centralising its offices to save money. But instead of leaving a giant hole in the town centre, the district council is selling the civic centre and adjoining theatre for £1 to a community consortium consisting of the town council, the regeneration agency Stourport Forward, and The Civic, a theatre charity. The aim is to create a new community complex housing the library, coroner's court, skills advisers, the job centre, the town council, police and local charities. The project also seeks to keep the theatre open and increase use of the town centre, linking it with a scheme to develop the nearby canal basin.

Stourport has consciously adopted a 'whole town' approach to its public buildings, concentrating uses in the civic centre to anchor the town while alternative uses are sought for other buildings that will become surplus to requirements. As David Thain, a county councillor involved in the project, noted, "the local authority cannot just offload its worst buildings and run". But rethinking public services on this scale, even in a small town like Stourport, demands time, patience and a commitment to work together. It also requires a recognition that no town can sustain an unlimited number of multipurpose hubs: bringing services together in one location means that new uses must be found for the buildings being vacated.

From public service to co-production

As the political and financial pressures on public services grow, the drive to redesign places for people will take on an increasing urgency. Effective services and successful places go together: a service revamp which saves money within a council budget but blights the town the council serves cannot be regarded as fit for purpose.

The Commission on 2020 Public Services, established by the RSA, has outlined three principles it considers vital to the future of public services: a shift in culture from 'social security to social productivity'; a shift in power, from central government to citizens; and a shift in finance, 'reconnecting financing with the purposes of public services'. All three of those principles need to engage with places. Social productivity relates to communities of locality as well as communities of interest; devolution of power requires an assessment of the appropriate scale at which decisions are taken; and reconnecting finance with the purposes of public services demands, at the very least, that the public who are served become more involved in how and where financial choices are made.

Recognising the importance and power of digital technology, the Commission has proposed using interconnected '21st-century town meetings' as a way of enabling citizens to play a fuller role in decision making. Citizens could come together online and hear from others in different localities about the impact of proposals similar to those they are considering, or gather information from expert witnesses (Cumming, 2010).

Another possibility is participatory budgeting – an approach that hands over financial decisions about particular pots of money to a citizens' panel, who make their own choices about how the cash is spent rather than leaving it to chief financial officers or politicians. In Govanhill, Glasgow, where £200,000 was allocated to a local action group to spend as they saw fit, a study found that 'within a neighbourhood where community engagement has proven especially challenging, the participatory budgeting process has enabled purposeful and reciprocal dialogue between community members and the public and third sectors' (Harkins and Egan, 2012).

This idea of citizens and the state working together to design and to steer public services is often described as co-production: 'delivering public services in an equal and reciprocal relationship between professionals, people using services, their families and their neighbourhoods' (Boyle and Harris, 2009, p 11). The thesis is that services are better in quality and in value (including value for money) when the recipients are also the creators, designing and delivering services tailored to the needs that they can uniquely understand.

Such notions aren't just the fancies of academics. In Croxteth, one of the poorest estates on the edge of Liverpool, a community trust has brought together a library, sports centre, and education and training services that are geared to the needs of local people. Alt Valley Community Trust calls itself a 'Communiversity' – a university of life, if you like, but without the school of hard knocks. Led by local people since the 1980s, the Community Trust has turned an elderly people's home into a lifelong learning centre, revived the failing library and refurbished the sports centre as a holistic health centre in an area where poverty-related ill health is a serious problem. In an area of high unemployment it provides apprenticeships and vocational training.

A different model is the 'cooperative council' approach pioneered by Lambeth Council in South London. Here the council is seeking to work with local residents to design the future of public services together. Among the ideas being explored is the Young Lambeth Cooperative, involving young people in decisions about a range of children's and youth services, including running adventure playgrounds. The council says that in future it will 'do things with local people instead of doing things to them' – an admirable aspiration, but one that demands a radical change of culture in a short space of time.

Doing things with people rather than to them requires a different set of relationships. Physical space is symbolic: the council office, with its security screens, waiting rooms, queuing systems and locked doors protecting the professional officers, turns citizens into supplicants and encourages adversarial interactions. A move towards more relational public services, where citizens and service providers work as equals alongside elected representatives, means rethinking the places public servants occupy and where they meet the public. Places where people can simply drop in, like the Work Shop in West Norwood, help to generate a more equitable dynamic between professionals and the public – and at the same time can create a new and sustainable use for high street premises.

There are three big and interconnected challenges ahead: to recognise how public services affect the physical places and buildings people value; to acknowledge that the buildings and spaces that public services use are often valued by the public, who would like a say in their future; and to join forces with local people to think strategically, as people in Stourport are beginning to do, about the best use of local assets. It's a lot better than mounting midnight raids on libraries.

8

The space in between

Jamaica Street 10 years ago was a road most Bristolians would avoid. Warehouses and homes had been left to rot. If you were on your uppers in Bristol, this street in Stokes Croft is where you might end up – as a squatter if you were lucky, as a client of the Salvation Army or queuing for methadone at one of the local drug advice services if your luck was out.

One day brightly painted signs appeared, proclaiming the Stokes Croft neighbourhood Bristol's cultural quarter. Striking murals decorated a wall fronting the street. A while later, another notice declared Stokes Croft a Britain in Bloom winner, twinned with St Ives and Montmartre. Today murals and street art are everywhere.

Among them a visitor might find the slogan of the People's Republic of Stokes Croft: 'We make our own future'.

It's a blustery April afternoon, and down at the Bear Pit Jas, selling his Indian masalas, greets every stranger as a long lost friend. "I haven't seen you here for ages," he says. "How are you doing? Are you still in work? We're doing a special offer for the end of the day, five starters for £5. Have you tried our pakora?"

"It's a good spot, but trade is slow," Jas muses. You can see his point. The Bear Pit is a pedestrian underpass surrounded by the giant roundabout of St James Barton. Around its concrete concourse are raised turfed areas, a few trees and daffodils punctuating the dreariness. Holding the roundabout in a stifling double embrace are a giant Holiday Inn and a Debenhams. Down below, the enterprising energy of Stokes Croft is labouring to create a new market, with crafts and street food, an antidote to the tedium of Bristol's 'shopping quarter'. In the tunnels leading to the Bear Pit, buskers banter with street drinkers and the walls host a gallery of local artwork.

A month later the Bear Pit makes the local news as the city's mayor, George Ferguson, unveils Ursa, a striking black and white sculpture of a bear. A black-and-pink-clad wind band draws the crowds while stalls sell snacks and jewellery. At the heart of the city local people are beginning to make their own future.

The People's Republic of Stokes Croft isn't really a people's republic, just as Stokes Croft isn't really twinned with Montmartre. It's a statement of what could be, a projection of imagination into the urban streetscape. But it's a real entity too: a community interest company with a mission to turn the idea of a 'cultural quarter' into a reality. The People's Republic is the brainchild of Chris Chalkley, once a china wholesaler, and now the compere for a motley crowd of artists and activists. Chris Chalkley used to be too busy running his business to have time to do much about the area around him. But when his suppliers in Staffordshire went bust because it was cheaper to produce china on the other side of the world, and locals stopped buying his wares because they could buy cut-price crockery at Ikea, he started to wonder why the global economy was leaving his area in a worse state than before. The businessman morphed into an artistic agent provocateur:

'I got to a point where my businesses were forced to close and I thought, time to stop talking the talk and attempt to walk the walk. There's no point saying one thing and doing another. I'd become involved in the arts in this area and Stokes Croft six or seven years ago was seen as the sink of the South West, it was one of the worst places. What it really was, was one of the most interesting places.

'We had a derelict fence next door to where I'd moved the remnants of my business after it collapsed and I was busy painting the fence and decided to do an anti-consumerist mural on it at Christmas 2006, and while I'm painting it people kept coming up to me and saying, "Are you allowed to do this?" I'm going, I should think so, it's my wall. And it became very apparent that the role of the state was seen by people in this area as to stop stuff happening. There was a strong graffiti culture here, and the council spent much of its time painting grey squares over the graffiti.' (interview with the author)

From these beginnings came a surge of unofficial and uninvited improvement, Chris Chalkley says.

'It started by looking at all the derelict buildings that were so filthy and so grotty and sweeping them up with brushes and brooms and painting them beautifully, and encouraging the council to attempt to convict you for making the area better. By boxing clever you put them in a position where you show them up.

'So when they said it would be far too complex to have recycling on the street we made our own recycling bins, painted them, put them on the street and encouraged people to use them, and we said to the council we've done this, now can you sort out your end? What the council actually did was confiscate them. So for the last six years we've had one thing after another, just pushing, pushing, pushing ideas.'

The People's Republic of Stokes Croft is nothing if not aspirational. Chris says people "pissed themselves laughing" when the first cultural quarter signs went up. But by intervening in the neglected in-between spaces that nobody else wants or is prepared to care for, places can start to change – and in ways that might never happen if we wait for officialdom to get round to it.

Stokes Croft has had no shortage of officials drawing up plans and spending money on well-meaning proposals. In February 2006 Colin Buchanan, a firm of consultants, was funded by Bristol City Council and the now defunct South West Regional Development Agency to draw up what they called the 'gateway enhancement project', consulting community organisations and putting together a comprehensive plan to preserve the area's architectural heritage and revive the local economy. Little of it got further than a 72-page report (Colin Buchanan, 2006).

Contrast that with what happened at the Bear Pit, where there is now a Bear Pit Improvement Group supported by Bristol City Council – but only, as Chris Chalkley recounts, after a battle:

> 'We fought and fought by painting things in areas where we weren't allowed to paint and then they got scrubbed off and it culminated in a criminal damage conviction for myself. I got nicked but it completely changed things – suddenly the council was interested in walking round the Bear Pit. The reason this sunken 1960s area had nothing going on is that there were five different government agencies charged with looking after the space and they couldn't organise a piss-up in a brewery.
>
> 'It's a massive piece of real estate in the centre of the city and if we can make it work it has the possibility to become an autonomous zone. If we can get a market to work in there, and it's not an easy ask but we've started, if we can get that to happen that could be a model for everywhere.'

By bringing unloved corners to life, a place's prospects can begin to change. In Melbourne, Australia, the laneways or back alleys once used for servicing city centre shops and offices have become one of the city's main tourist attractions since street artists began to use them as their canvas. These once neglected spaces are now full of eateries and coffee shops, some wedged into the tiniest of corners, bringing bustle and business to turnings that were once avoided. In Bristol, the See No Evil festival in 2012 brought street artists from around the globe to redecorate the drab office blocks of Nelson Street. What was once illicit is now seen as a way of putting the city on the world stage.

Such constructive anarchy in public places comes in all shapes, sizes and colours. Bristol's is influenced by hip-hop culture and can be stridently political. In East London, Steve Wheen, otherwise known as the Pothole Gardener, is strictly about fun, creating miniature gardens in potholes around the capital. "It's about making people smile and giving them an unexpected moment of happiness," he told the *Daily Mail* (Webb, 2012).

A couple of hundred miles to the north, a more ambitious form of gardening anarchy is being practised. In Todmorden, West Yorkshire, a run-down former mill town has been turned into an unlikely tourist centre with the help of chard, fennel and sweetcorn, planted judiciously and frequently without permission.

At the derelict Abraham Ormerod Health Centre where the serial killer, Harold Shipman, once worked, gardener Nick Green began by planting runner beans and artichokes. Around the same time fruit trees mysteriously started to appear on patches of public land. What started as guerrilla gardening soon became official: it was not long before the nearby community college and police station, both on the busy Burnley Road, had their own conspicuous raised beds.

The canal, too, which is popular with boat users and walkers, is a showcase for planting. The Canal and River Trust now welcomes planting beside towpaths, having seen what happened when local people went ahead and did it without asking. As Pam Warhurst, co-founder of Incredible Edible Todmorden, put it: "We don't ask permission. It takes too long and anyway we're improving the place."

By planting in strategic places and creating clear links between them, Incredible Edible Todmorden has turned what could be seen as random outbursts of enthusiasm into a form of organic planning, putting the town on the map by mapping the town. Walk around Todmorden now and you'll find a 'green route' of walkways with edible and bee-friendly plantings, designed to bring a unity and identity to the town and encouraging people to circulate, discovering its market, cafes and independent shops as they do so.

The town, at the top of the Calder Valley on the border between Yorkshire and Lancashire, has traditionally been split into three segments, divided by the Burnley, Rochdale and Halifax roads. The green route creates a pedestrian circuit from the railway station, along the canal, through the modern NHS health centre with its fruit trees and 'apothecary garden', past the Hippodrome Theatre and back towards the market in the town centre – itself now becoming a showcase for local produce.

This is destination management without the use of expensive consultants or the creation of endless strategies and official documents. It is local people deciding what kind of town they want to create and building an identity and reputation around that, starting with small actions and joining them up to create coherence. As Pam Warhurst says, it's not just about growing vegetables: it's using vegetable growing to grow people. In the phrase coined by Jaime Lerner, mayor of Curitiba in Brazil, it's 'urban acupuncture' – small interventions that make a big difference.

Incredible Edible Todmorden is a demonstration of what people can do if they decide to take action for themselves. It's a touchable, feel-able explanation of the importance of local food networks; it's a set of activities that brings unlikely friends and neighbours together; and it's a model for community resilience in the face of climate change. It is changing schools by putting local food on the curriculum and getting kids growing, and it is changing business by creating new networks that link producers and consumers.

Incredible Edible has always worked from an understanding that people respond to simple shared ideas rather than heavy-handed persuasion. It has grown from its early unauthorised experiments with planting in public places, and is now spinning off its own food-growing businesses. Once the seeds of change are sown, the possibilities can seem limitless.

A garden, a promenade and a stage

This anarchy is the opposite of the lawlessness of the 2011 riots. It is people literally becoming a law unto themselves: defining and agreeing boundaries, working with respect for each other and the place they live in, coming together to decide what needs to be done and then getting on with it. In an environment where the powers that be are often unwilling to exercise their powers, it is powerful. And contrary to the popular view of anarchy as chaos, it can be a force for order.

Whether it's done with paint or with plants, it can be a catalyst for change, and for changing the mindsets of institutions. In some cases the guerrilla gardeners and street artists never get beyond the plants and paint. The actions may be symbolic, but their effectiveness is limited. For others, like Chris Chalkley and Pam Warhurst, it is impossible to take action without engaging with wider issues.

Painting derelict buildings means confronting or engaging with the owners of property, and challenging their ideas of what creates value. A painting that delights passers-by might be seen by a property owner either as an encroachment that devalues the bricks and mortar and subverts the principle of ownership, or as a free good that increases its attractiveness. Planting edible produce in neglected public spaces forces the owners of those spaces to justify their neglect and to explain why they are not making better use of their land. Spontaneous and impromptu planning rubs up against the bureaucracy of local government regulations.

Painting, planting or performing in public spaces highlights the worth of the in-between and transitional space. While it may not have commercial value or might be regarded by planners simply as part of the infrastructure, it can play a profound role in shaping perceptions. Todmorden and Stokes Croft both draw in visitors from around the world, and in doing so have created a dynamic that was never on their local councils' agendas. People have looked at the spaces in front of them and allowed themselves to imagine what could be done. As the fate of the Stokes Croft 'gateway enhancement project' shows, waiting for permission can be a recipe for blight.

Sometimes a brave council official will see the scope for small interventions that can radically change public space. After the fall of communism in Albania, the mayor of Tirana, Edi Rama, was in charge of a city where corruption was rife and infrastructure was crumbling. With the best will in the world it would have taken decades to deal with Tirana's systemic problems. But he felt he could lift the city's spirits by encouraging people to paint their buildings.

Tirana is now famous for its brightly painted apartment blocks. Painting the city was cheap, and it made a difference. Mr Rama – now the country's Prime Minister – said: 'When colours came out everywhere, a mood of change started transforming the spirit of the people.... People started to drop less litter in the streets. They started to pay taxes. They started to feel something they'd forgotten' (Ted.com, 2013).

Just as the interior of shops or public buildings can metamorphose into places of possibility, so, too, can the external environment. What was previously the preserve of highway engineers and traffic managers can become a garden, a promenade or a stage.

Greener towns for a changing climate

Todmorden has led the way in showing how communities can be changed by growing food in public places. Many other towns and cities are beginning to turn themselves into gardens. New York's High Line and the Promenade Plantée in Paris are well-known examples of former elevated railway lines that have been transformed into linear parks in the heart of the city. Chicago has a network of green roofs, with gardens on top of office blocks creating habitats for birds and insects. In Hackney, East London, a network of rooftop beehives is putting wildlife into the heart of a densely populated suburb. Green walls or vertical gardens can bring buildings alive, providing insulation for those inside and a more attractive environment for passers-by, absorbing pollution from busy streets including harmful gases such as nitrous oxide.

You only have to watch the way people use green spaces in towns and cities to understand how they lift people's spirits and provide a setting for socialising. Some of London's most popular gardens and squares are the relatively small spaces that punctuate the urban landscape, such as Victoria Embankment Gardens in Westminster and Gordon Square in Bloomsbury. Even in winter these oases are populated, creating a breathing space for office staff or students, restaurant workers or builders; the moment the sun shines and a hint of warmth breaks through, they are packed.

Contrast them with the hard landscaping you'll see in many town centres, from Luton to Wolverhampton. Designed for ease of maintenance and flexibility, these places often reflect the sterility of much of the built environment around them. They are functional and people will use them if there is nothing better, but they are cheerless. Given the choice between a grassy space surrounded by trees and plants, with moveable chairs as you'll see in the parks of Paris, and a hard surface with fixed seats and benches, most people will head for the grass.

That tells us something significant about how we can bring our town centres to life. If people love parks and green spaces, let's bring them into our city and town centres. In Bradford, the hole left while Westfield prevaricated over its shopping centre plans became a temporary urban garden, planted with wildflowers and surrounded by artworks. From being a screened-off development site touting a flatulent promise of retail-led regeneration, it became a place to stroll and sit.

As the amount of space we need for shops, offices and public buildings decreases in many towns, there will be opportunities to be more creative. In Cleveland, Ohio, the glass-covered Galleria at the Erieview mall, built in 1987 and now redundant as a shopping centre, has become an urban greenhouse growing salads and vegetables. Some of Britain's flagging indoor shopping centres could follow suit, becoming winter gardens and meeting places rather than filling up with the retail flotsam of Greggs and Poundland.

As shopping areas shrink, more vacant sites will open up. Some buildings won't be worth saving; others are already standing idle and have no obvious use. Instead of turning them into car parks or simply surrounding them with boards and leaving them, as happens in many towns, these could become temporary community gardens and urban parks. Cleared sites could be turned into wildflower meadows or become play areas for children, creating social value in places where commercial value is absent. Instead of putting barriers in front of members of the public who want to put empty spaces to use, planners should lean on landlords to provide good reasons why vacant spaces should not be lent to local people.

The reasons for greening our towns go far beyond simply making them nice places to visit and relax in, although we shouldn't underestimate the value of that. Making high streets greener also makes them more able to withstand the vagaries of climate change and creates a healthier environment.

Flooding is one of the greatest risks to urban areas. The results can be devastating to businesses and homes, as the floods in Hull in 2007 and Hebden Bridge in 2012 demonstrated. Even those who are not directly affected pay a price in the loss of local services and in higher insurance premiums. Green spaces and planted areas help to absorb water run-off, while hard surfaces increase the severity of flash floods. Sustainable urban drainage systems use natural landscape features to hold and filter stormwater, countering the worst effects of heavy rainfall. Pavements can be constructed of porous material made from recycled tyres, reusing a waste product that might otherwise end up in landfill to make streets more resistant to the effects of storms. In Curitiba, Brazil, the Municipal Secretariat of the Environment has developed a network of open spaces as a response to problems of flooding and overcrowding. It has its own legislative powers and financial resources, which amount to 4 per cent of the city's total budget, partly raised through fines on polluters.

It isn't just the rain we need to watch out for. In hot summers, heavily built-up areas create 'urban heat islands' – hotspots, literally, where the temperature is higher than in the surrounding area. Buildings and tarmac absorb and radiate heat, so much so that some pioneering companies are now examining how this energy can be converted to power homes and offices. The US Environmental Protection Agency reckons that urban heat islands can be up to 3°C warmer than surrounding areas during the day, and up to 12°C warmer at night – increasing the demand for energy-intensive air conditioning and the risk of heat-related illnesses (US EPA, nd). Planting trees on our streets helps both to reduce the ambient temperature and to absorb pollution.

Greening our town centres can help build our 'green infrastructure', the network of natural spaces – parks, woodlands, fields and watercourses – that preserve biodiversity and limit the negative effects of climate change. This infrastructure is at least as important as our roads and railways, but receives far less care and investment. When the UK government announced an investment of £100 billion in infrastructure in 2013, there was not one mention of green infrastructure or its role in underpinning all the other services we rely on (HM Treasury, 2013). In Hamburg, by contrast, the city authorities are planning a green network covering 40 per cent of the municipal area (Braw, 2013). Healthy high streets need to be connected to our green infrastructure just as they are linked to the 'grey' infrastructure of roads and sewers.

Green networks are essential for wildlife too. As intensive farming practices threaten biodiversity, it becomes more important that towns and cities play their part in providing habitats for plants, birds and insects. The Lawton review of Britain's wildlife sites described green spaces as a network within which different elements support and sustain each other. Not only must we look after each site, the review concluded, but we also need to create connectivity between them. This enables species to move from place to place, increasing their chances of surviving floods or droughts, and helps to reduce the negative impact of human activity (Lawton, 2010).

There are also powerful health arguments for providing green spaces in town centres. Greenspace Scotland, which examined 87 separate studies, found that better health was linked to green space regardless of socioeconomic status: rich or poor, your health is better (Greenspace Scotland, 2007). The more time people spend outdoors the less stressed they feel – an important consideration given the cost to the economy of depression and mental illness, which has been calculated at £26.1 billion in the UK (McCrone, 2008). A study of 345,143 GP records in the Netherlands, quoted by the Faculty of Public Health, indicated that the annual prevalence rates for 15 of 24 chosen disease clusters was lower where there was more green space within 1km. This correlation was strongest for anxiety and depression, and among children (Maas et al, 2009). Green your town centre, and people will feel better.

These streets are made for walking

If the idea of the town centre as a garden doesn't come naturally to planners and developers, they should be more comfortable with the concept of the town centre as a promenade. After all, that's been one of its key functions since ancient times. It's only in the last hundred years that through traffic has routinely squeezed out those who want to linger, and motorised transport has been given priority over those on foot.

In recent decades planners and engineers seem to have gone out of their way to make the ritual of *la passegiata* – or its less stylish British equivalents – something that is daunting or physically impossible.

Walkers are pressed onto narrow pavements and hemmed in by railings. The old-fashioned zebra crossing, where the driver must stop when the pedestrian crosses, has frequently been replaced by the pelican crossing, where the pedestrian must push a button to ask permission to cross. Britain has not yet descended to the North American extreme of making jaywalking a criminal offence, often accompanied by on-the-spot fines, but in most of our main streets, there's no question that the car, not the walker, is king. Signposts, bollards and street clutter are crammed onto pavements to enable vehicles to get through unimpeded.

In modern Britain we've had an odd love–hate relationship with walking in town centres. For decades, traders in small towns on major routes campaigned for bypasses to free their towns of congestion. Now motorists travelling along those bypasses find signposts beseeching them to take a detour to enjoy the services of the towns that have been bypassed. In larger towns, pedestrianised shopping streets and multistorey car parks were seen as the solution for many years: the streets were car-free but nobody would have to walk far. Now some of those pedestrian streets are being handed back to motorists on the assumption that, as Welsh butcher Michael Turner told a TV reporter, "we need cars".

> 'Pedestrianisation does not work, it's not rocket science, we need cars. At the end of the day, if you could allow cars onto the high street and get back to how it was you could turn major towns and cities around and it wouldn't take a lot, because the car is here to stay.' (quoted on ITV Wales, 2013)

There is surprisingly little research to justify or to disprove such heartfelt views. The arguments for pedestrian streets are obvious: they encourage sociability, make it easier for visitors to access facilities and shops, and invite people to linger. The street becomes a place for strolling and sitting, and walking is a pleasure rather than a chore. A study by the traffic consultants Ecolane in 2001 concluded that pedestrianised streets attracted more visitors and brought more business to retailers – although increased turnover was partly offset by rising rents and rates as landlords and local authorities sought to cash in (quoted in Baker Associates, 2010).

There are alternatives to the complete segregation of cars and people that can still encourage walking and lingering. New Road, Brighton, became the first of a new generation of 'shared spaces' in 2007. A shared space gives pedestrians priority: road surfaces are changed to soften or remove the divide between people and traffic. In New Road, restaurants and cafes now set out tables and chairs on the street, which has seen a 62 per cent increase in pedestrian traffic, 22 per cent more cycling and, according to the designers, a 600 per cent increase in 'staying activity'.

The Civic Trust, which selected the scheme for a special award in 2009, commented:

> By adopting the concept of a shared space the scheme has transformed a traditional, motorist dominated street scene incorporating rigid features such as kerbs and crossings into one where pedestrians are able to move freely over the whole area and have priority over other users. The inclusion within the design of attractive features such as bespoke seating and lighting has improved the experience of many people who use the area, and has created a new café culture with a lively, welcoming atmosphere which is pedestrian friendly both during the day and in the evening. (www.civictrustawards.org.uk)

'Shared space' thinking has also influenced the redesign of Seven Dials in London's Covent Garden and Kensington High Street, removing clutter and putting the needs of walkers before drivers. Cars and trucks slow down because drivers are more aware of the needs of other road users. In the Netherlands, thanks to the pioneering work of the traffic engineer Hans Monderman, many town centres have now adopted the shared space approach.

A street that puts the needs of walkers first will tend to be busier and more welcoming. The Danish architect and urbanist Jan Gehl calculates that a street with two pavements 11.5 feet wide can handle 20,000 people per hour. Two cycle lanes, each six feet wide, can carry 10,000 cyclists an hour. By contrast, a two-lane, two-way street can carry at most 2,000 cars per hour – and it is much harder for a motorist to stop and linger than it is for a pedestrian. In Melbourne, a programme to improve conditions for pedestrians led to a 39 per cent increase in the number of walkers in the city centre between 1993 and 2005, and three times the number of people staying; after a decade of action to make Copenhagen more bike-friendly, well over one third of journeys to work or educational institutions was by bicycle (Gehl, 2010).

Just as a greener town centre is a healthier one, so is one that is good for walking. Britain's National Institute for Health and Care Excellence (NICE) reckons that only 6 per cent of men and 4 per cent of women manage the recommended 30 minutes' 'moderate or vigorous' activity on at least five days a week; illnesses related to physical unfitness, such as coronary heart disease, strokes, cancers and diabetes are on the increase. Air pollution, largely caused by motor traffic, reduces life expectancy in the UK by an average of seven to eight months, and causes 50,000 premature deaths each year. More people on foot and fewer in cars makes for a healthier society (NICE, 2012).

To make a high street, town or city good for walkers there needs to be plenty to see and do. Life at three miles per hour is dull if all you see is blank facades and if shop units are designed according to national and multinational retailers' preferred standards of efficiency, which dictate maximum street-level floorspace for ease of access and profit per square foot. No amount of window dressing will compensate for the fact that for yards and yards, there is only the same gigantic store. Public buildings are often even worse, the contents and activities hidden behind monumental facades designed to impress visitors with their civic vanity. Variety, invitation and permeability need to be the watchwords of a walkable town.

People as performance

As well as being a garden and a promenade, a good high street is a stage. It is a place to see and to be seen, to watch and to participate. For that you need both performers and an audience. Jane Jacobs recognised this in her description of the ballet of the streets (see Chapter 1); William H. Whyte's film, 'The social life of small urban spaces', records the serendipitous performances of New Yorkers' use of parks and street corners and the unconscious rituals of people-watching (Whyte, 1980).

Britain's towns have got into the festival spirit in recent years, recognising that town centres offer an ideal venue for everything from fine art to fine food. Sheffield's Tramlines music festival, which draws up to 80,000 people into the city centre for three days in July, uses indoor and outdoor spaces to showcase local and international music, as well as street theatre, children's activities and even a science festival. London's Southbank Centre hosts the capital's culinary expertise with the Real Street Food Festival, while most major cities now have Gay Pride parades. The Lambeth Country Show, staged every year since the early 1980s, mixes urban music with a more bucolic line-up of farm animals and traction engines.

You don't have to put on a festival to turn your town into a stage. Indeed, if you're going to put on a festival it helps if your town is a stage already: a place where people feel comfortable sitting, being with friends, and whiling away the time. Watching the way children use town centres can be instructive. If they have corners to sit in, open space to run around in, objects on which they can climb and engage in imaginative play in the ordinary streetscape rather than in special pens designated as official play areas, the street meets the first requirement of an effective performance space: it's a place people are happy to stay in.

The sport of parkour, or freerunning, shows how the urban environment can be used as a platform for gymnastic feats, just as skateboarders have always used ramps and obstacles such as benches and steps to demonstrate their prowess. Officials often view parkour enthusiasts, like skateboarders, as antisocial and dangerous – because they are young and lippy or because of a fear of litigation rather than because of the physical damage they might inflict on themselves or anyone else. After 93 parkour enthusiasts attended a training workshop in Guildford, Surrey, the Safer Guildford Partnership decided the safest way of following it up was to tell them to stay away. The local police sergeant advised: 'We urge participants to think very seriously about coming to Guildford and indulging in this dangerous pastime which poses a serious risk to themselves and to others' (see http://forums.worldwidejam.tv/showthread.php?t=2586). But by seeking to eliminate risk, there's a high chance of eliminating theatre too.

In other towns, councils have taken a more enlightened attitude. Nantwich in Cheshire, for example, has opened a public freerunning park, supported by environmental charity Groundwork and Nantwich Town Council. The famous skatepark at London's Southbank Centre has been declared an 'asset of community value' under the Localism Act, forcing the centre to reconsider plans to move it.

Thinking of the town centre as a performance space helps to make it fit not just for special events but also for everyday life. A stage needs comfortable places where you can sit and watch. It must be adaptable to a variety of activities. It ought to be easy to get to and to get away from. There should be plenty to do between performances, the equivalent of the drinks during the interval of a show; and accessible toilets and enough of them. Lighting and acoustics matter too: a town where you can have a conversation without having to shout over the roar of traffic, and where both natural and artificial light are used to best effect, is a good place to be.

Most of the time, the performances people watch are not those of events and festivals, but the everyday theatre of other people. It's hard to people-watch on a street where there is nowhere to stop or pause without getting in someone else's way; it's hard, too, if the view is blocked by a cavalcade of buses. The more space there is for pedestrians, the more they are likely to hang around, to watch and even to perform – consciously or not – for others.

One of the best indicators of a good town for people-watching is the proliferation of pavement cafes and restaurants. The passers-by become part of the entertainment, as do the other customers. The coffee may well be secondary. People aren't drinking more coffee than they used to because coffee is so much better than it used to be. Neither can you put the spread of street cafes down to huge increases in disposable income. What you're buying with your latte or macchiato is a comfortable breathing space, a place to chat, an opportunity to observe others or to take part in the social rituals of meeting colleagues or contacts.

Jan Gehl observes:

> Coffee is probably the ostensible reason for someone to be seated at a sidewalk café, but it is also an excuse to watch city life go by ... in almost all cases staying times are considerably longer than the time it takes to drink a cup of coffee. The real activity is recreation, time off and pleasure in city space. (Gehl, 2010, p 146)

Between 2001 and 2008, the number of pavement cafe chairs counted in Philadelphia grew from 1,208 to 3,380; in Stockholm the figure rose from 3,400 to 5,750 between 1990 and 2005; and in caffeine-addicted Melbourne, from 1,940 in 1993 to 12,570 by 2009.

In a pickle about parking

Thinking of the town centre as a garden, promenade or stage leads us straight to one of the most fraught debates about the future of the high street: access, or, as many would prefer to describe it, parking. That framing of the debate in itself is revealing, privileging the motorist above other users of urban space. The real issue is how the greatest number of people can gain the maximum enjoyment and use of town centre spaces for as long as possible and at the most reasonable cost.

Parking can't be airbrushed out of the picture. A lot of people have to use cars – including many people with disabilities, elderly people or those travelling from locations that aren't served by public transport. Some, including families with children, often find it much more convenient to use a car. And few things are more guaranteed to enrage motorists, whether they need to use their vehicles or simply prefer to, than the cost of parking – a cost that many see as a punitive tax on a facility that they can enjoy free of charge at most out-of-town shopping centres.

In recent years an urban myth has developed that free or cheap parking will save the high street. It was a view consistently expressed by shopkeepers and market traders during the course of researching this book. The Federation of Small Businesses has campaigned hard for town centre parking to be viewed as an 'essential service' (2008). City of Chester MP Stephen Mosley told Parliament his town's 'free after three' parking scheme had increased footfall by 23 per cent. Never one to turn down a crowd-pleasing opportunity, Eric Pickles, Secretary of State for Communities and Local Government, grabbed the chance in 2011 to blame the previous government's 'anti-car restrictions' for 'ghost town' high streets, declaring: 'We want to see more parking spaces to help small shops prosper in local high streets and assist mums struggling with their family shop. We are standing up for local high streets' (DCLG, 2011a).

In the columns of local newspapers and in social media discussions, residents and traders regularly reinforce the sense of injustice. One commentator in a discussion on parking price rises in Horsham, West Sussex, was so outraged he suggested direct action: 'We should hold a protest day: everyone use a bus, take the train or walk in but not give the council any income on parking' (www.facebook.com/horsham.uk/posts/10150507309704139?comment_id=20729700).

If only. And contrary to the received wisdom, traders might welcome it. A study for London Councils, the collective voice of the capital's borough councils, found that shopkeepers routinely overestimated the proportion of their customers who travelled by car, in some cases by as much as 400 per cent:

> In London, as well as other cities, the share of those accessing urban centres on foot or by public transport is much greater. Walking is the most important mode for accessing local town centres; public transport is the most important mode for travel to international centres, such as Oxford Street. (Tyler et al, 2012, p 5)

While car drivers spent more per trip, the study found pedestrians and bus users spent more over a week or a month in London's town centres, splashing out £147 more per month than motorists in 2011. This echoes earlier findings cited in a review by Professor Greg Marsden, Director of the Institute for Transport Studies at the University of Leeds. He noted that the data 'present a challenge to the orthodoxy that providing good car access is the main factor in encouraging shopping in an urban context' – a challenge that policymakers continue to duck (Marsden, 2006). International evidence adds more grist to the mill: a study by San Francisco's Municipal Transportation Authority found that in Polk Street, one of the city's main shopping and leisure areas, half the visitors arrive on foot and only 15 per cent by car (Streetsblog San Francisco, 2013).

As Professor Marsden observes, 'parking policy is at best an opaque balance between a revenue raising activity for local authorities, a desire to avoid deterring visitors and therefore damaging urban vitality, and a need to manage transport demand'. That balance needs to become much more transparent.

A common assumption, reinforced by Eric Pickles, is that cars are required to carry shopping home. But the kind of people who shop in bulk for groceries, white goods, clothes or gifts are already more likely to use supermarkets and out-of-town malls, which are built precisely for the purpose of enabling customers to buy and take away as much stuff as possible. Town centres, on the other hand, will increasingly host a much wider range of activities, relatively few of which will involve carrying large quantities of goods. If shoppers stop using supermarkets and malls for bulk shopping, it won't be because they've gone back to the town centre; it will be because their bulk shopping is migrating online.

It's certainly true that supermarkets and out-of-town malls enjoy an unfair advantage in the UK because they can provide free parking, but that's only one of their unfair advantages – and this particular horse has bolted. The opportunity to charge for out-of-town parking was lost a quarter of a century ago.

If it's too late to prevent out-of-town stores offering free parking, what about making town centre parking free? Doing that, of course, is a cost to the local authority providing the parking spaces. It's a direct cost in terms of maintaining the car parks and payment systems, and it's an opportunity cost in that the spaces used for car parking could be used for something else – new developments or open space in the case of off-street parking, or wider pavements or cycle lanes instead of on-street parking. If parking is provided gratis, the cost must be levied directly on local taxpayers (many of whom won't be motorists at all) or town centre businesses, or taken from other budget headings.

Motorists' sense of unfairness is often fuelled by a perception that council finance chiefs see them as a cash cow. Smart technology could enable a shift to dynamic pricing, which would be more transparent. The cost of a parking space could change in real time according to the available spaces and the length of time spent there: a motorist arriving at 9am on a Sunday might find a space available at a nominal cost, but the same space might cost £5 an hour at the same time on a weekday. That might create a better match between supply and demand, effectively letting the market dictate its own price, but it also creates more uncertainty for motorists, traders and the parking authority. Los Angeles and San Francisco are starting to experiment with dynamic pricing, but it will take time for the impacts to be clear.

There is some evidence that reducing parking costs can provide a short-term boost to town centre shops. A scheme by Vale of

White Horse District Council to offer two hours of free parking in Abingdon, Faringdon and Wantage town centres brought many more cars into town. While it wasn't clear whether or not there was a direct correlation, 70 per cent of traders said the scheme had been good for their businesses (Vale of White Horse District Council, 2013). Other towns have reported similar results, but few councils are in a position to afford long-term subsidies for town centre parking. And while this mitigates one problem, it can magnify others.

A better way to frame the debate is to pose the question in terms of access for all. How can as many people as possible use the town centre easily and conveniently, ensuring nobody is excluded because of age or disability, and that when they get to town the quality of the experience is as good as it can be? Creating as many parking spaces as possible might tick the right boxes for the motorist, but not for anybody else. By contrast, a town that encourages walking and cycling is better for everyone, including those who arrive by bus or car: the air is cleaner, the streets are quieter and more attractive, and it's easier to move around. And that's without considering the arguments for carbon reduction or the possibility that increasing fuel costs and the growth of car sharing will begin to limit the rise in car ownership.

To create civilised, healthy and active town centres, priority has to go first to pedestrians and people with mobility difficulties; then cyclists and those using public transport; then those who have to use a car because of where they live or special circumstances; and finally to other motorists. There needs to be differentiation between motorists, too: commuters who leave their cars in town all day contribute less to the town centre than tourists or shoppers. Smart pricing systems driven by real-time data, and incentives for commuters to use bikes or public transport, can help to remove many of the vehicles that simply take up space. A further option is to link preferential parking rates to spending at town centre stores or use of public buildings. Smartcard technology could be used to log the use of local facilities and award points that could be used in exchange for parking.

Motorists may fume, but if what's on offer is worth visiting, people will visit it. London's Regent Street welcomed visitors to four Sundays of car-free 'summer streets' in July 2013: nearly two million people joined the fun. In New York nearly seven miles of city centre streets were car-free on three consecutive summer Saturdays, bringing in 250,000 people in 2012. Bogota in Colombia turns its streets into cycle lanes every Sunday, and hundreds of thousands of people take advantage of the open space for the weekly 'Ciclovia' events. Venice is famously free of cars, and nobody complains about their absence. The international PARK(ing) Day event turns on-street metered parking spaces into urban green spaces on one day a year, transforming boring bits of asphalt into pop-up urban farms, bike repair shops, and even wedding venues (see http://parkingday.org).

Car parking, despite the protestations of traders and motorists, is neither a universal right nor a free good. As research by the British Parking Association and Association of Town and City Management noted, 'in reality there is no such thing as a free parking space; someone, somewhere is paying for it' (Macdonald, 2013).

The challenge, as the National Assembly for Wales recognised in a recent inquiry, is to think about the future of the whole place, not just about parking in isolation or as an instant fix. It noted:

> We understand that parking in town centres is a complex and highly charged issue, but we have found the evidence in this inquiry to be mostly anecdotal. There is a need to grasp the nettle by planning for the much longer-term so that town centres can be resilient in the face of rising fuel prices and energy scarcity. (National Assembly for Wales, 2012, p 27)

The aim of transport policy in town centres shouldn't be simply to get people from A to B as rapidly as possible; it should be to bring places to life and keep them alive. That means investing in facilities and improvements that prioritise quality of life. As we consider in the next chapter, this is a must if the town centre is to become a place to live in as well as to visit.

Restoring the common wealth of cities

Transport policies and habits can be critical in enabling town centres' in-between spaces to come to life, or in squeezing the life out of them. Much of what has been achieved in places like Bristol and Todmorden has been done despite the traffic, but when it's been possible to create walker-friendly environments, like Bristol's Bear

Pit and Todmorden's Green Route, the scope for changing the atmosphere and activity in a town expands enormously.

Places like London's South Bank function as promenade, garden and stage. So do some unexpected parts of the urban fabric, like Regent's Canal in North London, which works as a social street, a place to relax and a pleasant commuting route for walkers and cyclists. Around the world city leaders are recognising the importance of such places to the urban economy: in Seoul, Korea, the Cheonggyecheon river, once culverted and covered by an elevated highway, has been restored as an open stream surrounded by a linear park, bringing nature and pleasure back into the heart of the capital.

Projects like Cheonggyecheon restore the common wealth to the city. They replace spaces that are exclusively used by traffic with public places open to all, turning the ugly into the pleasurable. But towns don't need to wait for gung-ho mayors with massive budgets to do huge projects. They can begin changing neglected and unappreciated spaces into gardens, promenades and stages by recognising and encouraging the efforts of helpful troublemakers like Chris Chalkley, facilitating them and joining them up. Every town has a few. Given space and support, they can spearhead the rediscovery of the common good in our town centres.

9

A place to live

At Waterloo Bridge, the Thames turns 90 degrees, flowing from Westminster to the City of London. Go into any of the pubs and bars on the north side of the river and the talk is likely to be of politics or finance, while most of the prominent buildings and public spaces represent the interests of one or the other. In between are the cloisters of the Temple, the seat of Britain's legal profession, where the marriages of convenience between politics and finance are sealed or dissolved.

Cross the river and a different atmosphere prevails. South Bank has often put two fingers up to the interests of Westminster and the City, or has catered to their less respectable tastes. In the 16th and 17th centuries it was known as the haunt of vagrants and pickpockets, prostitutes and – naturally – performers, including William Shakespeare's own Lord Chamberlain's Men. Today Southwark still has its seamy side, but the long sweep of the South Bank of the Thames is characterised by officially sanctioned culture, in a procession that begins with the Royal Festival Hall, takes in the National Theatre and British Film Institute, scoops up the television temple of London Studios, and whose rearguard is the Tate Modern gallery in the former Bankside power station.

This long cultural high street, embracing popular attractions such as the London Aquarium at the former County Hall and the London Eye with its panoramic views of the capital's landmarks, is connected by an extended riverside walkway. Halfway between the Festival Hall and Tate Modern you'll find Gabriel's Wharf, an eclectic mix of designer shops created from former garages. At first sight it's the kind of visitor-focused shopping area you might find in any capital city, with bars and eateries for those seeking a civilised break from their cultural tourism.

A little further downstream you'll find the slightly more refined shops of Oxo Tower Wharf, with artists' studios, fashion and furniture designers, a dressmaker and a ceramicist, an art gallery and more restaurants. In between, for anyone wanting a rest without having to spend money, is the green space of Bernie Spain Gardens, a little oasis amid the bustle.

Cast a quick eye over the lawns on a warm day and you might assume that everyone there is a tourist, perhaps taking a break between watching a show and spending the evening at a nearby restaurant. You certainly wouldn't guess that some of them are among the poorest people of London, living in the apartments and houses around Bernie Spain Gardens because the local council has given them priority for housing.

This enclave on the South Bank is home to Coin Street Community Builders, one of the longest-established and most successful community organisations in the capital. It is thanks to Coin Street Community Builders that the riverside walkway links the South Bank's cultural attractions; thanks to them, too, that Bernie Spain Gardens, named after local campaigner Bernadette Spain, exists; and it is thanks to Coin Street Community Builders that the riverside has been animated with the shops and restaurants of Gabriel's Wharf and Oxo Tower.

At the heart of these developments is a housing project designed to offer affordable homes to ordinary people – people who 40 years ago faced having to move to make way for yet more riverside offices. In 1977 the Coin Street Action Group was formed to oppose plans to turn the largely derelict 13-acre site into an office city featuring Europe's tallest hotel. The action group's alternative plans included affordable homes, a riverside park and walkway, workshops and leisure facilities. Today much of that vision has been realised, with four housing cooperatives on site offering more than 200 affordable homes, a neighbourhood hub providing childcare and space for events, a sports centre and meeting spaces.

The South Bank demonstrates many of the qualities of a successful high street discussed in Chapter 8: it is a garden, a promenade and a stage. These attributes are brought to life because ordinary people can use them. They use them not only because they have permission to enter a public space: they use them because the public space was created on their behalf and belongs to them. The community has created the commons.

South Bank is good for tourists and visitors because, far from being led by commercial interests, the areas owned and managed by Coin Street Community Builders have been designed as a good place to live. Bernie Spain Gardens exists because people living in the housing cooperatives need access to green space on their doorstep. The riverside walkway benefits local tenants and residents as well as commuters and sightseers. The neighbourhood centre puts affordable childcare and meeting spaces at the heart of the community. The refurbishment of the landmark Oxo Tower provides an income that can be reinvested in new projects, such as plans for new homes and a leisure centre with a swimming pool at Doon Street, a site next to the National Theatre that has been derelict for half a century.

When we turn our town centres into places to live and that are worth living in, the benefits spill over for everyone. People who live in a place are more likely to have a sense of responsibility for it than those who are just passing through. They want it to be a good place for their children and relatives; they invest their own time and money in helping it to look good and work well. Something as simple as a pot of geraniums on a balcony can make a difference, adding the human touch that comes when people call a place home. When everyone puts a pot of geraniums on their balcony, the whole place takes on a different character. And when people work on behalf of the community to create better places, the benefits spread far and wide.

South Bank is an exceptional location, and some exceptional people have been involved in Coin Street Community Builders. But it is not the kind of exception that proves a contrary rule. The sorts of changes that have taken place in Coin Street have been seen elsewhere.

Notting Hill is now thought of as one of West London's prime locations – so prime that the term 'Notting Hill set' was used to describe the circle of people surrounding Conservative Party leader David Cameron before he became Prime Minister (*Daily Telegraph*, 2006). Fifty years ago it was associated with the activities of slum landlords and was a place of last resort, full of poor quality accommodation often rented to London's new immigrant communities. 'No blacks, no dogs, no Irish' was the traditional welcome from many English landlords, pinned to front doors across West London. Notting Hill Housing Trust, established in 1962, set to work to provide good quality affordable housing, and in doing so tackled the problems of the high street too.

Part of the trust's strategy was to convert homes over shops. But simply providing accommodation wouldn't work on its own. Peter Redman, the trust's former chief executive, explained what happened in the street by the trust's office near Portobello Road:

> 'It was a pretty run-down street some years ago. The police had closed the pub for criminal activities. Staff were frightened to witness prostitution and drug dealing in broad daylight outside their office. Not many people wanted to live in this street.
>
> 'What businesses there were, were struggling and most properties were being boarded up. It was quite a vibrant area in other ways, with floats for the Notting Hill Carnival assembled in the street and made ready and huge costumes were put around people to move into the parade. So it perhaps had some life in it. My predecessors took a decision that we were going to take control of this street. So steadily over a period of years we bought up half of it....

'We took that pub and turned it into starter workshop units and got a bit of sense into the place that something was possible. That encouraged people to say that they wanted to live there; not families, as you can imagine; retired people, young people, young couples, people who found the cosmopolitan nature of the Notting Hill area of North West London attractive to them.' (Redman, 2001, p 1)

Bringing people to live in the street helped to provide new uses for the shops and commercial premises. By working with local residents, Notting Hill Housing Trust embarked on an active strategy to influence and change the neighbourhood. An area once seen as a no-go zone became valued.

Living in the workplace

Venture into cities like Belfast or Bradford on a typical weekday evening and you can see what happens when town centres become shopping ghettoes. The main streets are often deserted: even the city centre pubs are quiet. If you're not there to drink or eat, or to go to a show, there's little to do. Contrast that with Manchester, which has seen a revival in city centre living, much of it sparked by the emergence of the city's Gay Village in the 1990s. Today Manchester city centre is a mixed community of young and old, many living in apartments converted from former cotton warehouses, and as a result the streets are well used and many shops and cafes stay open into the evening.

Our towns and cities aren't short of property that could be turned into homes. In virtually every town centre the blank windows of the upper storeys above shops display wasted and under-used space. In many cases these spaces were once lived in; in others they could provide good quality accommodation in rooms previously used as offices or for storage. But often the owners or retail tenants of town centre buildings have regarded residential accommodation as simply too much hassle, seeing the spaces above shops as liabilities rather than assets. In Halifax, flats above the town's historic covered market have been left empty for decades. Sometimes landlords or occupants deliberately remove access to the upper floors, closing rear entrances and blocking or removing staircases in order to declare the spaces 'void' and avoid paying business rates. More often, landlords and lenders are simply unwilling to approve a mortgage or tenancy, assuming that the vast majority of the value of a property lies in its ground floor uses and that tenants inevitably mean trouble. By acting in what they think is their own individual interest, they close the door to public benefits.

While this may have been understandable at a time when retail was booming and house buyers could get easy credit for mortgages, the continuing crisis in Britain's housing demands an urgent rethink. The National Housing Federation puts the scale of the challenge starkly: 232,000 new households are forming every year, but only 109,020 new homes were completed in 2010-11. Private rents have risen 65 per cent since 2001 while average earnings have increased by 35 per cent, and mortgages are increasingly unaffordable (National Housing Federation, nd). A study by the London Planning Advisory Committee in 1998 estimated that 73,000 extra homes could be created by re-using empty or under-used shop space.

The following year the Urban Task Force, led by the celebrated architect Richard Rogers, called for government help to bring more empty space above shops into use, recognising that in many cases an intermediary was needed to provide a bridge between prospective occupants and absentee landlords. As the Task Force pointed out, the potential rewards were well worth the effort: 'Bringing these properties back into use not only creates additional housing, it also attracts a mix of residents back into the commercial hearts of our urban neighbourhoods, creating the critical mass vital to economic and social regeneration' (Urban Task Force, 1999).

The response to the call was half-hearted at best. Since then demand for homes has risen, credit for prospective homeowners has become harder to obtain (except where bankrolled by government) and the amount of vacant space has increased.

A decade-and-a-half later, the experts are still knocking at governments' doors to bring town centre premises back into use. Malcolm Fraser, chair of Scotland's town centres review, argues that more than 10,000 retail properties in Scotland's town centres could be turned into homes.

'We have a situation where there's a lot of young couples and single people who can't access mortgages. At the moment government initiatives are about kick-starting distressed diddy-box sites on the edge of town. These people – do they actually want to go and live there? They're going to have to find the money to buy a car, they're going to drive round the ring road and shop at Asda, maybe they'd actually prefer to be in town in their existing communities.' (interview with the author)

Far from being obsolete in a rapidly changing world, our historic town centres offer the kind of accommodation that, with a little will and imagination, could be effectively repurposed. For people on pensions or low incomes, those just starting their careers or in training, living in town offers the possibility of living within walking or cycling distance of work, shops, leisure facilities and friends.

As the world of work changes, with a growing proportion of activity being done online and a rising number of self-employed or freelance workers, bespoke live/work accommodation offers an alternative to the costly 20th-century model of separating home and work. Live/work is not the same as working from home; it involves creating studio or office accommodation in the same building as the home, but designed and equipped as workspace. Such accommodation can be purpose-built or converted from existing premises, especially buildings that have previously had a history of conversion from residential to office or retail and back again.

The key advantage of live/work accommodation is that it is affordable and flexible. In South West England the Live/Work Network has pioneered the approach as a solution for rural areas where house prices are high and traditional workplace-based jobs are increasingly scarce and involve long commutes. Several housing associations and commercial firms have already built live/work developments, and the Heartlands project in Cornwall, reviving the site of the county's last working tin mine, includes 22 live/work units designed for artists.

By clustering live/work accommodation together rather than simply converting individual homes, it is possible to create a sense of neighbourhood and workplace collaboration. Think of it as a 21st-century version of the artisan and craft quarters that traditionally existed in and around town centres, from the Huguenot weavers of Spitalfields in East London in the late 17th century to the Jewellery Quarter in Birmingham 200 years later. Living and making never used to be very far apart. In Burslem, in the heart of the Potteries, Victorian buildings next to the Burslem School of Art have been extended and turned into live/work accommodation as a way of stimulating creative activity in a town where one fifth of the historic core lies empty.

The need for such accommodation is growing as more people choose to work from home or become 'accidental entrepreneurs', setting up their own businesses after being made redundant from traditional jobs. According to the Live/Work Network, one in 12 workers in the UK now runs a business from home, an increase of 80,000 in 2011-12 to a total of 2.43 million. In the decade to 2011, the total rose by more than 28 per cent, and it continues to increase (Live/Work Business Network, 2012).

While live/work in town centres offers obvious advantages in terms of workspace and transport costs, one potential downside is the difficulty in replicating the networking and cross-fertilisation that can happen in multi-tenanted offices or business districts. This is where work hubs can come in: flexible, adaptable and professionally serviced spaces that can offer everything from business administration services to informal meeting and collaboration areas. The Old Church School in Frome, Somerset, is a good example, a converted listed building with shared workspace, studios and meeting rooms. As founder Gavin Eddy said, 'By the time your visitors find out that you're a freelancer working in the corner occasionally, it doesn't matter. The impression's been created and they see you as a serious company' (quoted in Dwelly et al, 2010).

One of the biggest hurdles for people looking to live and work in town centres is the cost. There is a shortage of high quality developments or refurbishments of existing property. The people who need studios and workspaces are often on low incomes or just starting their own businesses, so tend to be short of capital or collateral against which they can borrow.

In Tower Hamlets, East London, Bow Arts Trust joined forces with a social landlord, Poplar HARCA, to provide affordable 'short life' live/work accommodation. While longer-term development plans for the area were being implemented, many buildings were available on short leases. Left alone, they would become liabilities, with rising repair or maintenance costs and a risk of vandalism or being used for criminal activities. Poplar HARCA agreed to make unused flats available to artists as living and studio space, recognising that by occupying them they would reduce the landlord's security and maintenance costs and bring benefits to the local community.

Bow Arts, acting as an intermediary, rented out the flats to artists and took responsibility for basic repairs, bringing the flats up to a liveable standard. Rents were charged at affordable rates and one third of the rent went into a 'community arts chest' to fund local projects. More than 100 artists took part in the scheme (Self-help-housing-org, nd, a).

Whether the initiative is temporary or permanent, flexibility and imagination is the key. In 2013 the UK government brought in long-mooted changes to planning laws in England to make such flexibility easier, allowing unused offices and commercial premises to be converted into residential accommodation through new 'permitted development' rights. To make it easier to bring shops back into use, new retail businesses were given rights to start up, in many instances without seeking planning permission for a change of use.

Such moves can help to counter a perception that the roadblock to regeneration is the regulatory role of local planning officers, more concerned about dotting i's and crossing t's than with bringing life back into their high streets. But flexibility without creativity can generate as many problems as it solves: indeed, without positive planning for town centres' future and a consideration of the wider impact of each change, it may simply make it easier for lowest common denominator uses to proliferate, with developers and landlords using the argument that any use is better than none.

A tale of two storeys

Imagining a better future can be hard work. For nearly 20 years Ann Petherick campaigned to bring empty space above shops back into use. Everybody could see the potential, it appeared, but few had the interest or the will to bring it to fruition.

From one survey in Stockton-on-Tees, Ms Petherick calculated that 300 homes could be created in space above town centre shops, housing up to 500 people. In Chichester there was scope to house 275 people. These calculations disregarded buildings where access had been blocked or there were other physical obstacles to conversion. From her research she was convinced that the issue was neither a shortage of supply nor a lack of demand, but rather a lack of confidence:

> Owners need not just grant but a solution – a package of complementary measures which will enable them to unlock the value of vacant space and generate an income from it. Changing long-held attitudes is a slow process, which proceeds at an unpredictable rate and is affected by unpredictable outside influences. (Petherick, 2001, p 6)

Her project, Living Over The Shop (LOTS), proposed a simple but effective approach: to transfer responsibility for potential residential space to an intermediary organisation that would deal with the landlord and arrange refurbishment and lettings, providing both landlord and residential tenant with an expert agent who would manage the property and guarantee the income from it. Normally this intermediary would be a housing association or a non-profit organisation such as a university or health trust, taking the property on a commercial lease from the owner and letting to the occupiers on assured shorthold tenancies, allowing the owner scope to terminate the tenancy if the building were to be sold or redeveloped. The approach was designed to be particularly attractive to national retailers or property companies that wanted a model that could be applied across a portfolio of premises, rather than negotiating each conversion separately.

As Ms Petherick pointed out in her report for Chichester District Council, owners of commercial premises tend to be much more interested in the income stream from a property than in the activities that take place within it. It can be far easier to deal with a single tenant than with several, but retailers often only need the ground floor of a building. By using a third party to handle residential lettings, property owners could receive additional income for little extra effort.

Ann Petherick comments:

> 'Nobody had addressed the issue of ownership and this is absolutely an ownership issue. It's not a property issue, it

certainly isn't a housing issue, because you can't approach
it from that end, it is an ownership issue.' (interview
with the author)

In other words, instead of focusing on the physical details of
converting space above shops into homes, the challenge was to
convince the owners of such spaces of the benefits – and the most
effective way to do that would be to work on a national scale with
organisations that owned large amounts of property.

LOTS had some successes. The biggest was with NatWest bank,
now part of the Royal Bank of Scotland (RBS), whose property
director, Peter Armstrong, heard about the idea and contacted Ann
Petherick. Over several years, she estimates around 10,000 people
were housed in properties created above NatWest branches – but after
the bank was taken over by RBS in 2000 the momentum evaporated.

The fate of LOTS exposed one of the many contradictions of the
UK property market: that while investors might be willing to take
huge speculative risks on the capital appreciation and potential rental
uplift of properties, they turn out to be remarkably risk-averse at
the very local scale. Left long enough, the risk-averseness becomes
a self-fulfilling prophecy as the state of upper floors deteriorates and
the cost of refurbishment rises. But LOTS also exposed the failure of
both central and local government to understand what was required
to bring the upper floors of town centre shops back into use. A
succession of funding initiatives ran into the ground because, Ann
Petherick argues, they were directed at individual local authorities
rather than working nationally with major property owners.

Despite the advocacy of the Urban Task Force, the New Labour
governments at the turn of the millennium proved incapable of
grasping the nettle. By 2005 consultants Grant Thornton were
telling the Office of the Deputy Prime Minister that in spite of its
'significant potential', the idea of creating homes above shops carried
many risks. 'The market is wary of this programme,' they reported,
warning that it could cost up to £2 million to run an advisory agency
for three years (Cooper, 2008). Nearly a decade on, our high streets
are paying the price of that wariness and of governments' habit of
bowing to the markets' supposed wisdom.

In the boom years of the early 2000s there were easier ways to
make money. Property values were rising and towns were investing

in new retail developments. Ann Petherick's project came to nothing. She told *Inside Housing* magazine: 'I am getting owners of properties approaching me and I am having to turn them away. There is nothing I can do to help them as I haven't got the resources. The whole thing has collapsed in a heap' (*Inside Housing*, 2005).

Occasionally someone does demonstrate what can be done at a small scale. DISC, one of the largest charities in the north of England working with ex-offenders and substance misusers, converted a flat above a barber's shop in Holderness Road, Hull. The repairs cost £10,000 and the charity will lease the property for 10 years. The two volunteers who worked with a local builder to do up the property are now able to live there – so they have a home, construction and repair skills that they learned during the eight-week project, and better job prospects. What the experience of LOTS shows, however, is that a much more concerted approach is required to bring any significant amount of our wasted town centre space back into use.

Lifetime town centres

The 'can't do' approach of successive governments, commercial investors and even housing organisations stands in stark contrast to the practice in many European cities, where commercial uses of ground floor premises with residential apartments above are the norm. In the UK, a culture of only investing where returns are easy has produced the dead zones of uninhabited town centres and monofunctional retail districts; elsewhere a wider mix of ownership and a far-sighted approach to investment has created centres that are alive throughout the day and where property is more likely to be used to the full.

In Tübingen, Germany, an approach has been developed that could help create town centres that are places to live and not just shopping areas with redundant space above them. In the town's Südstadt, a former French military base, new homes are being designed and constructed by 'building partnerships'. Development plots are made available to groups of individuals who come together to decide what kind of accommodation they want; they must then select a partner to use the ground floor for commercial or community purposes. The land is acquired by the city council and sold on to the building partnerships that typically consist of groups of families, individuals and associated business partners. If the council approves a partnership's plans, the group then commissions its own architects and builders. The result is that each plot is developed to satisfy the long-term needs of its users rather than as a speculative venture driven by short-term returns. There is a mix of uses and architectural styles, reducing the area's vulnerability to economic and demographic changes and avoiding the uniformity of so many British and American developments.

Contrast this with the unimaginative approach deployed in many British towns, where 'urban villages' or 'city centre living' in the first decade of the 21st century focused on the building of apartment blocks, often designed to look fashionable on the outside with wiggly roofs or curvy walls, but poorly fitted out and sold off-plan to buy-to-let investors. It has brought people to live in town centres, but not turned them into communities: the occupants are often people in transition, students and young professionals who stay a year or two and then move on.

That's not to naysay the importance of students to town centres. Many university towns have built or leased huge quantities of student accommodation in recent years. In Exeter a study found that international students alone contributed an estimated £88 million to the local economy in 2011-12, supporting more than 2,800 jobs in the city and surrounding area (Oxford Economics and University of Exeter, 2012).

But building student flats on their own can create places that only serve the needs of a particular demographic. To turn town centres into communities, we need to think of them as neighbourhoods and not just business or educational districts. Some of London's more successful high streets still work in this way. Strutton Ground is a surprisingly traditional street at the heart of Westminster. Behind the glass and concrete offices of the government departments and corporations that line Victoria Street are housing estates built by the Peabody Trust and other housing charities, catering for people on low incomes or state pensions. The shops reflect that, with a fish and chip shop, a discount shoe shop and a Costcutter as well as the more upmarket establishments you might expect within spitting distance of Westminster Abbey.

Creating living space, whether above shops, next door to them or around the corner, is only part of what makes a town centre a place to live. To attract a wide range of people a town centre needs to provide all the essential services, from doctors' surgeries to parks and gardens, from children's play areas and nurseries to social centres and meeting places for elderly people or people with disabilities. A town centre will never be a fully functioning community if the schools and colleges have all been moved out; nor will it work if there is nowhere to take part in sports or leisure activities.

In recent years the idea of 'lifetime neighbourhoods' has started to infiltrate the discussions of civil servants and policymakers. It was born out of a recognition that Britain is becoming an ageing society and will need to adapt rather than assume that people will fit their lifestyles around infrastructure designed for younger, more mobile people. In 2008 there were 1.3 million British citizens over the age of 85; by 2033 that figure is expected to reach 3.3 million.

A government report in 2011 set out a range of principles for creating neighbourhoods that work for everybody at all stages of life, including old age (DCLG, 2011b). Top of the list was the idea of resident empowerment – that people should be involved and have a say in planning, developing and maintaining the communities in which they live. Next was access, connecting people with each other and enabling them to get out and about, to use local services and socialise. Lifetime neighbourhoods, the report argued, should have a broad range of services including banks and post offices, should be safe, have plenty of green spaces, and provide a wide range of social activities. Accessible and affordable housing, flexible enough to meet residents' requirements throughout their lives, was seen as essential.

These principles should apply to town centres too. Lifetime neighbourhoods without lifetime town centres leave less mobile residents or those with health problems disconnected from the heart of their communities. Town centres where people have a say in what goes on, can easily reach events and facilities, have good local services and green spaces, have social centres and can obtain flexible and affordable housing, will be good for everyone. As the 2011 report argues, this means combining good urban design with good service design, linking the physical environment with 'an understanding of the social factors and events that promote active participation in community life' (p 12).

Lifetime town centres are not only good for residents; they are also good for local businesses. People who struggle to travel far will use services that are near them. And if town centres work for an ageing population, they are more likely to be suitable for families too. Places that are walkable, with plenty of spots to stop and sit, convenient and well maintained public toilets and welcoming green spaces will be suitable for parents and carers of small children. The 'five Cs of walkability' – connected, convivial, conspicuous, comfortable and convenient – are a good rule of thumb for town centres that will work for everyone.

Communities in control

Creating liveable town centres means thinking about the whole place, not simply encouraging the conversion of individual properties from one use to another or changing the mix of uses allowed within a building. Planning legislation is ultimately only as good as the people who use it: our towns need changed attitudes, not just changed rules.

There are still traces in the not-too-distant past of the kind of attitudes and approaches that can change a neighbourhood or a high street. The housing association movement in the 1960s and 1970s, fuelled by the popular outrage sparked by Ken Loach's film 'Cathy come home', had a sense of dynamism and urgency about it that is missing from the quasi-corporate approach of many of today's mega-landlords.

With their roots in squatters' groups, concerned church congregations and 'short life' campaigns to bring unoccupied homes back into use while awaiting redevelopment, the housing activists of the time had few resources. But they had energy and a determination to tackle the desperately poor quality of rented accommodation in post-war Britain, and to counter official attitudes that stigmatised and patronised people who found themselves homeless.

Their concerns soon spread beyond the immediate problem of repairing individual properties or helping individual families. It was obvious to the people who set up organisations like the Notting Hill Housing Trust that there were wider issues at stake: poor housing, crime, a depressed and blighted environment and economic hardship were all interlinked. The holistic approaches that ultimately found their expression in the concept of neighbourhood renewal championed by the UK government at the turn of the millennium were seeded by these local activists.

Turn the corner of an ordinary-looking street just off Harrow Road in West London and you can still see the results of this kind of action. The Walterton and Elgin estates were once run-down and neglected, a triangle of Victorian terraced homes next to a modern estate pierced by two asbestos-riddled tower blocks. Westminster Council, which had inherited the homes from the Greater London Council, wanted to sell them to developers in the late 1980s as part of a strategy to move more affluent people into the area to bolster the council's Conservative majority – a strategy that soon became known as the 'homes for votes' scandal and ended with the council leader and Tesco heiress Dame Shirley Porter being castigated by the district auditor for 'disgraceful and improper gerrymandering'. Local people resisted the plans, putting forward their own proposals to take over the estates and run them for the benefit of the community. The idea came to fruition in 1992 with the formation of Walterton and Elgin Community Homes (WECH), which now owns more than 600 homes in the area – including new housing built on the site of the condemned tower blocks.

Two decades on, we can see how community control of housing can work at a significant scale. A survey of residents found that 84 per cent feel the landlord helps them to meet their neighbours; 79 per cent say there is a good community life in the area; and 85 per cent say the landlord plays an important role in fostering community and voluntary activities (Rosenberg, 2012). WECH takes family life seriously, too: tenants' grown-up children are given priority for rehousing, building what it calls 'co-located family networks'. In a cosmopolitan area with a high turnover of population such networks bring communities together and provide a web of informal support. WECH found that 12 per cent of its tenants had relatives within the community, in networks of between two and four houses.

Starting with the people and their priorities has led to some unusual and pioneering decisions. One WECH tenancy has been offered to a local police officer; in return, he plays an active role in the community and responds to requests for help and information (Rosenberg, 2011). WECH believes community ownership helps people to feel healthier and happier because it gives them more control over their lives and environment. It gets the basics right, providing affordable and secure homes in one of London's most deprived areas. As Anne Power, one of Britain's foremost housing academics, has commented, 'the efforts of ordinary people to gain control of their lives are indeed the watershed in making cities and communities work' (quoted in Rosenberg, 1998, p 5).

If the achievements of WECH look impressive, a project on the other side of the Atlantic shows how much more can be done. Over a period of 30 years the Dudley Street Neighborhood Initiative has turned the burned-out and abandoned heart of one of Boston's poorest districts into a thriving and culturally diverse community, led and managed by local residents. This was an area that had seen devastation on a scale comparable to the Bronx in the 1970s. Owners of empty buildings – and many that were still occupied – would routinely arrange for them to be torched in order to collect insurance payments and clear the way for speculative development. Journalist Holly Sklar described the situation as 'an escalating unnatural disaster of government negligence, banking discrimination, racism, and arson for profit' (Sklar, 2009).

The author and urbanist Kaid Benfield put the story in a nutshell:

> Plagued by severe disinvestment, illegal dumping of all sorts of waste, and with more than a third of its lots vacant, the Dudley residents over a period of several years got rid of the trash, stopped the dumping, gained control of the vacant properties, and undertook long-term planning based on the community's own vision of an 'urban village'. (Benfield, 2012)

Like WECH, the Dudley Street Neighborhood Initiative began with opposition to plans that would have bulldozed local residents' homes and moved out some of the poorest people in the city. Its organisers contrast their homespun vision for the future with the urban competitiveness theories of Harvard economist Michael Porter, whose view of cities' life and functions has strongly influenced city leaders worldwide. Economic development in conventional business terms, they point out, is a far cry from economic power for local residents, and from the networks of families and festivities that bring life to a metropolis. Their idea of an urban village is to provide 'a living example of how a community can successfully achieve social and economic goals while maintaining control over its destiny' (Benfield, 2012).

Today, despite the continuing challenges of poverty and unemployment and the social stresses that go with them, Dudley Street has become a model for 'development without displacement'. By setting up a community land trust, which vests ownership of the land in a non-profit trust in perpetuity, it has been able to provide the only permanently affordable housing in the city of Boston. Astonishingly – and only after years of legal challenges – it has managed to acquire 'eminent domain' powers, the equivalent of compulsory purchase powers in the UK. This has enabled Dudley Street Neighborhood Initiative to force negligent landowners to sell abandoned property within a 60-acre triangle to the community. The land trust, known as Dudley Neighbors, Inc, has been able to build 400 new affordable homes, a 'town common', schools and community centres, parks, gardens and a community greenhouse and orchard. By saving and restoring the area as a place in which to live, it has been able to improve public spaces and revive commercial activity.

If places facing the challenges of Dudley Street or the Walterton and Elgin estates can be turned into thriving and sustainable neighbourhoods, one has to question the poverty of vision and lack of ambition that characterise so many high street and town centre improvement plans. An assumption that local authorities know best and that development needs to follow the money has resulted in a slurry of off-the-peg masterplans touting the same bland blend of ersatz urbanism and uniformly 'vibrant' pastiche public squares.

We can do much better than this. But to do so we need a framework in which people can create their own places rather than simply purchasing the conveyor-belt products of housebuilders and developers. This needs to couple a long-term vision with short-term action. Genuine transformation takes decades: that's the lesson of Dudley Street, WECH, and Coin Street. But it also demands action: you have to start somewhere. In all three cases what began with protests turned into planning, and from planning to land acquisition, and from land acquisition to the creation of community assets. The immediate led to the temporary, and the temporary to the permanent. That's the model for change.

By working with the weft of the urban fabric, identifying buildings and places that have value and meaning within local communities and refitting them for contemporary needs, we can preserve the essential character of our town centres without fossilising them in uses and activities that are no longer appropriate. The concept of self-help housing, currently being tested in a range of locations across England, encourages housing groups to lease or acquire local properties to meet the requirements of people who might not be needy enough to qualify for local authority or housing association homes, but who would struggle to afford current rental or ownership costs. By setting up or working with an existing charity or social enterprise, people who need homes can negotiate with property owners to use existing property on a temporary or permanent basis. Funds for improvements are raised against the rents that will be charged over the expected life of the property (Self-help-housing.org, nd, b).

On a wider scale, housing associations, local councils or community land trusts (see Chapter 11) can repurpose and convert larger commercial buildings or groups of buildings. In the past it was common to declare 'housing improvement areas' or 'enveloping' schemes to improve the physical fabric of groups of buildings. This could be done with a mix of ownerships in the improvement zone; private or commercial owners would contribute the costs of the repairs to their own properties while benefiting from the economies of scale achieved by refurbishing several at once. Where a streetscape has become tired and neglected, such approaches can give an immediate lift to an area. By using a non-profit agency or public body to manage the work, improvements can be done when they are needed rather than when a private developer judges that a speculative gain can be made.

From the small-scale interventions of Notting Hill Housing Trust's early years and today's self-help housing projects to the transformative work of Coin Street and Dudley Street Neighborhood Initiative, there is ample evidence that ordinary people, with determination and support, can effect lasting change and create value both for people who need somewhere to live and for the wider residential and business community. But to preserve that value so that these achievements are preserved for future generations to build on, we must open one of Britain's biggest cans of worms: the question of ownership and access to land.

10

Reclaiming the land

Anyone looking for a microcosm of middle England should take a trip to Letchworth Garden City, nestling in the placid undulations of Hertfordshire. Places don't come much more middling than this.

Match the local census data against the national picture and the fit is almost perfect. There are a few more Sikhs, the population is a notch or two above the average age range, there are more people who've bought their homes from the local council. But if you're looking for Mr and Mrs Average in their three-bedroom semi, you'll probably find them here.

You wouldn't expect this to be the legacy of a revolution. A century on from the radical vision of Ebenezer Howard's first garden city, the result seems to be a not untypical English country town, with signs pointing to the A1(M) and neat hedges protecting residents' semi-detached modesty. In the town centre the focal point includes a railway station, three banks, a pub, a chip shop and a job centre. If anywhere could be called unassuming, it's Letchworth.

Down the Broadway, past the hotel on one side and the housing office on the other, the grand vista opens out to display a park, a fountain, a church – and then gentle waves of low-rise houses. Meander back through Eastcheap, Garden Square Shopping Centre and Leys Avenue, and you'll find a museum that's closed; an Art Deco cinema that's the envy of the county; vacant shops that used to host La Senza, Clinton Cards and Blockbuster; and David's, a treasure trove of books and vinyl LPs.

In the Letchworth Garden City museum there's an exhibition about the Spirella Company, the corset manufacturer whose motto was 'Happy healthy workers are the best workers!' It's somehow appropriate that the prime company in this town was once a firm whose purpose was restraint. Restraint is everywhere in the town's history, from the Skittle Inn – the original 'dry' pub – to The People's House, a temperance social club that is now a job centre beckoning the town's unemployed to opportunities in pound shops. The buildings display an endearing diffidence, a far cry from the bombast of Victoriana or the austere lines of modernism, and are set back so as not to encroach on green spaces and pavements. Letchworth seems determined not to get in anybody's way.

Ebenezer Howard, founder of the garden city movement, would have been happy that his legacy appears so ordinary. In many ways it is what he wanted: a healthy, open environment without the filth of the city or the loneliness of the country. His was above all the middle way. The garden city, he believed, should be the 'third magnet', drawing people into a new life of quiet enjoyment and moderate prosperity.

But for all its exterior decorum, Howard's approach has achieved something few others have managed. While Jane Jacobs – who loathed Howard's petty-bourgeois principles – had to take to the streets to prevent her beloved Greenwich Village from being carved open by an expressway, First Garden City Limited and its subsequent incarnations ensured (notwithstanding a few narrow escapes) that what belonged to the garden city stayed with the garden city.

Howard's seminal work, *Garden cities of to-morrow*, first published in October 1898, was billed as a mission to tackle the squalor and poverty of urban overcrowding. The garden city, he imagined, would have a communally owned park at its centre, showcasing civic buildings such as the town hall and municipal gallery. Around the central park would be a 'crystal palace', a circular arcade where people would walk and shop. Among the garden city's concentric rings would be residential areas, schools, places of worship and, at the perimeter, industrial areas, surrounded by green fields and woodlands (Howard, 1902).

Industries would provide local jobs for residents, but without the danger of the 'smoke fiend': they would all run on clean electricity, and be served by railways that would keep heavy goods off the roads. The result, Howard argued, would be good for all. His scheme would seek to 'find for our industrial population work at wages of higher purchasing power, and to secure healthier surroundings and more regular employment' (p 13). The talent of manufacturers and professionals would be better rewarded in such an environment, while farmers would find a new local market for their produce.

To prevent land-grabbing by developers, the green space surrounding the garden city would be communally owned. If the population looked set to increase beyond the ideal of 32,000, a new satellite town would be set up at a suitable distance. Eventually these clusters of towns would become what Howard called the 'social city', an urban centre with a maximum of 58,000 people, with six surrounding garden cities, all linked by a rapid transit system.

Ebenezer Howard was fortunate enough to have the chance to put his ideas into action. Influenced by the workers' towns of Bournville in Birmingham, created by George Cadbury, and Port Sunlight on the Mersey, instituted by W.H. Lever, he set up the Garden City Association in 1899. In 1903 First Garden City Limited was formed, with Howard as Managing Director and prominent shareholders including Cadbury, Lever and Alfred Harmsworth, owner of the *Daily Mail*, and land was bought at Letchworth. Helped by the Cheap Cottages Exhibition of 1905 – an effort to stimulate the supply of affordable housing using new building methods – Letchworth began to take shape. By 1917 the population totalled just over 10,000. It took until 1951 to reach 20,000, and it was not until the late 1980s that it achieved its target size of 32,000.

Howard's vision and legacy may seem unprepossessing, but in its approach to land ownership and the creation of shared value it was far ahead of its time. Letchworth today has its share of empty shops, but the decisions about what happens to most of them are taken locally. The land and commercial property assets of the town are looked after by a charitable trust set up by an Act of Parliament in order to generate benefits for the community. Every year several million pounds are channelled back into local services, community activities and physical improvements, in line with the original garden city ethos.

John Lewis, chief executive of the Letchworth Garden City Heritage Foundation, explains:

> 'We're 110 years on and it's happily carrying on and arguably getting stronger because our whole strategy is for the long-term benefit of the town, it's not from a developer's perspective. The whole structure is such that there's no opportunity to spend elsewhere. We are tied by geography and so just by the clever structure of the set-up you're guaranteed that whatever is created has to come back here.
>
> 'Yes, we can control timing, emphasis, scale – but there's no opportunity to say we've got a bit bored with Letchworth, let's go somewhere else. I think when you have that geographical tie-in and asset-related approach to where you're working you can't but take a long-term view. Anything we do we've got to live with.' (interview with the author)

That may be modest, but for the people of Letchworth it's a much bigger deal than many of them know. It's also a much better deal than most other middling towns in middle England are likely to get through the investment activities of property developers and landlords.

The ownership of the land and property in our high streets and town centres matters. It determines who can get access to premises and on what terms. It can facilitate or frustrate plans for improvements and development. The interests of property owners can either support or undermine the long-term interests of the communities who live in and use a place. If property owners stand in the way, any attempt to bring an ailing high street back to its previous vigour risks being stymied. Jess Steele, Director of consultancy Jericho Road Solutions, has catalogued numerous examples of what she calls 'irresponsible ownership', including the case of Plymouth's Palace Theatre, allowed to fall into disrepair while its owner serves a nine-year prison sentence for drug dealing (Steele, 2013).

In most historic towns and cities the street names tell you a lot about who owns or has owned the land. Names like Grosvenor, Cavendish, Devonshire, Norfolk or Surrey are like the graffiti tags of the landed gentry, signatures of an aristocracy that despite appearing anachronistic continues to own large tracts of real estate. The Duke of Westminster's company, Grosvenor, owned £2.5 billion of property assets in the UK and Ireland in 2012, a portfolio that began with the acquisition of 300 acres of what is now Mayfair and Belgravia in 1677 (Grosvenor, 2012). Fans of the board game Monopoly might be fascinated to know that the exorbitant rents charged on the highest square on the board are simply a reflection of real-life flows of money towards the traditional landowning class. Grosvenor owns a big chunk of Liverpool, too, through the Liverpool One shopping centre: Liverpudlians once known for their militant leftism are, in their own small way, helping to keep the Duke in the style to which he is accustomed.

But dukes and duchesses are relatively small fry when it comes to owning Britain's town centres. The total stock of commercial property in the UK, which includes offices, business parks and out-of-town shopping centres as well as traditional high street shops, was worth £569 billion in 2012. Of that, a quarter is town centre retail property – the same amount as in out-of-town retail parks and shopping centres (BPF, 2013). Institutional investors – insurance companies and pension funds – own 22 per cent of all commercial property, which means that household savings are heavily exposed to fluctuations in the property market. Increasingly, however, foreign investors are moving in, fuelling price increases in 'hot' markets like London and South East England. More than half the offices in central London are now owned by overseas investors, compared with less than one tenth in 1980; between 2008 and 2011 the average investment by an overseas buyer in London was £91 million (Lizieri, 2011).

On the face of it, rising land and property values might seem to indicate a successful economy. But the higher prices rise, the greater the polarisation and the harder it becomes for those without resources of their own to get a foot in the door. The higher the purchase price, the higher the rent required to repay the investment or to service the debt. The result is exclusivity: cities that become playgrounds for the well-heeled rather than shared spaces.

The property booms of the late 20th and early 21st centuries have reinforced inequalities. The wealth of the top 10 per cent of British households is now more than four times the wealth of all the bottom 50 per cent combined, and 850 times greater than the bottom 10 per cent (ONS, 2012b). The less you have to start with, the harder it is to do well. You have fewer assets to borrow against or none at all, and finance is more expensive or impossible to obtain.

As well as the institutional investors and what the trade likes to call 'high net worth' individuals, there is another group with large portfolios of commercial property. In many cases, however, these people never intended to get their hands on it. They are the owners of last resort: the banks and lenders who used property as collateral on their loans, and who have been left 'holding the baby'. In the 10 years to 2009 the use of debt to buy property increased five-fold, and in 2012, according to the British Property Federation, there was a total of £235 billion of debt secured on UK commercial property – a sum larger than the total value of retail premises in Britain. A study by De Montfort University in 2013 found that around £45 billion of the commercial property debt owed to banks had a loan-to-value ratio of 110 per cent – in other words, it was worth less than the money lent out to buy it (Maxted and Porter, 2013).

When it comes to irresponsible ownership, the banks take some beating. In 2013 a report by entrepreneur Lawrence Tomlinson uncovered allegations that RBS, owned by taxpayers since the bail-out of 2008, had been deliberately asset-stripping viable businesses in order to increase its own profits. In some cases bank officials were said to have changed their lending criteria in order to put borrowers in breach of their covenants; their businesses were then put in the hands of RBS's Global Restructuring Group (GRG), which sold the assets at significant discounts. Often these under-valued assets were snapped up by West Register, another RBS enterprise, and re-priced at much nearer the original valuation. Tomlinson commented: 'There is a clear risk of a perception arising that the intention is to purposefully distress a business to put them in GRG and subsequently take their assets for the West Register, at a discounted price' (Tomlinson, 2013).

The age of irrational exuberance

In his acid assessment of the culture preceding the great stock market crash of 1929, the economist J.K. Galbraith noted the phenomenon of 'preventive incantation'. 'By affirming solemnly that prosperity will continue, it is believed, one can help insure that prosperity will in fact continue,' he wrote. 'Especially among businessmen the faith in the efficiency of such incantation is very great' (Galbraith, 2009, p 44).

The British property market, both residential and commercial, sets its compass by such incantation. Another boom is always around the corner. In 2007, the respected Urban Land Institute published an assessment of 'emerging trends' in European real estate. Noting that observers were already questioning the hyperactive property markets of countries such as the UK, Spain and Ireland, it commented:

> ... few of those interviewed think that European real estate is in the grip of completely irrational exuberance. "There are no indications of madness ... yet." "The assumptions people are making may be optimistic, but not fundamentally ridiculous or irrational." "There's no comparison with the dot.com bubble. People are investing in assets that have cash flow and can be managed." (ULI and PricewaterhouseCoopers, 2007, p 4)

We all know what happened next. Fast forward six years to a very different economic climate, and we find property agents Savills once again rehearsing the incantations of prosperity, hailing the start of a 'long, slow climb out of the recent swamp of negativity', evidenced by new interest in shopping centre transactions and a slowing down of the number of retailers going into administration. The industry is nothing if not optimistic (Savills World Research, 2013).

Economists and politicians like to quote a simple mantra, attributed to two very different US presidents, Ronald Reagan and John F. Kennedy: 'a rising tide floats all boats'. If the economy is doing well, everyone does well. But for a boat to float it has to be seaworthy. The truth is that the tides, whether they are flowing or ebbing, always and inevitably expose the differences between the haves and the have-nots. The holes in many town and city centres, the derelict buildings and boarded-up shops, the empty spaces and the 'To let' signs, the development briefs still on the drawing board and the low-value uses of the premises that are occupied, reveal the consistent and continuing failure of the commercial property market to operate in the interests of the wider community.

The reality is a dysfunctional market, dominated by narrow pecuniary interests and short-term thinking, in which planners, politicians and investors combine to perpetuate the age-old confidence trick: if we say things will be all right, then things are all right. Occasionally a shaft of light reveals that all is not what it seems. In April 2013 Tesco suddenly announced that its UK property holdings were worth £804 million less than it had previously calculated. More than 100 sites, many bought at the height of the property boom, were no longer needed and would not be developed (Tesco PLC, 2013). The wealthier you are, it seems, the more notional the idea of value appears.

Tesco at least had the honesty to admit that the worth of its properties had been over-egged and did something about it. The banks holding the 'distressed assets' of retailers that have gone bust tend to be much more opaque about real values, as the Tomlinson report highlighted. In some cases banks grossly undervalue assets; in others they would rather sit on an empty property than release it at the discount required to bring it back into use.

The boom-and-bust culture of Britain's commercial property market has a direct impact on high streets and town centres, forcing up prices when times are good and blighting communities when they are hard. The long-term care and investment that would enable high streets to ride out the market's ups and downs is missing: investors would rather surf than sail, forgetting that every wave breaks sooner or later.

The Bank of England doesn't like to use common or garden words like 'madness' or 'folly'. The nearest the property industry comes to it is that peculiar phrase, 'irrational exuberance'. But as the Bank made clear in a recent report, not only does the market lack sanity; it also lacks both the capacity and the desire to learn from its mistakes. In the last 50 years Britain has seen three boom-and-bust property bubbles, in the 1970s, from the late 1980s to the early 1990s, and in the first decade of the 21st century. In the 1980s, 'when the bubble burst, prices fell by over a third, and there was a "near crisis" with 25 banks failing or closing down' (Benford and Burrows, 2013, p 49). In 2007-08 the global financial system was only saved by unprecedented government and international bail-outs, effectively passing the consequences of all that 'irrational exuberance' on to the public through higher taxes and swingeing cuts in public services. The Bank of England reported:

> The backdrop to the recent crisis involved yet another build-up in valuations and debt levels, with CRE [commercial real estate] lending exceeding 20% of annual nominal GDP, double the previous peak.... As the crisis unfolded, valuations fell sharply, with real commercial property prices almost a half lower than their 2007 peak by end-2012. (Benford and Burrows, 2013, p 49)

The Bank of England, like the De Montfort researchers, suggests that many of the outstanding loans on commercial property are highly risky. It poses three conceivable explanations for swings in property prices. One is a 'feedback loop' of easy credit leading to higher purchase prices, creating more notional equity against which investors can borrow more; like a Ponzi investment scheme, the house of cards inevitably collapses. The second explanation is irrational exuberance: investors allow themselves to imagine that the gravy train will never stop. The third is a mismatch between property companies' investment in fixed assets that are hard to sell in a downturn, and the ability of their own investors to withdraw funds at short notice, forcing the companies to sell at a loss. The first two in particular reflect a prevailing business culture, not just business errors.

The former Wickes and Iceland boss Bill Grimsey put it more bluntly: 'Property developers and retailers became too greedy about putting too much space down and went too far, creating far more than we ever needed.' With an over-supply of space and inflated asking prices, the bubble was bound to burst (Grimsey, 2012).

If investors and property industry experts learned from their experience, there might be a case for turning to them for solutions and new ways of thinking. But as the Bank of England observed, there is a repeating pattern at work. Liz Peace, until recently chief executive of the British Property Federation, is frank about the nature of the industry:

> 'The trouble is the property industry has always been cyclical and the boom and bust cycles encourage people, frankly, to rash behaviour. So if you see lots of people around you making a huge amount of money on the back of very easy debt, you'd probably tell yourself you'd be a fool not to take advantage of it. I know one or two of my members said they could not believe the length of time prices rose, and the last year that they rose before the crash, that was the year that with hindsight people wished they hadn't [invested] – they'd started to level out before that. I suppose you have to conclude that real estate businesses like many other businesses took advantage of what was on offer. You could say they were a bit rash to think it was going to go on forever. I think it's the way of the world, really. I don't see how you get people to move out of that way of looking at things.' (interview with the author)

A few landlords take a longer view. They might be private companies like Grosvenor, where the aim is to pass on assets to future generations within the family, or new investors with a more sober view of the nature of property. Mark Robinson, chief executive of the asset management company Ellandi, talks of a need for 'a clear-out of the busted structures to allow new owners to come in', basing their models on income rather than capital growth (Robinson, 2013). Overall, however, we should ask ourselves whether the people who got us into the hole are best placed to help us out of it. And if the evidence tells us they are not, are there better ways to manage the land and property in our town centres so that they bring genuine and lasting benefits to the communities they serve?

The inspiration of the interim

Get the experts together to discuss town centre land and property, and the discussions almost invariably start in the wrong place. They might begin with the question of how to get more development going. They might focus on margins and yields and rates of return for investors. Bring in the architects and built environment professionals, and you might get a smattering of how to improve particular streetscapes or why bits of heritage are important.

Hardly any of those conversations begin with the question of how to make better places. If we start there, then there are three compelling issues that should dominate discussion of property: how to use it well, how to care for it, and how to spread the benefits as widely and as far into the future as possible – whoever is the legal owner of the land.

In short, it is a question of stewardship. People who are trying to make a quick buck tend to be poor stewards. If you don't think you'll hang around long, you don't invest in maintenance or make long-term plans; the temptation is to see such things as costs and liabilities, and shuffle them off onto the next owner. Even those who do invest in their properties tend to think little of what lies beyond their particular purlieu.

To steward a building or piece of land well, you first have to ensure it can be used. Walk down many of our high streets and it's obvious that this first rule of stewardship is constantly broken: buildings stand locked and barred, not only to long-term commercial users, but also to those who might bring them to life now.

In the last few years an explosion of 'pop-up' and 'meanwhile' activities have begun to redress the balance, bringing temporary activity into vacant spaces. They include pop-up retail, arts and events, workshops and community activities. Pop-ups, like fairs and markets from time immemorial, create a splash of activity and colour in spaces that otherwise lie unused. They create spaces for the fleeting and the fragile. Inside an empty building, they can help to keep a place functioning and maintained, protecting it from vandalism and preventing it from blighting its neighbours. For a few days or weeks, they turn private liabilities into public assets.

'Meanwhile' activities take the idea a stage further, providing short-term and transitional uses for vacant premises. Enthusiastically supported by the government at the height of the 2008-09 recession, they were viewed by many as simply a stopgap, something to be allowed until the market returned to normal. After five years of economic stagnation coupled with seismic shifts in the nature of retailing, it became clear that whatever 'normal' would look like in future, it would be very different. 'Meanwhile' activities will be needed for many years to come.

Some of the earliest projects under the 'meanwhile' banner were, literally, window dressing: using dead shopfronts to showcase artists' work in towns such as Margate and Scarborough. All that was needed was access to the shops' display frontages. These days, projects tend to be more ambitious, involving the use of premises over a period of weeks or months as workshops or arts centres. In Newmarket a shop was opened up as a training hub for prospective retailers; in Hastings, a derelict cookware shop hosted a programme of activities, from a pop-up architects' practice to a skittle alley. In Willesden Green, North London, part of a library scheduled for redevelopment was turned into a 'Library Lab', attracting 3,000 visitors a month over the course of a year to enjoy craft workshops, a crèche and adult education events.

For such uses to take place, there needs to be trust between the users and the building's owners. Voluntary organisations or local councils can act as brokers, negotiating a temporary lease of the premises, providing guarantees to the landlord in the event of the property being sold or let, and covering issues such as insurance and fire safety. Packages of support have been developed to match people wanting premises with owners of empty property, reducing the risk on both sides. As awareness grows that 'meanwhile' may sometimes be years rather than months, the need for such brokering and support becomes greater.

In Peckham, a busy multicultural suburb of South London, the Bussey Building shows how a run-down site can become a hive of creativity. Sitting in the angle between the railway line to London Bridge and the ever-packed Rye Lane, it was once a factory churning out cricket bats for the sports manufacturer George Bussey, who supplied it with willow from his farm in Suffolk. For years it was scheduled to be demolished to make way for a tram depot, until those plans were reversed by the mayor of London, Boris Johnson. In the meantime the Bussey Building and nearby former industrial premises were bought by a commercial company, Copeland Park. Space is let out to artists, faith groups and voluntary organisations; the CLF Art Cafe nightclub has been described by *Time Out* magazine as 'simply one of London's best venues', and a rooftop film club operates during the summer. It is a classic illustration of Jane Jacobs' maxim that new ideas need old buildings.

The Bussey Building is also home to Peckham Vision, a group of community activists determined to promote arts and cultural activity and the sympathetic regeneration of the town centre rather than the demolish-and-rebuild approach favoured by Southwark Council, the local authority. The creative short-term use of a single building is supporting imaginative ideas for the long-term future of the town centre.

This is the inspiration of the interim: it creates futures that emerge organically rather than being superimposed to satisfy the grand schemes of mayors, planners or developers. The paradox is that the fluid and ephemeral can often make a more important long-term contribution to the value of towns and cities than the fixed and supposedly permanent.

To allow the short-term use of a building is not a favour that landlords offer the users, but one the occupiers provide both for the landlords and for the surrounding community. Their work turns dingy and dusty places into bright, cheerful ones; it turns empty boxes into living rooms filled with conversation and exchange; it turns dead ends into curious turnings. As Jess Steele, former director of the Meanwhile Project, says: 'Meanwhile projects can ... be catalysts for innovation and energy, converting empty spaces into opportunities to generate enterprise and employment, to trial and develop ideas and to provide new creative, community uses in unexpected places' (Meanwhile Project, 2010).

Ownership for common benefits

To use property wisely and for the broader public benefit, it needs a wise owner: one with an understanding of how that property contributes to the wider townscape, a view of success that stretches beyond the balance sheet, a willingness to reinvest and an openness to new ideas and opportunities.

For nearly a century, public ownership was assumed to be concomitant with public benefit. The response of left-leaning politicians to the profiteering of landowners, particularly in rural areas, was that land should be nationalised: this, it was believed, would stop it lying idle and unproductive. Since then the political pendulum has swung in the opposite direction, with an underlying assumption that private ownership is more conducive to productive use. After the arrival of the coalition government in 2010 pressure increased on public bodies in the UK to divest themselves of assets in order to raise ready cash. Across the country, 'For sale' signs went up on land and buildings that had been bought on behalf of the community or gifted to local authorities for the benefit of the public.

The experience of the last century shows that neither public nor private ownership in themselves guarantee public benefits. While the private property industry has been plagued by greed and short-termism, public landlords have often proved poor asset managers, remote from the street-level effects of their management decisions and slow to respond to challenges and opportunities. Both public and private landowners have been guilty of focusing more on their revenue streams than on the wellbeing of the places where their property is situated.

A good steward operates at the right scale, either through direct ownership or by using managers who have the authority to take decisions at an appropriate level. Just as a council-owned park works better when it has a regular park-keeper who knows local people and is a recognised figure in the community, buildings work best when it is clear who is responsible for them. Ownership, finance, maintenance and use go hand in hand.

Where existing models of ownership fail to deliver the benefits of stewardship to the wider public, or where they limit or prevent the productive use of buildings, there's an urgent need to examine alternative approaches. This is where community-based organisations have a growing and creative role to play. Instead of relying on the market to act in the best interests of a town, or expecting a local authority to work as an effective and responsive asset manager, asset-owning community organisations can bring buildings back into use or keep them open in ways that meet local social and business needs.

In the late 1960s and early 1970s Britain's road-building boom was at its height. New motorways snaked across the countryside, spidering out of London and finally surrounding it. In West London, a US-style elevated freeway, the A40(M), carved its way through the historic neighbourhoods of North Kensington. Although the protests of local residents failed to halt the roadworks, there was a small compensation: the North Kensington Amenity Trust was set up to manage the mile-long strip of land under the motorway's concrete stilts for the benefit of local people, holding it in trust so that it could not be taken away.

The shadow of an extended flyover is hardly the most promising land asset, but the trust was determined to show it could be put to good use. Today one fifth of the land has been occupied by commercial developments, bringing rental income to what is now the Westway Development Trust. There are community facilities such as gardens and sports clubs, business premises and social clubs, and the trust runs the world-famous Portobello Market. The trust has a 10-year plan to refresh older buildings and develop new ones, forming partnerships with private investors to fund improvements.

Westway Development Trust's plans are constantly evolving and responding to changes in the economy and the property market. The difference is that its land and property is managed for its returns to the community, not just its returns on capital. There is no pressure to sell or develop at the wrong time in order to maximise profit or avoid losses, and the trust can think of the land in its care as a whole, not just as individual sites. This means that a balance is struck between community and commercial needs, between buildings and green space. At the heart of it all is the courage and determination to imagine a better future for local people.

In Caernarfon, North Wales, another community trust is changing the face of a very different town. Caernarfon is a historic market town, a far cry from the melting pot of North Kensington. Unlike Westway Development Trust, Galeri Caernarfon has not been gifted a site to develop: instead, it has worked bit by bit to acquire assets, creating a patchwork quilt of change within the town's medieval walls. Since 1992 it has bought 20 previously empty or derelict shops, offices and homes, refurbishing or redeveloping them. In 2005 it opened Galeri Creative Enterprise, a £7.5 million development with a theatre and cinema, 24 business units, rehearsal and meeting rooms and a cafe bar. This is asset management for the long term, and the difference shows when you walk down the street.

In Hebden Bridge in Yorkshire's Calder Valley, the town's former town hall, deserted and neglected when the council moved to bigger premises in nearby Halifax, has been refurbished as a community hub. Under local authority control it lay idle even though on paper it was held for the public good; now, as the first community-owned town hall in the north of England, it provides events and meeting spaces, workspace for creative businesses and a cafe.

Developing, taking over and managing local property for community benefit isn't easy. There are many buildings that are more millstone than cornerstone, dragging weights that demand endless maintenance and are not easily converted to contemporary uses. But given the right people, skills, funds and time, community asset ownership can be a creative and sustainable solution for buildings that matter to local people, ensuring property is managed sensitively, at the right scale, and with local needs in mind.

From gunboats to crowdfunding

To begin to understand the possibilities as well as the challenges of community ownership, it is worth taking a trip to the Highlands and Islands of Scotland. Here the legacy of the worst aspects of absentee landlordism is still felt in many places, where properties were acquired as sheep farms or 'sporting estates', with little thought of the welfare or prospects of the people living there. The memory of the brutality of the Highland Clearances, spanning a century-and-a-half of evictions and forced removals, is also strong. So, as a consequence, is the tradition of campaigning for land reform, which reached its height in the Land League of the late 19th century and was revived with the establishment of the Scottish Parliament at the end of the 20th.

In the far northwest of Skye is one result of those early campaigns. Glendale is a collection of crofting hamlets centred on a small village with a shop, post office and community centre. It's the kind of rural settlement tourists find idyllic, with red deer roaming the hillsides and fishing boats moored at the edge of sea lochs. At the top of the hill on the road into Glendale is a memorial to the Land Leaguers who confronted their landlords in 1883 with the message, 'We want more land and there is plenty of it in the country.' Prime Minister Gladstone's response was to send a gunboat to Loch Pooltiel to defend the interests of the property owners; but 21 years later, the Glendale estate was acquired by the Congested Districts Board, a government body designed to address the grievances of crofting communities by giving them the right to buy their land on 50-year purchase agreements. By the 1950s Glendale was fully owned by its inhabitants. In a neat historical footnote, Glendale Trust bought Meanish Pier, where Gladstone's marines landed, from Highland Council in June 2013 to develop it as a community asset.

Cross the Minch to the Outer Hebrides and you'll find community ownership at work in Stornoway, the main town on Lewis. The island was bought by Lord Leverhulme, owner of the soap company that has now become Unilever, in 1918, but his plans did not work out and he got out after five years. Unlike most landlords before or since, he offered to give the island to its residents. While rural crofters turned down his offer, Stornoway's town councillors set up a trust to take over the 70,000 acres in and around the town. Ninety years on, the trust has survived numerous difficulties and continues to provide homes, business premises and jobs for local people. Its developments include a sawmill, a business park, a quarry, and even a seaweed company.

In the last two decades community land ownership has gathered pace, from Assynt in the far north of Scotland to Gigha, the most southerly of the Hebrides. The renovated homes of Gigha, the unique local electricity grid of the Isle of Eigg, and the community-owned golf course on South Uist that has even been lauded in the pages of *New Yorker* magazine, all bear testimony to the ability of locally owned and accountable organisations to steward their resources effectively and to harness the energy and enthusiasm of local residents. As the writer and historian James Hunter observed:

> [M]ore than three-quarters of all the people living in the Outer Hebrides live today on land they themselves own collectively. That is remarkable. In under ten years, an ownership pattern which appeared to be forever fixed had been changed in a manner little short of revolutionary. (Hunter, 2012, p 149)

Community ownership and land transfer isn't a panacea and it may not always be workable. But compared with the get-rich-quick approach of many commercial owners, and the get-shot-quick desperation of many public bodies, it offers a far more sustainable and responsive long-term approach to land and property. The challenge is to transfer the learning from remote parts of Scotland

and isolated urban projects into the way we think about the heart of all our towns and cities.

There is a growing range of tools and methods available to enable this to happen. In Scotland, the Land Reform (Scotland) Act gave communities the right to buy property being sold by landowners, and further legislation has been promised. South of the border, the coalition government's Localism Act (see Chapter 7) created a series of 'community rights', which, while weak, recognise in law that local people have an interest in the physical environment around them and should be given the chance to take over buildings that they value.

Go to any historic town and you'll find memorials and public buildings with foundation stones or plaques declaring that they were 'erected by public subscription'. The idea of raising funds from local people for civic buildings went out of fashion in the 20th century, but has returned in the form of crowdfunding – an appeal for funds, either as investment in an enterprise or as support for a community project. The UK now has its own internet-based version of the traditional public subscription model in the form of Spacehive, an online platform for crowdfunding buildings and public spaces. You pitch your idea through the Spacehive website, and if people like it, they can sign up to support it. Successful projects have included a free Wi-Fi zone in Mansfield town centre; a memorial in Stratford, East London, to the theatre director Joan Littlewood; and public food growing spaces in Rochdale.

Another take on the old idea of public subscription is the community share issue. Just as anyone buying shares in a public listed company owns a fraction of the business, so community shares enable people to invest in local projects and become part-owners of them. Unlike the idea of crowdfunding or sponsorship, community shares can provide owners with a return on their investment – although this is unlikely to be an investor's main motivation, given that most community share issues are for projects at a start-up phase.

There is a growing list of successful community share issues in the UK. What is particularly interesting is the willingness of investors to sacrifice the prospect of quick returns for the possibility of long-term change. In the North Yorkshire village of Hudswell, 202 investors have put more than £250,000 into a cooperative to buy the local pub, the George and Dragon, for the community. The pub has not only been kept open: it has developed a range of other services, including a library with free internet access, a shop selling local produce, and allotments on land behind the pub. In the village of Slaithwaite, near Huddersfield, a community share issue helped save the local greengrocer's shop when the owner decided to retire. More than 100 people raised £18,000 to keep the shop open by buying shares. Four years on, the shop is profitable and eight jobs have been created.

As well as raising finance to get things going, ways need to be found to preserve community assets for future generations. Community land trusts (see Chapter 9) are one promising approach, acquiring property and preserving it in trust to prevent speculation. A community land trust might buy a site and build homes or workshops to be sold or rented to their occupiers, with the trust retaining the freehold of the land with a provision that it should always be used for a social purpose. A buyer purchasing a house on a community land trust site would pay for the use of the building, but not the site on which it sits. When they sell, they would have to sell to somebody qualifying for membership of the community land trust at a purchase price agreed by the trust rather than at open market rates. In cities like London, where it is estimated that up to half the price of a house is the value of the land, this could substantially reduce the cost of accommodation.

To ensure the homes or business premises they provide are affordable, community land trusts seek to acquire their land at less than market value. The organisation is run as a non-profit entity and controlled by a locally accountable board. Community land trusts have been seen as an important way of providing affordable housing in rural areas where house prices are high and local people are often on low incomes, but there is also increasing interest in urban projects. A community land trust on the site of the derelict St Clement's Hospital in Bow, East London, was a key element of the 'Olympic legacy' following the 2012 Olympic Games.

There is international evidence to show the viability and success of community land trusts. The Champlain Housing Trust in Vermont has been operating for 30 years and now manages 1,800 apartments and more than 500 owner-occupied homes. A study in 2008 found that the trust had achieved 'larger social goals like the preservation of affordability, the stewardship of public resources, and the stabilisation of residential neighbourhoods' (Davis and Stokes, 2008).

The challenge with most forms of community ownership developed so far is that they are a relatively small-scale response to issues that are national as well as local. They can take an age to come to fruition, and often feel like spitting in the wind in the face of hostile trends. It is not surprising, then, that many people would prefer bigger, faster actions.

One of the more common large-scale responses is to set up a joint venture between civic and commercial interests to develop land and property. This can involve pooling resources into what is known as a 'local asset-backed vehicle' (LABV). A local authority might agree to put in a parcel of land, private companies would raise the finance, and between them they might develop a site over a period of 10 or 20 years. These ventures have included some ambitious redevelopment plans, including a £500 million partnership between Torbay Council and developer McAlpine covering nine town centre sites, and a deal worth at least £350 million between Bournemouth Council and Morgan Sindall Investments to deliver the council's 'town centre vision' across 17 sites.

Although the intention is to form long-term partnerships and to share the proceeds, the approach has tended to favour standard models of commercial development that are of questionable value for today's town centres. In Tunbridge Wells, Kent, a £150 million partnership between Tunbridge Wells Borough Council and developer John Laing ended in tears after four years with not a single project delivered. The centrepiece of the scheme, the replacement of the town hall with a shopping centre, proved hugely controversial and was abandoned – along with the partnership – after public consultation.

The difficulty with LABVs, as Alex Thomson, Director of thinktank Localis notes, is that in a commercial deal between a local authority and a developer, the partners' notion of public benefit might prove very different to that of the local community (Thomson, 2012). That said, there may be occasions where such a long-term arrangement, properly accountable and developed in partnership with a wider body of local residents as well as councillors and industry executives, may provide the kind of long-term property ownership and management town centres need.

Liz Peace at the British Property Federation has expressed interest in using a similar kind of pooling arrangement to buy and bring back into use empty high street properties or assets owned by companies in administration; the approach would be to create a single entity to own problem properties, allowing them to be managed actively rather than waiting for the market to pick up or the owner to accept a devaluation.

A joint venture approach could also be developed to include community involvement and ownership, suggests Annemarie Naylor, Director of the consultancy Common Futures:

> 'If you're trying to do a LABV model between public assets and the community instead of the private sector, the problem in poor areas is the money isn't around to make that an investable proposition at the same rates and the same timeframes. But I do think LABVs that use social finance or community finance through shares or whatever may well have some legs, because they demand a more patient return and timeframe.' (interview with the author)

By combining councils' property assets, sustained commercial finance from institutions such as pension funds and insurance companies, and the community trust model developed in Scotland and elsewhere, a foundation could be built for the long-term management and improvement of town centres. What is needed is a shared vision for the future and a commitment to shared value for all – a 'commons' as well as a common purpose.

A duty of stewardship

Back in Letchworth, John Lewis is outlining his ideas to create shared value in the town centre. It's a centre that doesn't really work as a shopping destination, he admits – most of the big stores are in Stevenage, Milton Keynes or Welwyn Garden City. People wanting the quirky or high quality independent offer of a traditional market town will go to nearby Hitchin. So is Letchworth doomed? Not a bit of it, he argues. He believes that by focusing on arts and culture, Letchworth can develop a different kind of town centre, one that creates a buzz because of what there is to do rather than what there is to buy.

The architect and academic Nabeel Hamdi argues that the practice of placemaking is 'about making the ordinary special, and the special more widely accessible' (Hamdi, 2010). In the ordinariness of Letchworth and other towns, making the ordinary special is an important first step towards putting the heart back into our high streets. To keep it beating requires the kind of vision of shared value that inspired Ebenezer Howard and his supporters to create Letchworth Garden City in the first place.

It is time to create a new generation of garden cities. Not through the pastiche executive newbuild schemes on Home Counties greenfield sites favoured by politicians, but by rethinking the places where we already live. We need to find a way of retrofitting the principles that guided the Garden City movement to our existing environments.

To achieve that, we need to put a duty of stewardship at the heart of property law and practice. A duty of stewardship would require all owners – whether public or private, family businesses or community trusts, charities or government bodies – to look after their assets and have regard to the value they add to or remove from wider society, the 'commons' of our towns. In practical terms, owners should be required to maintain their properties, keep them in use and do their best to ensure their use benefits the local community.

Such a proposal will be fought tooth and nail by those who believe that ownership should allow people to act irresponsibly – who want to own a place, as the former laird of Gigha, Malcolm Potier, remarked, 'much as a child yearns for a train set' (Hunter, 2012, p 124). But without such a requirement banks will continue to allow empty buildings to blight our towns, investors will use high street landmarks as game counters as they play the property market, and local councils will allow assets gifted by public-spirited citizens to fall into decay because they can't find the resources to look after them.

There is already a legal right in England to take action against public bodies that neglect this stewardship role. The 'community right to reclaim land', announced in February 2011, enables individuals or groups to appeal to the Secretary of State for Communities and Local Government to order the disposal of public land that is vacant or unused. The process is longwinded and there is a long list of exceptions, but it is a step in the right direction.

The 'right' is an extension of the Public Request to Order Disposal (PROD) process, which applies when a public body is holding land and property assets that could have an alternative public or community use. The government has pledged to publish regular lists of the land it owns and manages via the Homes and Communities Agency (see www.homesandcommunities.co.uk/land-and-property-assets).

The PROD mechanism creates a potentially powerful method for citizens to bring vacant property back into use by triggering an order that the owner should dispose of it. The scheme covers a range of public bodies set out in Schedule 16 to Part X of the Local Government, Planning and Land Act 1980. These include all local authorities and a handful of quangos (quasi-autonomous non-governmental organisations), but not central government departments. If ministers think the evidence supports a request, they can serve a disposal notice on the owner (or, in the case of bodies not covered by Schedule 16, write a letter recommending disposal).

To make a significant difference in our town centres, we need a much more radical extension of the right to reclaim land. It needs to apply to private property and land held by charitable trusts and non-governmental organisations (NGOs) as well as public bodies, using the same principle that land that is neglected should be made available. Additionally, there should be a right of first refusal for community or public organisations, so that land earmarked for disposal is not simply snapped up on the cheap by speculators.

This would be a step towards ending the right to blight – the assumption in land and property law that ownership trumps use, and that buildings or sites can be left idle for years on end as long as they are not a health hazard or a public nuisance. Even when places have been allowed to deteriorate so far that they have become dangerous, the process of forcing an owner to take action is often expensive and tortuous, and therefore one that hard-pressed local councils tend to avoid. Although councils have powers under Section 215 of the Town and Country Planning Act 1990 to force landowners to repair derelict properties, these are seldom used and cannot be activated by the public; even when a council does decide to take action under this or other existing powers, the process is time-consuming and often costly.

So a fortified right to reclaim should be automatically triggered when a property or site has been left unused for a year or more, and the local authority has not been informed of viable plans for its re-use or development. Given the time it takes to go through the planning or development process, this would allow local communities, businesses or public bodies to put forward alternative proposals which the municipality would be required to consider. Rather than going through central government, a request to order disposal should be determined locally in the first instance, with an appeal process if the decision is considered to be against the public interest. To avoid using the right to reclaim to fuel profiteering, a duty of stewardship should apply to any handover: the new owners would be expected to put forward long-term plans for use and maintenance.

Where properties have been seriously neglected, the sale price should reflect the cost of bringing them up to a usable standard. One of the bugbears of transferring assets to community organisations has been that landmark buildings – and historic buildings in particular – tend to need far more maintenance and repair than envisaged by their original owners. To avoid overburdening new users with liabilities, such properties should be made available at a price substantially below their book value; in exceptional cases they should be transferred with a 'dowry' reflecting their negative value. A similar process was used in the late 1990s to transfer run-down housing estates to new landlords through a government programme, the Estates Renewal Challenge Fund (ODPM, 2005).

Alongside a reinforced right to reclaim should be a 'right to try': a right to gain temporary access to vacant buildings in order to test alternative uses. This would enable businesses or community organisations to take over premises in the short term, with a requirement that they maintain them and fulfil the usual tenants' obligations, and the option of ultimately purchasing the premises at a discount mirroring the value of their role as caretakers and improvers. The thinktank ResPublica has suggested that this could be used as a preventive measure to preserve valued local shops or markets (Schoenborn, 2011).

As well as creating and gaining access to property, we need to address the failures that result in a succession of boom-and-bust market cycles that encourage unnecessary speculative development in the 'good' times, and bring everything to a standstill when times are hard. Instead of accepting these cycles as a fact of life and leaving the wellbeing of our communities to the luck of the market, we should explore how to harness the market, making the trade and exchange of land and property a beneficial activity.

Speaking in the House of Commons in 1909, Winston Churchill highlighted how private landowners extracted and privatised the value created by public activity:

> Roads are made, streets are made, services are improved, electric light turns night into day, water is brought from reservoirs a hundred miles off in the mountains – and all the while the landlord sits still. Every one of those improvements is effected by the labour and cost of other people and the taxpayers. To not one of those improvements does the land monopolist, as a land monopolist, contribute, and yet by every one of them the value of his land is enhanced. (quoted in IFS, 2011, p 371)

What is needed, then, is a way of redistributing that value without suppressing beneficial economic activity. *The Mirrlees review*, an expert panel convened by the Institute of Fiscal Studies, revived the idea of land value taxation as a solution. A land value tax costs the owner of a property in an expensive area more than if they owned an equivalent property in a cheap or run-down area. It penalises speculative acquisition of land, but not the business carried out on that land or the services the land or the buildings on it provide. It helps to shift the idea of value from the capital cost of an asset to the way the asset is used. As *The Mirrlees review* puts it: 'Economic activity that was previously worthwhile remains worthwhile. Moreover, a tax on land value would also capture the benefits accruing to landowners from external developments rather than their own efforts' (IFS, 2011, p 371).

If a property is empty under current rules, it can be cheaper for a landowner to knock it down in order to avoid business rates than to maintain it. When it is occupied, the cost is more often than not borne by the occupier rather than the owner. This is a disincentive to activity, penalising the more economically productive. By levying a land value tax on landowners, those who are not using their land would have an incentive to sell it – or, if it has no perceived value, to give it away. This is a simpler and more equitable approach than systems such as 'tax increment financing', where local councils are able to borrow against expected future uplifts in land values in order to finance infrastructure or services. Far from inflating land values that are already too high, we need a system that dampens speculation and rewards the use of land rather than the hoarding of it.

Governments have always shied away from land value taxation, largely because of pressure from landowners who did not want their wealth devalued. It very nearly became law in Britain as part of the famous 'People's Budget' of 1909, but was overruled by the House of Lords. Land value taxes have been introduced in New South Wales, Australia; Pennsylvania in the US; and Denmark and Estonia in Europe.

As the current system of property taxation in the UK becomes increasingly detached from any realistic valuation of land or property, the need for a new approach is becoming more urgent. Domestic property taxation – the Council Tax system – is fossilised with valuations set in 1991; the system of business rates is stuck with valuations set in 2008, and that are likely to be a decade old before they are revisited.

A land value tax, as *The Mirrlees review* suggests, could replace these clunky and inequitable systems with a tax that is transparent and helps to counter the wilder fluctuations of the property market. With a little adjustment, it could also be used to create a stream of funding that could support community organisations wishing to take over and revitalise neglected public and private land and property. In 2009-10 business rates raised £24 billion in the UK, while Council Tax raised £25 billion after deducting Council Tax Benefit. A 1 per cent fund drawn from a revenue-neutral land value tax would create a pot of nearly £500 million a year that could help to put property in the hands of the people: not just remote expanses of Scottish wilderness, but the land and buildings at the core of the towns and cities where most of us live.

A further reform could help to boost economic activity in our poorest areas, directly or indirectly supporting high streets. A Community Reinvestment Act would oblige banks to reinvest a proportion of their profits in the localities where their customers are based. In the US, such legislation was introduced in 1977 to combat the practice of 'red-lining', where banks refused to provide loans to individuals and businesses in particular areas.

In the UK a Community Reinvestment Act could channel a percentage of banks' profits to community development finance institutions – intermediary bodies that lend funds on to social enterprises and new businesses, particularly in poorer areas. This would help ensure finance reaches the new ventures that need it; it could also be used to finance asset purchases by community organisations. Both would help to counter the effects of an increasingly polarised nation where everything from land values to concentrations of retail spending favour the haves at the expense of the have-nots.

First steps in stewarding

A duty of stewardship, land value taxation and a Community Reinvestment Act are measures that could work wonders in our urban landscape, giving communities the resources to take ownership of their towns and the confidence to plan for future generations. But all of these will upset vested interests that have done well out of the current system. The battle of ideas will be hard-fought.

There is much that can be done in the meantime. None of it will address the underlying defects of the property and investment market. But just as interim uses of high street shops are better than leaving them empty, so 'meanwhile' approaches that build the practice of stewardship will be helpful.

Four broad areas of work should be considered. The first is to recognise, and account for, social value as well as market values. The second is to give local organisations more opportunities to develop their own ideas and projects. Third is to involve communities more closely in planning, both at a strategic level and in individual projects; and fourth is to make better use of existing assets and to explore ways of building community benefits into asset management.

A common complaint among local organisations wishing to take over properties or land is the owners' insistence on payment of a full open market price. This fails to acknowledge the value that is created when an empty property is brought back into use or a local eyesore improved. While it may be understandable (if counterproductive) for private owners to demand as much cash as possible for their property, there is no excuse when public bodies fail to consider the wider public benefits.

A typical response is that public bodies are forced by Treasury rules to demand the highest cash price. But the Treasury itself has a more nuanced view of value. Its *Green Book* makes it clear that policymakers should value 'non-market impacts' of policies or projects (see Chapter 8). Recent guidance on accounting for environmental impacts outlines how 'total economic value' – including wider public benefits or externalities – can be used as a methodology for decision making (HM Treasury, 2012).

There is now a legal requirement, through the Public Services (Social Value) Act 2012, for public authorities in England to consider 'social value' when tendering for public service contracts. This social value, arguably, should include the effect on a town or a high street of the relocation or development of services such as one-stop shops, advice centres and libraries.

The second thing that can be done now to mitigate the impacts of a skewed and dysfunctional property market is to give local people more help in putting forward alternative proposals for use and ownership. The 'community rights' trumpeted by the coalition government as part of the Localism Act take a small step in the right direction, allowing local organisations to list local landmarks or properties, such as a historic pub or a well-loved park, as 'assets of community value'. This means that if one is put on the market, community organisations are given a breathing space of up to six months to prepare a bid. But six months is a very short time to form an organisation from scratch, to agree proposals for the future use of a site, and to raise the finance to compete for it on the open market.

To help communities make the most of these rights, they need practical help and financial support. The Royal Institution of Chartered Surveyors' Land and Society Commission has called for 'pause agents' – intermediaries to act as holding bodies for assets that would otherwise be sold before community organisations can develop their plans (Land and Society Commission, 2011).

At a more strategic level, councils can make sure local people have a meaningful say on the future of their towns by adopting community-led planning. The Land and Society Commission estimates that more than 4,000 communities have already done so, going through an 18-month process of weighing up the different social, economic and environmental challenges facing their areas and agreeing priorities. Local authorities and property owners need to take this process seriously, responding positively when people set out their concerns and vision.

Neighbourhood planning is a more formal process, introduced through the Localism Act. It provides a statutory right for people within a defined area to adopt their own planning process, deciding – within limits – where homes or shops should be built and what they should look like. The plans can be produced by town or parish councils, or neighbourhood forums established by local people. In Chatsworth Road, Hackney, traders and residents are setting up a neighbourhood forum to plan the future of a London high street. In Ivybridge, Devon, a neighbourhood plan has been produced to help protect and revive the town centre.

The fourth thing that can be done now is to manage existing assets better, ensuring there is a return to local communities as well as to the asset's owners. Several private property companies, including Grosvenor, run charitable trusts to finance community activities; these could look at ways of giving community organisations access to unused buildings or sites.

Britain's landed establishment could set the pace in ensuring its profits help to finance the creation and maintenance of community assets. The Crown Estate, which owns Britain's coastal seabed, more than 350,000 acres of farmland and forests, and has a huge property portfolio including 15 retail parks and shopping centres in Exeter, Oxford and Worcester, has come in for particular criticism for its failures in this respect.

In 2012 the Crown Estate turned a profit of more than £252 million. Of that, nearly £38 million funds the Queen's spending as head of state, while the rest goes to the Treasury. As a government body you might expect it to have a greater concern for local communities' interests than a private corporation of a similar scale. A parliamentary inquiry into its activities in Scotland found otherwise.

The House of Commons Scottish Affairs Committee heard a litany of complaints about the Crown Estate Commissioners' management of their responsibilities for the Scottish seabed and foreshore, and the impact on coastal communities. It criticised 'the lack of accountability, the lack of communication and consultation with local communities … the cash leakage from local economies

... together with the limited benefits in Scotland from the CEC's involvements'. The only solution, it suggested, should be to end the Crown Estate's responsibilities in Scotland (House of Commons Scottish Affairs Committee, 2012).

Belatedly, the Crown Estate is now exploring how to use its assets to support local communities, building on initiatives such as the coastal communities fund, which provided £27.8 million in 2013-14 to support the regeneration of seaside settlements. Organisations in Portree, Skye, and Lochmaddy, North Uist, are piloting 'local management agreements', enabling them to develop their own proposals to manage the estate's marine assets for the benefit of local people.

While the Crown Estate has yet to apply this thinking to urban areas, it is a start that other traditional landowners should note. The Duchy of Lancaster owns 44,500 acres of land in England and Wales on behalf of the Queen, with a capital value of £428 million and profits of £12.5 million in 2012. Its holdings include prime office and shopping land in central London, parts of Harrogate and the North York Moors village of Goathland. Its charitable activities include providing affordable rural housing, but it could do much more to reinvest in the places it profits from.

The Duchy of Cornwall, owned by the Prince of Wales, has even more extensive landholdings, totalling more than 131,000 acres. These are held in trust and Prince Charles and his family receive an income from them, totalling more than £19 million in 2012-13. From the surplus the prince funds many of his charitable activities, with interests in sustainable farming and preserving the historic built environment. Again, more could be done.

In certain respects these bodies already fulfil a duty of stewardship, looking after their estates for the long term rather than for speculative gain. What they could do better is to use their assets to support the self-reliance and economic empowerment of the communities affected by their interests. This in turn could offer a model for commercial businesses: instead of focusing on self-serving public relations exercises in corporate social responsibility, they could reinvest a proportion of their profits to endow local communities with assets in land and property, and create economic opportunities through temporary uses of vacant buildings.

Another form of local reinvestment is the idea of business improvement districts. Known as BIDs and originating in the US, these work through a voluntary levy on business occupiers to fund local improvements. Their advantage is that they can provide a recurring income within a specific locality – sometimes as limited as a single street – to support initiatives such as events, physical improvements in the street scene or shopfronts, or paying the salary of a town centre manager or local wardens. In Bedminster, Bristol, traders voted for a BID that will bring in £80,000 a year to support the local 'town team', replacing a one-off grant of £100,000 from central government when the area became a 'Portas pilot'.

BIDs can be an effective way of creating a dedicated income stream for a local high street. But they are more likely to work in prosperous areas where traders can see the benefits in paying extra for improvements. In England very few of them involve the landlords and property owners whose activities have done so much to blight many towns; and they do nothing to address underlying inequities in terms of access to land and the cost of owning it (the rules in Scotland are more inclusive and democratic). Their lack of accountability and appropriation of powers previously exercised by local government is also a cause for concern.

That's why, for all the ordinariness of Letchworth Garden City, it presents a far more powerful approach to the future than anything the property or retail industries have advocated in more than a century since Ebenezer Howard presented his plans. Howard's bourgeois vision has proved more sustainable than both the irrational exuberance of the property market and the post-war municipal socialism of many local authorities that are now desperately dismantling their achievements in a quest for ready cash.

Howard understood that the only way to guarantee a community the benefits of local land and property management is to make them the managers. As the Scottish writer and land reform activist Andy Wightman put it: 'The real issue remains as it has always been – that of power – how it is defined, who has it, how it is exercised, how it is transferred and how it is held to account' (Wightman, 2013, p 2).

But the issue is not only about power. It is about care too. Power without care creates blight. Care without power fuels helplessness and frustration. This is why stewardship needs to be at the heart of any vision to reclaim the land for the people.

11

If we had a little money

It's a bright, fresh day in Bedminster, just south of Bristol city centre. On shopfronts and house walls along North Street are brightly painted giant insects, the Bugs of Bedminster. It's a Friday morning and the street is starting to stir.

At Mark's Bread, the independent bakery, an aroma of fresh loaves combines enticingly with the coffee brewing in the attached cafe. Across the road, the Tobacco Factory, home of Bristol's largest independent theatre, is still quiet, a flower seller using the entrance as an impromptu stall.

The Tobacco Factory is the pride and joy of George Ferguson. Architect, property developer and now independent mayor of Bristol, he sits in the bar in his trademark red trousers, patiently explaining his vision for the city to a procession of journalists who have come to find out why Bristolians seem to have turned their back on traditional political leaders.

It's not just politics that have been shaken up since George Ferguson's election in November 2012. The former president of the Royal Institute of British Architects is a passionate supporter of the city's independent culture, from street artists to artisan foodstores, from Bristolian beer to neighbourhood high streets. He made waves, too, by announcing immediately after his election that he would take his entire mayoral salary of £65,700 in Bristol Pounds.

If this was a gimmick designed to generate national newspaper headlines, it certainly worked. A pay packet consisting of money that could only be spent locally, and even then, only in a relative handful of independent shops? Jaws dropped. But for those who had never heard of the Bristol Pound or were tempted to dismiss it as Monopoly money, the fact that the most prominent citizen had decided to be paid in local currency suddenly got people to take it seriously.

The mayor is still enthusing about this little declaration of independence from the global financial system:

> 'I think the Bristol Pound's absolutely great. It would be great if it represented 10 per cent of our economy in the long term. It's not going to represent the majority of our local economy, but I think it's got everything going for it. It's probably done more to market Bristol than almost anything else and the fact that I take my salary in Bristol pounds gave that a bit of a boost. I can spend it on everything from bread to rates and council tax.
>
> 'The funny thing is I think Tesco in Stokes Croft actually approached the Bristol Pound to see whether they could accept it and they said no, that's not quite the point, the point is to encourage independent businesses. And I think it is a great message. Beyond the actual use of the Bristol Pound will be the benefit of the message that it's about spending locally.' (interview with the author)

Local money like the Bristol Pound is currency that can only circulate within a particular area or among a specific community. The value is pegged to sterling, and while UK financial rules mean that a sterling reserve must be held in a bank or credit union to guarantee the local currency, the aim is to use the Bristol Pound as an alternative to encourage Bristolians to spend their hard-earned cash with local suppliers rather than national chains. When they accept Bristol Pounds, traders either use them to buy from other Bristol-based businesses – strengthening local business relationships and networks – or to pay bills such as business rates, with the council converting the currency back to sterling. This is what is known as a complementary currency: not an alternative means of exchange, like bartering, but a way of helping to influence the local economy by using a sterling equivalent that is restricted to a particular market.

Just over 100 miles away in South London, another enthusiast is waxing lyrical about local money. In the covered market of Brixton Village and in the surrounding streets, reggae music is gently beating from shops whose wares spill out onto the pavements. The whole world has come to trade here: the Sierra Leone stores selling dried fish, the patty stall with its Jamaican specialities, Fish & Wings & Tings with its secret-recipe Tabasco sauce, the picture framer, old-fashioned fishmongers and those shock troops of gentrification, the cupcake sellers.

You wouldn't think this is the suburb where a quarter of a century ago the police feared to tread, and where the local council defied Margaret Thatcher's government by refusing to set a budget. The famous Nuclear Dawn mural on Coldharbour Road, now faded, is more a historical artefact than a message of defiance. And if the Brixton Pound is a continuation of that struggle for independence, it's fighting its corner in the nicest possible way with the nicest possible people.

Look at the shop windows in Brixton Village and now and again you'll see a sign saying the stallholder accepts Brixton Pounds or 'pay by text'. Sitting outside one of the market cafes, Mehul Damani, smiling and earnest, spreads out on the table a selection of colourful notes featuring local heroes such as David Bowie and Chicago Bulls basketball star Luol Deng. While campaigners had to make Herculean efforts to persuade the Bank of England to put the uncontroversial Jane Austen's face on a banknote, Brixton's notes have embraced the area's multi-ethnic heritage and won a hipster accolade into the bargain in the form of a design award from *Marketing* magazine.

Like George Ferguson, Mehul Damani recognises that the intangible rewards of a local currency can be as important as the direct trading benefits. He quotes a survey by Lambeth Council suggesting that the launch of the Brixton Pound was worth the equivalent of £100,000 in terms of positive news coverage for the area and the local council (interview with the author).

Creating a new currency from scratch, with all the accompanying hassle of meeting financial services and banking regulations, and then selling the idea of a complementary currency to householders and businesses, can seem a lot of effort simply to promote a locality and the independent shops and services it offers. While you can spend your Brixton Pounds at more than 250 businesses and your Bristol Pounds at more than 500 shops, as a proportion of the local economy, both currencies are minuscule. A few brave souls at Lambeth and Bristol Councils have taken the lead in having part of their salaries in local currency, but they are a tiny minority. At present the value rests as much in the publicity, and as a conversation-starter about supporting local businesses, as in any direct economic benefits.

But local or regional currencies are not just a quirky experiment in some of the more alternative corners of the UK. There is a long history of complementary currencies being issued outside the traditional banking system, and it has often been driven by necessity more than by ideals.

Guernsey, now a bastion of the offshore financial services industry and a tax haven for the super-rich, was once much poorer. After the Napoleonic Wars in 1817 it was on its knees, with no money to invest in infrastructure and debts of more than £19,000 – at a time when the island's entire revenue came to only £3,000 a year. The island's government, the States, responded by issuing its own currency. Rather than borrowing from the banks at punitive interest rates or taxing citizens who had few resources, it printed notes that could be used as circulating currency or in payment of taxes, but with an expiry date after which they would no longer be valid – ensuring the island would not be flooded with worthless money. The funds were used to pay for the construction of a market hall near the harbour at St Peter Port, road building and schools. An initial issue of £6,000 was followed by two smaller issues in 1820 and 1821, another £5,000 in 1824 and £20,000 for school building in 1826. The Guernsey government was effectively borrowing against its own future revenue streams, but without increasing its debts or taxes (Holloway, 1958).

The Guernsey experiment was relatively short-lived and came to an end when the island's private banks decided to get in on the act and issue their own competing notes. But in Switzerland, a complementary currency, WIR Francs, has been going since 1934. WIR – German for 'we' – is a contraction of Wirtschaftsring, which means economic circle. The WIR Bank operates a mutual clearing system in which businesses lend to and borrow from each other, underwriting each other's negative balances rather than raising new interest-bearing loans when they need short-term finance. The system is effectively a closed loop, operating independently of, but alongside, the national currency, and is financed through transaction fees. WIR also provides traditional loans at competitive rates.

The purpose of the scheme, set up during the 1930s Depression, is to support small and medium-sized businesses that may find access to credit difficult or prohibitively expensive, or that are having problems with their cash flow. Trading in WIR Francs helps to smooth out the bumps in the wider economy, and builds a network of mutual support among independent businesses, reducing the requirements for ready cash or loan facilities. More than 60,000 businesses were trading in WIR Francs in 2010. The Bank's President, Jürg Michel, described this as a 'unique economic network' based on trust – a trust that has developed and been sustained over three quarters of a century (Kennedy et al, 2012).

Trust is especially important in communities that are marginalised by the global economy. Banco Palmas in Brazil is a complementary currency a bit like the Brixton Pound, set up to support the local economy in the shanty town of Conjunto Palmeiras. By combining the local currency with a micro-credit scheme, Banco Palmas has helped to create more than 1,800 jobs since 1998. The success of the local currency shows where the Brixton and Bristol Pounds might end up: the proportion of spending within the Conjunto Palmeiras community rose from 20 per cent to 93 per cent between 1997 and 2011. As researchers Margrit Kennedy, Bernard Lietaer and John Rogers argue: 'Micro-credit combined with a local currency keeps wealth local, and reduces transport costs, food miles and

CO_2 footprints. Local money works to protect the local and global environment' (Kennedy et al, 2012, p 27).

In Brixton and Bristol, the promise of local money is just that at the moment: a pledge that if people stick with it, there may be real benefits to the local economy in future. In 19th-century Guernsey, 20th-century Switzerland and contemporary Brazil, local and regional banks have shown they can fulfil the promise.

Till debt us do part

There is another kind of money available on most of our high streets, and it illustrates why initiatives like the Brixton and Bristol Pounds are important. It is driven by debt and it sucks value out of the locality.

The payday lender and the pawnbroker are the public, and least popular, faces of the debt economy. In any run-down town – and plenty of not-so-run-down towns – the pawn shop and the loan shop are the default occupiers, moving into the spaces vacated by the vanishing butchers, bakers and candlestick makers or their successors. Together with their cousins, the betting shops, the media typically use them to represent high street decline. And for all their protestations that they create employment and bring space back into use, there are good reasons for seeing them as a physical and social blight.

Objecting to a proliferation of activities commonly associated with working-class people and those on low incomes can smack of middle-class snobbery. But there are more serious issues. The pawn shops and payday lenders blight not only the streetscape but also people's lives. While the online lender Wonga.com has borne the brunt of negative publicity, with Archbishop of Canterbury Justin Welby famously vowing to compete it out of existence by supporting socially beneficial alternatives, the loan shops that line our town centres are just as harmful.

Promising instant access short-term finance, they foster a survival economy in which borrowers are constantly paying over the odds in order to get from one end of the month to the next. What is presented as an instant fix for an immediate shortage of cash can quickly become a trap: a borrower taking a loan of £500 for 28 days at a fixed rate of £25 per £100 borrowed would have to repay £625 on their next payday (see, for example, www.quicksilvercash.co.uk). But if their net monthly pay was £1,000, that would leave only £375 for the following month. If the borrower's monthly expenses averaged £900, they would need a new loan of £525 before the end of the second week – with a repayment due on the next payday of £631.50. Instead of saving £100 a month, they would be running to stand still, and any unforeseen expense would tip them into deeper debt.

The extent of the crisis is even greater than the rash of pawn shops and loan shops in our high streets would suggest. A survey by the government's Money Advice Service found that of 49 million adults in the UK, only 16 million had 'healthy finances'. Nine million were in urgent need of help with managing their money, 10 million were 'on the edge' and starting to struggle, and 14 million were 'focused on the now rather than the future'. A staggering 18 million people run out of money before payday – including one third of people with incomes over £30,000 (The Money Advice Service, 2013). The Money Charity, which compiles regular updates on the level of household debt in the UK, put the nation's total personal debts at £1.4 trillion in June 2014 – almost as much as the UK's entire economic output in 2012 (The Money Charity, 2014).

This means that money that could be spent in local shops or on generating local economic activity is instead going into the back pockets of loan companies and banks. To argue – as payday lenders do – that their activities create jobs is disingenuous: the jobs they generate simply accelerate the process of sucking money out of communities.

The same is true of betting shops. There has been particular concern over the proliferation of shops providing 'fixed-odds betting terminals', machines that contributed £1.5 billion to betting companies' revenues in 2012. The Association of British Bookmakers, citing a study by the Centre for Economic and Business Research, claims betting shops contribute £3.2 billion to the UK economy and provide 55,000 jobs (ABB, 2013). But a separate study by Landman Economics argues that every additional £1 billion spent on fixed-odds betting terminals actually destroys 13,000 jobs in the wider economy because the money spent on gambling is removed from other shops and services (Landman Economics, 2013).

There are two other common complaints about betting shops. One is that planning rules that put them in the same category as banks and estate agents mean that premises can be changed without planning permission, allowing uncontrolled clustering. Hence Mary

Portas' call (rejected by the government) for a separate 'use class' for betting shops. The other criticism is that betting shops drive up rents, as most are owned by national chains, thus pricing out independent retailers and reducing diversity. In just one South London suburb, Tooting, there were 22 betting shops by early 2014 and a 23rd was due to join them. The industry focuses on poorer areas: in 2013, a total of £13.2 billion was staked on fixed-odds machines in 2,691 shops in the poorest 25 per cent of English local authorities. For the richest 25 per cent of local authorities, the figures were £6.5 billion spent in 1,258 shops (Ramesh, 2014).

But it's not only individual debts and the activities of lenders and gambling companies that leach the life out of our towns. The bulk of our high street economy is dependent on debt and hobbled by the need to service loans. Just as indebted individuals must earn more than they would otherwise need to get by, indebted companies must make higher profits than would otherwise be required. A retailer saddled with interest-bearing debts, renting a property acquired using interest-bearing debt, must find ways to increase its margins. Its options are to drive down its own costs by employing fewer people or squeezing its suppliers, or to pass the costs on to consumers who may themselves be stretched by the need to service their personal debts. Who lends wins – until the system falls in on itself.

All of this is tied up with the banking crisis that exploded in 2007-08 but has been latent for far longer. While in the US this was linked strongly to sub-prime mortgages – loans given on residential property to people on low incomes or with poor credit histories – the UK's own banking crisis was more closely linked to speculation in commercial property such as shopping centres and offices. In an important speech in September 2011 Adair Turner, then chair of the Financial Services Authority, identified a root cause of the failure of both HBOS and RBS in 2008 as losses on 'old-fashioned loans' on commercial real estate. He observed:

> Credit extension to fund the purchase of assets whose supply cannot rapidly respond, such as property, or cannot respond at all, such as land, drives rising asset prices, but those in turn stimulate both credit supply and credit demand in a self-reinforcing cycle. (quoted in FSA, 2011)

The consequences are felt on our streets. The British Council of Shopping Centres noted in 2010 that more than £10 billion of shopping centre assets were at risk. Among the problems it identified was the behaviour of investors who took on large loans in the hope of quick profits:

> The most recent period of investment (2004-2008) saw the emergence of the private investor seeking high returns from assets held for very short periods of time (sometimes only 24 months). This 'flipping' of assets has led to chronic under investment in some centres. (David, 2010, p 5)

The debt-dependent nature of the town centre economy, far from encouraging caution and long-term thinking, has stimulated riskier behaviour. With huge loans to service, investors put their faith in being able to sell at a premium and make a tidy profit, passing the unexploded bomb to the next buyer. The detonation was both inevitable and hugely destructive. Yet the only positive future that governments, retail and real estate experts and financial gurus appear able to envisage for our towns is one where the wheels of the gravy train are re-greased and the whole shambolic jalopy is set in motion once again, with the same predictable consequences.

In his 2011 speech, Adair Turner pinpointed the prime function of banks in the UK economy as the creation of credit, which in turn becomes spending power. But to service the loans the wheels of economic growth have to spin faster and faster. As Turner explained, the financial universe created by the banks must always expand: '… they don't just allocate pre-existing savings, collectively they create both credit and the deposit money which appears to finance that credit' (quoted in FSA, 2011).

Appearances of finance can be deceptive. The equation works as long as there are returns to service the debt and to create a surplus. When the activity supported through loans is essentially speculation on the future sale values of shopping centres or the trading performance of a company, the bet is far from safe. The more distant the financial system becomes from real production, the more unstable it becomes and the more dependent it is on continuous and disproportionate levels of growth. As the Conservative MP Jesse

Norman observed, 'only one-tenth of UK bank lending goes directly to real, productive companies. UK banks have some £6 trillion in total assets and liabilities; most of these represent financial institutions trading with each other' (Norman, 2011, p 10).

It is a point underlined by Adair Turner: '... we need to challenge the idea that the bigger the financial system is the better. It may not be if the industry is involved in rent extracting rather than value-added activities' (quoted in FSA, 2011).

Because banks have come to support speculation in asset values more than investment in productive capacity, the economy in general and the economy of town centres in particular suffers from 'leaky bucket' syndrome: the money spent in a locality does not stay there. Money that services debt goes to the lender; money for rent goes to the landlord; and money paid to a national or multinational company is less likely to be re-spent within the community than money spent with local businesses. By contrast, when you do business with your neighbour, not only is your neighbour more likely to do business with you in the future, but they are also more likely to spend what you've paid them on the products and services provided by other neighbours.

The effect of that local spending, or recirculation of money, is known as the local multiplier, and underpins the thinking of schemes such as Totally Locally (see Chapter 5). It is the opposite of the multiplication of credit, where more and more money funds less and less real activity. The local multiplier is to do with the same amount of money being used to support an expanding range of activity. Instead of trying to put new money into the local economy by borrowing it (and paying interest), it keeps existing money in the local economy by prioritising local producers and service providers.

No economy, local or otherwise, can thrive by becoming a closed system trading only within itself. There needs to be a balance between local trade and wider national and international exchange. But in many communities, that balance is seriously out of kilter. A study in Knowsley, Merseyside, found that only 8 per cent of spending by the local authority reached local people, with the rest going to outside contractors, corporations and consultants (Boyle, 2009).

Rewards for loyalty

You don't have to be a government or a bank to create a currency. The trick is to be trusted. Air Miles started as a reward scheme offered by airlines to frequent flyers, but are now handed out by companies as diverse as Apple, eBay and Amazon as incentives to buy products and services. You can exchange them for flights, but you can also swap them for points from entirely different loyalty programmes through websites such as points.com. Effectively Air Miles are a complementary currency, sitting alongside national currencies and used to incentivise particular types of purchasing or trade.

In 2013 Amazon announced its own virtual currency in the US, the Amazon Coin. Anyone who buys a Kindle Fire tablet computer gets 500 Amazon Coins, the equivalent of US$5, to spend on apps or games. While the initial application of the currency has been very limited, it doesn't take much imagination to see how Amazon can offer discounts and promotions throughout its range using Amazon Coins − the catch, or joy, depending on your viewpoint, being that they can only be re-spent within the Amazon store itself. The objective is to keep customers enclosed within a corporate ecosystem with a currency that is worthless outside it.

Such reward schemes are nothing new. In the 1960s and 1970s you couldn't fill up your car at a British petrol station without being offered Green Shield stamps, which customers would then stick into dog-eared collection books and exchange for items from a catalogue. Tesco offered Green Shield stamps as a reward for supermarket shopping until 1977, when it dumped them as part of an aggressive price-cutting strategy. Today it has its own version, Clubcard points, which are far more sophisticated and allow the store to collect reams of data about its customers. Green Shield suspended sales of its stamps in 1983, merging the business into Argos, the catalogue retailer established in 1973 that has now become a staple of British high streets.

Green Shield stamps still have a value, but only as collectibles traded on eBay. Today's virtual currencies, whether Tesco Clubcard points or Amazon Coins, are created out of nothing and at little cost other than that of marketing and information management. Their purpose is to encourage loyalty and repeat business.

In the struggle for the future of the high street, loyalty and repeat business matter more than anything. They matter to retailers, obviously; but the broader idea of loyalty to a place or community matters to everyone who has an interest in its future. Some public services, like libraries and leisure facilities, survive on loyalty as much as on need. And loyalty generally involves putting your money where your mouth is.

For towns that want a more secure and sustainable future, there are two issues at play here. One is to encourage people to spend more with local traders and businesses, maximising the value to the local economy. The second is to reduce the dependence on debt finance that locks us into a system that inexorably ratchets up costs and risks.

The simpler part – unless you're going the whole hog and creating a new currency – is to build local loyalty. Totally Locally has demonstrated that a very basic message can work wonders, both in terms of raising awareness of what's on offer in a community and as a way of enabling people to feel they can make a difference with small actions. Others have developed more sophisticated and complex approaches, ranging from marketing programmes to smartcards intended to rival the big stores' loyalty cards.

An idea doesn't have to be complex to be effective. We're all familiar with the cards issued by railway station coffee outlets: get them stamped five times and you get your sixth coffee free. But while such grab-and-stamp cards can be an easy way to encourage repeat business or build a sense of connection, they tell a trader nothing about who their customers are, why they're coming back and what they're buying when they arrive. If the objective is to keep money within a community or to boost a particular business, it's hard to know how well it's working – are the users people who would have been repeat customers anyway?

Alternative approaches can be costly in terms of both finance and time. The WiganPlus loyalty card, developed using the same technology as Transport for London's Oyster travel card, enabled shoppers to earn points and enjoy discounts at more than 140 outlets in Wigan. By late 2012 it had attracted more than 5,300 members, and the WiganPlus team had helped keep a failing shopping centre, The Galleries, alive by offering exhibition space for local artists and craftspeople. But resources ran out before the project could be developed to a sufficient scale to make a significant impact. Other schemes have faced similar problems.

A different take on local loyalty is the 'high street as department store' idea, where traders join forces to present a unified approach, encompassing branding, activities and discounts or special offers. In North London the Crouch End Project (see Chapter 5) brings shops and community organisations together with a single online presence, a smartphone app, a 'What's on' guide and a loyalty card. Done with flair and professionalism, such schemes can create a buzz about a place and tap into residents' sense of local pride. They help plug the leaky bucket, keeping money within the town's economy, and without some of the complexities of complementary currencies.

On their own, however, they don't address the wider issues. Indeed, a really successful town branding exercise might ultimately prove counter-productive if the result is to drive up property prices and rents, squeezing out the independent and niche businesses that have helped to create the buzz and excitement in the first place. So local loyalty needs to do more than keep existing traders afloat. It needs to fashion the building blocks of a different kind of future for our high streets: one that minimises dependency on a broken financial and property system and maximises local people's ability to keep money, and therefore influence, in their own hands.

Banking on local

Standing sentinel at the junction of North Parade and Manor Row is one of Bradford's many impressive listed buildings. Topped by an octagonal clock tower and with a balcony suitable for state occasions, it is testament to the wealth and confidence of the Victorian city. But far from being a preserve of the well-heeled, the gilded wrought-iron letters above the entrance proclaim something for everyone. This was the Yorkshire Penny Bank, where any worker could open an account with just one penny.

The Penny Bank, built in 1895 and designed by architect James Ledingham, trumpets Yorkshire pride as brashly as a brass band. Above the entrance are the carved faces of Colonel Edward Akroyd, founder of the original West Riding Penny Savings Bank in 1859; the general manager, Peter Bent; bank director John Ward; and factory owner Henry Ripley.

From 2009 to 2014 the building in North Parade stood empty. Like bank branches in virtually every city in the UK, it had found a new, if insalubrious, life as a pub before being raided by the police and subsequently shut down because of under-age drinking.

Long before the physical home of Bradford's Penny Bank fell on hard times, the Bank itself had to go cap in hand to the Bank of England for a bail-out. In 1911 it had reserves of £500,000 but depositors' funds were valued at £18 million. Recognising that it would collapse if there were any significant withdrawal of funds, the Bank of England brokered a takeover by a consortium of bigger institutions, including Lloyds and Barclays.

The new organisation eventually changed its name to Yorkshire Bank Limited, and continued to have a strong regional connection; during the miners' strike of 1984-85 it allowed many customers to defer mortgage payments until the strike was over. But since 1990 it has been no more Yorkshire than guacamole. It is now owned by National Australia Bank, alongside Scotland's Clydesdale Bank. National Australia Bank may know all about running an efficient global financial corporation, but it's a far cry from the vision of Edward Akroyd, a mill owner motivated by a desire to see his workers save money and buy their own homes.

The succession of financial crises in the 20th century, and the 1930s Depression in particular, saw the failure and closure of local banks across the world. The days when every customer knew the name of the branch manager and getting an overdraft involved being ushered into a wood-panelled office for a personal interrogation are long gone.

In many respects this is for the better. As banks have turned into global digital businesses, customers have swapped personal connection for convenience and a sense of control. But as Jesse Norman, Adair Turner and Lawrence Tomlinson have all spotlighted, that loss of connection has come back to haunt us. Banks have pursued the big numbers in financial trading and real estate, paying scant attention to the small fry of local entrepreneurs.

To bring money back into our towns, the pendulum needs to swing back again. We need an alternative to the Hobson's choice of unaccountable and unresponsive global institutions and vulnerable, undercapitalised local ones – both of which have proved unstable when disaster strikes. As well as keeping spending local, we need to find ways to re-localise the wider financial system.

The barriers to entry in the UK banking system are so high that it's hard to imagine every city having its own bank any more. But regionally based banks and financial institutions that are close enough to make individual decisions about investing and lending, and that have a strong local focus, are a step in the right direction.

In Yorkshire, perhaps the nearest counterpart today to the ethos of Edward Akroyd is the Key Fund, which invests in social enterprises across the north of England. In many ways it has stretched Akroyd's ideals further, combining the commercial nous of a lender with a commitment to social value and investment in some of the North's poorest communities.

The Key Fund combines the work of a grant funder with that of a commercial investor, ploughing more than £26 million since 1999 into enterprises ranging from music studios to nurseries through a mixture of grants, equity funding and traditional loans. Over the years it has supported more than 2,000 organisations and enabled 130 new businesses to start. Its investment in town centres has included £30,000 to help establish Bar Lane Studios, a contemporary art space with a gallery, studios and a cafe in the centre of York; and the conversion of the former tourist information centre in Garstang, Lancashire, into The Fig Tree, an educational centre and workspace complementing Garstang's status as the world's first Fairtrade town.

Projects like Bar Lane Studios and The Fig Tree are the kind of activities that bring life and interest to empty or under-used buildings. But they are fragile and often run by people with limited access to finance and few assets against which they can borrow. Organisations like Key Fund help to bridge the gap, applying the resources that enable enterprising individuals to turn their ideas into reality.

Key Fund is what is known as a community development finance institution: a locally or regionally based lender focusing on businesses and individuals with good ideas and social purposes who would struggle to get a loan from a traditional bank. There are around 60 such lenders in the UK, each serving specific client groups or localities, and between them they lent more than £200 million in 2012. They are funded through a mixture of public funds and repayments on loans, and this public support acknowledges the higher-risk nature of the business and the opportunities created for people in more deprived communities. Loans are generally small, but the demand is huge, and has been estimated by the Community Development Finance Association at between £5.45 billion and £6.75 billion (Glavan, 2013).

For lower-risk ideas, what most places need is the services of a traditional bank: the kind where the branch manager will sit down with you, look you in the eye and judge your business proposition by the kind of person you are and your business plan, not just by a computer algorithm determining your creditworthiness. This is precisely the kind of banking that has been disappearing from our high streets.

One way forward is for local councils to use their reserves and pension funds to reinvest in their localities. In Cambridge, the county council pension fund and Trinity Hall, one of the university's oldest and wealthiest colleges, have established a bank that does exactly that. Cambridge & Counties Bank was set up in 2012 and in its first year opened 900 new deposit accounts and lent £40 million to small and medium-sized enterprises in East Anglia and the East Midlands. Its activity is spread across the region to reduce the risk of concentrating all its energies in one locality, but it is already channelling loans to growing businesses whose development had been frustrated by the attitude of mainstream banks. Borrowers are vetted individually by bank staff rather than through automated credit scoring; they range from a restaurant that wanted to open a new branch to a solicitors' practice that needed funding to restructure its business.

As Cambridge & Counties' chief executive Gary Wilkinson commented on the bank's first anniversary: 'SMEs [small and medium-sized enterprises] account for the vast majority of UK businesses and the UK's economic recovery relies heavily on the ability of these firms to grow.... Our popularity shows that there needs to be more activity from alternative lenders' (Cambridge & Counties Bank, 2013).

In Australia the idea of local banking has gone further. Bendigo Bank developed the Community Bank idea in response to a rapid decline in the number of high street bank branches. Between 1993 and 2000 more than 2,050 branches closed across Australia, a 29 per cent fall in branch numbers (Bendigo Bank, nd). Many towns were left with no local branch at all – a situation mirrored in the UK, where 1,200 communities have now completely lost local banking facilities (CCBS, 2012). Unlike British banks, Bendigo decided to do something about the problem, enabling communities to set up locally owned and operated franchises covered by guarantees for depositors from a parent institution with more than a century-and-a-half of profitable trading.

The Community Bank idea works by sharing risk and revenue. The local company pays the branch operating costs and revenue is split between the local operator and Bendigo Bank. Once the branch is making a surplus it can reinvest its profits through dividends for its shareholders and grants to community organisations. By March 2013 there were 296 Community Bank branches, and between them they had paid a total of AUD31 million in dividends and more than AUD100 million in grants to community groups and projects.

Another system that puts access to finance in local hands and generates community benefits is the JAK cooperative savings and loans system in Sweden. Run like a credit union, where members deposit funds and are able to draw down loans, it is distinctive in eschewing interest-bearing debt. Savers do not get a return on their deposits, but can take out interest-free loans for a modest fee. The monthly payments are higher than with a traditional loan because the fees include payments into a savings account, which guarantees the borrower a lump sum at the end of the loan period. Since 1965 it has grown to 35,000 members with 30 local branches and more than £100 million of assets. Members are also able to set up 'local enterprise banks' to kick-start new businesses that might not qualify for conventional finance (Lewis and Conaty, 2012).

You don't need a localised banking system to raise local money, but it helps. There are other ways of plugging the leaky financial bucket: community share issues that raise equity from local people, crowdfunding, even local lotteries. BIDs can raise money for local projects without going to the bank. Each method has its positives and pitfalls; the prize in each case is to pump money into a locality without losing local control and piling up new burdens of debt.

Social supply chains

If ordinary people can help plug the leaky bucket by choosing to buy locally, supporting local fundraising, investing in community projects, or by using a complementary currency, think how much more the big spenders in an area could support local businesses and high streets through their spending choices.

A few years ago Nottingham's main hospitals, City Hospital and Queen's Medical Centre, did just that, sourcing most of their food from local suppliers. The 1,000 pints of milk required every day at City Hospital comes from a farm 11 miles away – closer than some of the hospital's patients. Ninety-five per cent of its meat comes from a local processor, which in turn sources its supplies from farmers within the region. Vegetables come from a wholesaler that prioritises local producers. Far from costing more, the initiative saved the hospitals £6 million compared with its previous contractors (Soil Association, nd).

A study in Manchester underlined the power of public services to support their local economies. In 2009 Manchester City Council was spending £900 million a year on services and capital projects; researchers found just over half the council's top 300 suppliers had a Manchester postcode, and one third of the next 700 contractors. Money paid to Manchester businesses is more likely to be re-spent with Manchester businesses (Jackson, 2010).

Public services are under pressure, but are still among the most important spenders in many towns. By seeking to develop social supply chains, where suppliers are chosen for their impact on the community as well as on cost, they can make sure their everyday decision making helps to keep towns alive. What better way to encourage local loyalty than by practising it at a civic level?

So we need to turn the leaky buckets into magnets: tools that attract and retain money rather than letting it flow out. Just as there are immediate and local responses to a broken property system as well as long-term and systemic solutions, so there are immediate and local as well as systemic responses to the challenge of finance. Both need to be addressed. In the long term, we need a banking system that is responsive to local needs and that reinvests in communities, and a network of viable alternatives to debt finance. In the short term, we need locally controlled methods of raising funds to meet immediate local needs, and to ensure that wherever possible purchasing choices, individual and corporate, achieve social as well as private benefits.

12

From 'me towns' to 'we towns'

At the tearoom in Bury Market there's a chalkboard with a cheery-looking rag doll beside it. The board advertises Jackson's rag pudding – 'a little bit like chippy pudding but better' – for a modest £3.50. Few people south of Lancashire have come across rag pudding. You wouldn't call it a delicacy, but it's substantial and filling, the kind of dish you'd need after a long shift at the mill. And that's exactly what it was made for: the rag pudding originated in Oldham, where cotton workers would tuck into a pie of minced meat and vegetables, wrapped in suet pastry and boiled in a cheesecloth rather than baked in a tin. A bit like the now ubiquitous Cornish pasty, it was a meal in itself, put together with whatever was to hand. You could make one even if you were too poor to afford a baking dish, which many people were 150 years ago. Lancastrians still vouch for its flavour and wholesomeness, although it's said to taste even better after a few pints of ale.

The rag pudding makers knew how to make a little go a long way. In a nation where the divide between boom towns and bust towns is becoming starker, it's a secret many of us will need to re-learn: how to value and apply the resources we have ourselves rather than wait for the wash of others' economic ripples to reach us. At the heart of that is a rediscovery of solidarity. 'Me towns' of takers must become 'we towns' of makers, with a shared ambition to create a common future. The ingredients at hand may look more suited to a rag pudding than a banquet, but we need not be helpless in the face of forces that seem beyond our control.

While the changes in our town centres will affect everyone, they will be felt hardest and sharpest in the places that are already falling behind. Hence the rag pudding analogy. We have to take our future in our own hands while we can, using the resources we have now.

The challenge of change is an opportunity to think and to act differently. It is a chance to rediscover and recreate the magic of place, the local shared value that makes every town distinctive and generates pride in the work of our hands and minds. The future of the high street lies not in campaigns to save this and to stop that, but in actively shaping what is to come: both literally and metaphorically to nurture, connect, forge, build, perform and celebrate. The town centre will not be as we or our parents remember it, and it will require less physical space as digital connectivity alters almost every aspect of our lives. But it can be a place that once again belongs to all of us and functions as the heart of a community, a pump that gives vitality to the whole.

To turn 'me towns' into 'we towns' requires new activism and new attitudes. Something must be done. But more importantly, and first, something different must be thought and felt and determined. If we plunge straight into activism without thinking through its purpose and impact, we may find very little has altered at the end of it. This is why it helps to think of town centres as a new form of commons.

Rediscovering the commons

For centuries people in Britain have used common land as places to walk and relax, graze livestock or forage for firewood. The earliest roads and footpaths were common land, existing long before the Romans turned road building into a state enterprise. Before the Highway Act of 1835 all paths and roads were the responsibility of 'the inhabitants at large in the parish' where they were situated.

The popular idea of common land is of a free-for-all, but it's more accurate to say that it is land where the rules of access and use are set locally and collectively. The idea of the 'tragedy of the commons', popularised by the ecologist Garrett Hardin, is that there is nothing to stop self-serving individuals from over-exploiting a common resource: over-fishing is a classic instance (Hardin, 1968). But it would be more accurate to describe that as a tragedy of individualism. When rules of access are determined and overseen locally, shared assets can be stewarded sustainably.

An enduring myth about the commons is that nobody is responsible for them. This is a long way from reality. The 257 acres of Tunbridge Wells and Rusthall commons in Kent, for example, have been 'common land' for almost a millennium. Far from being owned by nobody or everybody, they were given after the Norman conquest to the Lord of the Manor of Rusthall and are still owned by the manorial lord's successors. In the 19th century the commons' managers were known as Hogpounders because of the enthusiastic way they levied fines for animals grazing without permission – a far cry from Garrett Hardin's prophecy. The land is now enshrined as common land by an Act of Parliament and overseen by a management body, the Tunbridge Wells Commons Conservators. There isn't much to be said for feudalism, but by preserving the concept of common land it delayed the real tragedy of the commons, which was their appropriation for private profit.

The Nobel-winning economist Elinor Ostrom has shown how communities have found ways of writing effective home-grown rules to administer common resources. These include the management of grazing rights for pastures in the Swiss Alps and of fisheries by cooperatives on the east coast of the US. In Switzerland, village courts fine individuals who over-graze shared meadows (Ostrom, 1990). Elinor Ostrom's particular insight was that local management could achieve the sustainable use of certain natural resources far more rapidly and effectively than national or international legislation. Communities proved more effective stewards of forests or fisheries than government bureaucracies or private corporations. Trust, reciprocity and a degree of autonomy were more reliable safeguards than the law or the commercial market (Ostrom, 2012). This doesn't mean that everything should be managed at a hyperlocal level by communities setting their own rules. Ostrom argued for 'polycentric' approaches to governance and management, with different authorities working at different scales and acting as checks and balances on each other. Just as the local commons depend on reciprocity and trust, so does the pursuit of the public good at regional and national scales.

Most discussions of the commons, and of the public benefits they bring, have focused on the use of land and natural resources. But urban centres, too, are common resources that have an identity and value well beyond the individual benefits any family or business might draw from them. A historic town, for example, has a public value that extends beyond its own boundaries, its buildings and its story providing a shared asset for visitors from many miles away. A high street, even one that seems ordinary to an outsider, has a public value as a focal point of a community. The value is created by the massing of shops, services and places of interest, and by the combination of activities that happen within and around them, not by the individual hardware store or coffee shop.

So a high street, and the wider town centre within which it sits, is far more than simply a collection of parcels of individually or publicly owned land, shops and highways. It is the heart that keeps a place alive. A sense of belonging and connection, a web of stories, the character formed by groups of buildings and open spaces, and above all the atmosphere created by the people who bring it to life and the economic activity that arises from that, cannot be the preserve of private landowners, a town centre management company or even a local authority. They belong to all of us. The value of a town, unlike the value of a shopping mall, can't be privatised because it is created and enjoyed collectively, even though it is the consequence of the actions of many individuals. The sense of place is a shared good, and like the historic commons, needs to be stewarded and cared for in the common interest.

In her essay 'The comedy of the commons', property lawyer Carol Rose shows why the idea of the commons is important for commerce, an activity normally associated with private ownership. 'Customary' uses – such as the use of an open space for a market, fair or social gathering – create commercial value which would not exist without people coming together in the first place. Mary Portas made a similar point in her review of the high street, arguing that social capital creates economic capital. A high street full of shops which are left empty because of the rent demanded, or because the owner won't accept a reduction in the property's capital value, is an example of the tragedy of enclosure: the loss of social value because of the self-serving actions of individuals. Carol Rose uses the example of a traditional dance to show how it is the participants, not just the organisers, who create value: '… the more persons who participate in a dance, the higher its value to each participant. Each added dancer brings new opportunities to vary partners and share the excitement' (Rose, 1986, p 767). Charlotte Hess, founder of the Digital Library of the Commons, defines a commons as 'a resource shared by a group where the resource is vulnerable to enclosure, overuse and social dilemmas. Unlike a public good, it requires management and protection in order to sustain it' (Hess, 2008). In that sense, we should think of our town centres and high streets as commons: they don't sustain themselves, and they are vulnerable to the antisocial activities of private individuals or corporate bodies (public authorities included). The problem we face in many towns, however, is under-use rather than over-use.

So imagine a future where we think of our town centres as commons and our high streets as a public resource, places that get better when more people join the dance. The blame culture that surrounds current debates – every problem is the council's fault, the retailers' responsibility, the landlords' failure, the shoppers' fickleness or the government's neglect – would have to change, because shared enjoyment demands shared responsibility. Property and business owners, however distant, would not have the right to walk away from considerations of their wider impact. Councils would have to stop pleading powerlessness in the face of planning rules and corporate pressures. In these town centre commons, the use of land and space must be curated so that everyone can benefit. The performer or protestor, the trader or community organisation, all need somewhere to set out their stall. Buildings should be managed for their intensity of uses, rather than as speculative capital assets. The Countryside and Rights of Way Act 2000 gave the public the right to walk freely on areas of mountains, moors and registered common land in England: we should investigate what comparable rights of access could be granted for buildings and public spaces within towns and cities, with similar codes of good practice on management and use. If we considered our town centres as commons, decisions about developments and public services would be taken with the future of the whole place in mind, not on narrow technical or bureaucratic grounds. Historic and cultural value would be respected and nurtured.

In practical terms, this means establishing a body to take such decisions and ensure principles of stewardship and shared access are kept to the fore. It could be a town team, as suggested by the Portas review; a town centre commission, as envisaged in Bill Grimsey's high street review; it could be a local authority or town council, or even (if modified to become inclusive and accountable) a BID or business-led partnership. The issue is not which organisational form is best, but how the organisation views its role. The idea of the commons provides a framework in which shared value is emphasised and assets and resources are considered in terms of how they benefit the whole place.

If we borrow the terminology of 'commons conservators' to describe this town centre body, its overarching role would be to preserve and sustain the town centre in the best interests of current and future generations of residents and users. The conservators of common land are concerned with rights of use, the flora and fauna, biodiversity and protection against risks such as flood and fire. The conservators of town centres would be concerned with rights of use, the built environment, economic and social activity and protection against risks such as property speculation and profiteering as well as longer-term economic and environmental dangers.

Town centre commons conservators would need to identify which elements of the town's physical, social and civic infrastructure are most valued; ensure that property owners act as stewards rather than speculators; and support local people's efforts to improve and beautify the places they live in. This would not diminish the status of individual private owners or undermine the power of municipalities.

Rather, it would add to both, fostering a sense of shared endeavour and common cause.

Activities that add to the sense of place and commonality, from street festivals to community growing projects, should be given precedence. Traffic should be managed to encourage walking and lingering. Space should be made available for voluntary and charitable activities. Access would need to be managed to ensure there are neither too few nor too many activities going on at once.

Shared resources, shared responsibilities

To weave this tapestry of shared value we need to think socially, systemically and serendipitously. This doesn't come naturally to businesses focused on their own bottom line, to councils fixated on plans and processes, to activists who are frequently driven by threats rather than opportunities, or to residents bombarded with messages encouraging them to see themselves as consumers rather than citizens. The rethinking required is comprehensive, but the possibilities it presents are liberating.

Thinking socially involves more than joining forces with other people. It means working towards a culture where social benefits and common value are given priority. As that culture develops it will lead to more open and creative relationships between businesses, and between businesses and their customers; it will lead to more transparent and participative practice within councils and public services; and it will embolden citizens to develop a sense of ownership of the places they live in rather than an attitude of helplessness and fatalism.

The UK government's Community Life Survey shows how far we are from such social thinking, but also how fertile the ground is. People in England still have a strong sense of local identity: 79 per cent strongly feel they belong to their immediate neighbourhood, and 76 per cent to their local area. An impressive 84 per cent are satisfied with their area as a place to live. The survey shows causes for concern, however: only 10 per cent have any direct involvement in decisions about local services; and fewer than two fifths believe they can influence decisions in their local area (Cabinet Office, 2013). People love where they live, but often feel powerless to change it.

So the first stage in thinking socially is to strengthen the common values we share. The Community Life Survey is not the only evidence that people feel a bond with places and neighbourhoods as the geographic expression of community. In recent years behavioural economics and psychological studies have generated considerable evidence that human beings are more sophisticated and socially aware than the mythical *homo economicus*, driven only by self-interest and calculations of individual gain.

The economists' trick has been to dupe us into thinking that anything that is not material is immaterial. But even economists are now starting to think more roundedly about human wellbeing. Politicians such as the former French President Nicholas Sarkozy have dabbled in applying the idea of wellbeing to national economics, commissioning Nobel prizewinners Amartya Sen and Joseph Stiglitz to examine alternatives to the traditional totem of gross domestic product (GDP) (Stiglitz et al, 2009). Britain's own Office for National Statistics is seeking to develop measures of national wellbeing 'to provide a fuller picture of how society is doing by supplementing existing economic, social and environmental measures' (ONS, 2013). In a culture where media and politicians consistently use economic growth as the hallmark of success, it is worth recalling Robert Kennedy's famous observation that gross national product (GNP) 'measures neither our wit nor our courage, neither our wisdom nor our learning, neither our compassion nor our devotion to our country. It measures everything in short, except that which makes life worthwhile' (Kennedy, 1968). Economists and political leaders can be slow on the uptake in identifying and nurturing common values. They fail to notice the deep connections with land and location that have driven the community ownership experiments in the north of Scotland and the resident-controlled housing organisations of inner cities from London to Boston. This affinity is not only the result of being in a place for generations: it is often felt as strongly by newcomers who put down deep roots in a locality in a remarkably short space of time.

The search for common values is inseparably entwined with human beings' search for meaning and purpose. If physical places demonstrate and encourage qualities of generosity, celebration, mutual support, inclusivity, imagination, and creativity, then people who hold those values will be attracted to them and make use of them. If, conversely, they reduce us all to shoppers who are judged by what we consume rather than who we are, the first economic chill will expose the emptiness of the offer.

The second aspect of thinking socially is to identify and make use of common resources. A sign of a 'me town' is that problems and challenges are always someone else's responsibility; in a 'we town' everyone brings what they have to the table. These common resources include money and property, obviously: methods such as crowdfunding and community share issues can apply private money for the common good, while temporary uses of space can turn private buildings into public assets, albeit briefly. In a 'we town' organisations invest because it is good for the locality, not just for their own bottom line; they consider how others can benefit from their properties, people and skills. Such civic entrepreneurship came naturally to the likes of Joseph Chamberlain and Edward Akroyd; few of today's business leaders can compare.

A town's common resources also include time, talent and connections. In a 'we town' there is an honest and respectful conversation between the professionals who offer their services for a fee and the volunteers who work for love, each recognising the value of others' contributions. The town harnesses the 'sweat equity' of volunteers' practical skills, whether it's redecorating an empty shop to bring it back into use or organising children's activities for a festival. It values the networks and connections of residents and activists and the energy they can bring to physical places.

It is necessary to articulate common values and bring together common resources because we face common challenges. A communal mindset is at the heart of resilience. Being able to recover from shocks and setbacks involves knowing when to ask for help and who to ask, and being confident that the response will be positive. The mutual aid shown after the Hull floods shows that far from being a utopian fantasy, cooperative attitudes simply need to be stirred from their slumber. The stronger the local networks and the greater the practice of collaboration, the easier it becomes to call on others for assistance or to offer it when trouble arises.

This concept of shared responses to common challenges does not stop at the doors of institutions. Too often towns imagine they can address their difficulties by bringing together the great and the good – the council leaders and chief executives, the university professors, the captains of industry and the senior public servants. They fail to appreciate that economic development must encompass community development, and that it is only by overcoming suspicions and engaging as equals with people from all walks of life that genuinely shared visions can be developed.

This means learning from all kinds of people, not simply trying to explain or sell institutional ideas to them. It is where issues of race, gender and social class kick in as much more than gestures of so-called political correctness. Civic and business leaders need to be humble enough to learn – from the family networks and cultural pride of many minority ethnic communities, for example; or the determination, leadership and sense of responsibility often more evident among women than men; or the generosity and resourcefulness of many working-class neighbourhoods. By accepting everyone who cares at the table and sharing what is on it, we can start the journey from resilience to prosperity.

Whole-place thinking

As well as thinking socially, it is vital to think systemically to give our towns a better future. This means considering not only what kind of places we want to create, but how they are to be run and in whose interests: who will control or influence what can happen in 5, 10, 20 or 50 years' time, and how to ensure our towns are no longer at the mercy of decisions taken hundreds or thousands of miles away – or even behind closed doors in the local town hall or chamber of commerce.

Responses that fail to address the underlying issues – how to do business better, who has access to space and on what terms, how to create places where people want to live, who owns land and property and how they manage it, and who is able to access finance and how – will always be vulnerable. Today's initiatives might generate enthusiasm and even bring extra spending into local high streets, but until they begin to address the deeper questions rather than simply trying to keep broken systems sputtering along, the best we can hope for is to slow down the decline.

Thinking systemically demands a concept of the whole place. The town centre needs to be seen not just as a retail enclave but as the core of a community. How does it serve that community? Does it provide the facilities and the activities people need and will enjoy? Are there opportunities to participate meaningfully in decision making and planning? Does it serve all the people, or are some excluded because they have less income or are less mobile? Can the town centre be good for people from all backgrounds and at all stages of their life? Does it welcome children or people with disabilities?

Partnering a concept of the whole place should be a philosophy of stewardship. If a place is for everybody, all should be involved in its care, preservation and development. There will inevitably be differences of opinion about how that should be done and what should be done first. Community-led planning and community organising, where people are enabled to articulate their concerns and hopes, can help to bring those differences to light and generate a consensus about how to move forward. The idea of stewardship shouldn't be left to local authorities, which, despite their vital role, have relatively little leverage over private businesses in their locality and still less over the actions of distant property owners or national retailers. An effective council needs to act as a broker and facilitator, using its powers on behalf of the whole population, and ensure all in the community are welcomed to co-develop this stewardship role.

To act as a steward, the team responsible for the town centre – whatever its legal structure and whatever it calls itself – needs a vision that is both far-sighted and flexible, setting out a direction of travel. We need to move on from the make-believe world of much economic and physical masterplanning, the familiar mash-ups of propaganda and wishful thinking with statistics and projections leading to the same predictable conclusion that the good times are about to roll. Instead, planning needs to be agile, responding to immediate challenges and unexpected shifts in the wider economy, demographic trends or business opportunities. It needs to draw on and amplify the ideas and innovation that emerge from local people. One of the great unlearned lessons from the first decade of the 21st century was how seldom the starry-eyed visions of prosperity through swish new developments and inward investment have come to fruition. Bradford and Rochdale are far from unique in standing testament to the failure of the 'boom goggles' worn by council chief officers and property developers.

This is why putting land and property in the hands of community organisations and locally based businesses in the long term, and making it easier for local organisations and enterprises to access what is there in the short term, must be integral to our towns' future. As long as the levers are operated by people who have no personal interest or stake in the future of the place, short-term financial thinking will dominate.

At the same time, the main organisations in a town need to take a civic view of their role. Schools and further education colleges should be invited into town centre premises and public spaces to strengthen their teaching and learning, and landlords should work with them to turn unused shops and offices into performance, exhibition and enterprise space. Health services could use high streets for health education and promotion; employers could showcase their work and advertise recruitment and training opportunities. The more local institutions are encouraged to use the town centre for their own work, the more they will take an interest in its success.

Space for serendipity

We need to think serendipitously too. The immediate is important. Stuff happens. Often it will open up unenvisaged opportunities or connections. An entrepreneur will arrive with a use for a building that hadn't been considered before; a community organisation will come forward with a new way of activating town centre space to meet local needs; artists and performers will bring dead spaces to life with events and festivals, or see the visual possibilities in bland or neglected buildings.

The transformation of Melbourne's laneways was the result of serendipitous as well as strategic thinking. So, too, was the emergence of Hay-on-Wye as a book town. Serendipity includes the unpromising circumstances that gave birth to Handpicked Hall, the street art of Stokes Croft and the 'No to Costa' campaign in Totnes, as well as the imaginative temporary uses of many a high street shop.

A long-term plan shouldn't be a straitjacket that excludes these things. Rather, it should set a direction and then encourage all to contribute. You could call it a framework for mess, a melding of the visionary and the spontaneous. Serendipitous thinking is always alert for catalytic people and actions, leaving enough room in the field for experimentation and learning from failure.

Thinking serendipitously requires a brutal honesty about the gap between the current reality and the possible future, and a recognition that we have to start from where we are. That means being open to unlikely alliances and people of goodwill, whatever hat they may happen to wear. The supermarket store manager who wants to open up their premises to community organisations, the street artist with an idea for brightening up a blank wall, and the teenagers who appropriate street corners or benches as places to hang out can all be fellow-travellers on the same road. The much-abused traffic warden, target of motorists' ire and comics' jokes from time immemorial, may have a better understanding of how a place works than the planner or highway engineer because they walk the streets every day.

On Valentine's Day 2013 the Birmingham suburb of Stirchley came alive through just such a 'just do it' mentality. A local community interest company, Place Prospectors, dreamed up a festival called Love Stirchley More. A 'love seat' toured local parks, and users were invited to write their thoughts about love on it. A canal boat became a venue for an evening of comedy. Shoppers could buy a specially commissioned Stirchley Sauce (aphrodisiac effects not guaranteed). For a modest financial outlay accompanied by a lot of local energy and enthusiasm, people were encouraged to see their town as a place to celebrate, harking back to the carnival that took place every year until 1939. Finding a little local love isn't too hard. The experience of Totally Locally is that people want to support the towns they live in; they just need to feel their efforts will be welcomed and worthwhile. By tapping into this civic pride and encouraging people to express it in ways that are relevant to their own lives, civic leaders can start to align a shared vision with shared action. Serendipitous actions can be symbolic, signalling an intention and a direction of travel.

Mapping for change

How, then, can we get from here to there? Even if the destination seems similar in many places, the route taken and the stops on the way will be very different. But there will be some common features on the map, and some map-reading skills that can be applied across the board.

The discussion and examples throughout this book have highlighted four elements that will be crucial to any high street that prioritises shared value: commerce, community, culture, and civic action. Each is necessary in itself; each plays a role in supporting the others; and each helps create the town centre 'commons' that we all enjoy, benefit from and contribute to. If any are missing, it will be much harder to reach our goal.

The test of any plan for a town is how to use this civic, commercial, cultural and community topography, both pre-existing and latent, to navigate towards a shared objective. How will we know whether we are on track and when we need to take stock and rethink?

Failing to answer this question is the bane both of big regeneration plans and of ad hoc or pop-up projects. If we don't spell out transparently what we are trying to achieve, how we will know when we've achieved it and what indicators of success or failure we might expect to find along the way, disappointment and suspicion will be unavoidable. Our measures of success need to relate back to our ultimate objectives: whether people are using the town centre, what they are using it for, whether they are spending time and money there, who benefits, and – crucially – whether their influence over the town's future is growing or diminishing. Are buildings being brought back into use? Are people starting to live in the town centre? Are there more events and festivals? Are community-run organisations starting to take over and open up access to land and property?

To navigate effectively, it helps to have a theory of change – a plan setting out the steps along the way and what you think you'll find when you get there. A theory of change for community asset ownership, for example, could set a destination of having a strategic group of buildings or spaces held in trust and brought into productive use for the benefit of the public. To get from here to there we would need to identify the owners; find out whether or when the assets might be for sale or how they could be shared; discover what temporary uses might be possible in the short term; consider how funding could be raised to take them over in the long term if necessary; and plan the kind of activities that might ultimately take place in and around them. Measures of success might include engaging the owners in conversation about the future of the premises in the first instance; finding opportunities to test different types of temporary activity; brokering alliances with the local council and commercial partners; and finding new ways to provide services or accommodation that make the most of the properties and are financially viable.

The idea of 'theories of change' was developed in the US as a way of testing whether 'complex community initiatives' could work, and has sometimes been used in the UK to plan and evaluate government initiatives. It can help to ensure visions are connected with reality (The Aspen Institute, 2003). The equivalent of a theory of change, whether or not you call it that, is needed for every town centre. It is necessary first, because there are few situations more complex than the evolution of a town centre, and second, because it is astonishingly common for interventions to be justified without any attempt to check whether they will match the claims made for them. A particularly crude example was the suggestion by Eric Pickles, Secretary of State for Communities and Local Government, that allowing motorists to park in restricted areas for 15 minutes would help to keep high street shops in business (Swinford, 2013). Needless to say, no research had been done. A theory of change isn't a solution for the town centre, but a way of checking whether a strategy might work, and how well it is progressing. To return to the map-reading analogy, you examine the map throughout the journey, not just at the start and the finish; and if where you are doesn't appear to match where you think you should be, you stop to check and retrace your steps if necessary, or find an alternative route. One academic study has suggested that to be effective, such wayfinding needs to be plausible, doable, testable and meaningful (Connell and Klem, 2000). The objective needs to be realistic, however ambitious the ultimate vision.

Any town embarking on a journey to create its own future will need to test its progress. There is no shortage of models and approaches on offer, from a kaleidoscopic mix of thinktanks, expert practitioners, consultants, salespeople and charlatans. With so many people clamouring to be helpful or wanting a slice of the pie, it becomes even more important to develop a local vision that stresses the common and unique value of each town, rather than adopting an off-the-shelf recipe. The mindset matters more than the model.

Whatever model or legal form (cooperative, community interest company, town centre management company) is chosen, what matters most is that it facilitates imagination and action instead of stifling it. People tend to work best when they feel a sense of agency and autonomy, but are also in a supportive team where their efforts are valued and open to constructive challenge. Low control and high accountability should be the watchwords.

A sense of realism about the length and difficulty of the journey is required too. Not every town will make the transition from 'me town' to 'we town'. Many will prefer to continue as they are, comfortably or uncomfortably numb, putting their faith in failed solutions and false promises of prosperity. Some will indeed prosper, because an economy that polarises nations into winners and losers will always bring wealth to a few. Some will decline and imagine they can do nothing about it, or shy away from actions that appear too radical and disruptive and that threaten a culture of accumulating and speculating.

For many others, it will be a long road: it took more than 30 years for Coin Street Community Builders to create the unique place that London's South Bank has now become. But where people are ready to be open-eyed and open-hearted, working together for as long as it takes to create and nurture the new commons of our towns and cities, there is the hope of different trajectories and new possibilities.

Letting the light in

None of the thousands of journeys from here to there begin unless someone is prepared to make a start: to think a little bit differently, to dare to make a change. The difference might appear where you least expect it.

In an Asda supermarket in Shore Road, Belfast, the store manager heard a few years ago that the local community centre had been broken into and the presents for a children's Christmas party stolen. The manager gave the community centre £1,000 to replace the toys.

"For God's sake don't tell anybody, I'll work it out on my P & L [profit and loss account], I'll work it out," the manager told Paul Kelly. "It will come back to me in spades. I won't need to tell anybody I've done that, they will all know by the end of the day that Raymond at Asda rescued the Christmas party." Paul Kelly says Asda responded in the same way to the Tottenham riots of 2011:

> 'Within a couple of days we had a lorry there with 10 grand's worth of towels and clothing and bedding and crockery to help people who'd lost their homes. It just

happens. It doesn't need anyone to say, can I do it? It's the right thing to do. We don't give stores a budget – just get on and do what you think is right because that's what the community would expect you to do.' (interview with author)

His vision is for store managers to act as 'pillars of the community' and for the business as a whole to be seen as a positive force in the towns it serves:

> 'For me it's about how do you create that kind of three-legged stool in a community, which is the public, the private and the voluntary sector coming together to work on issues. We've got to earn the permission and the recognition to do that.'

Is it possible for supermarkets, so often the curse of the local economy and society, to play a positive rather than a predatory role? The hope lies in the fact that they are staffed and used by people with their own sense of what is right, who mostly live in the towns they serve, and who may have the sense of purpose and agency that turns a wish to do the right thing into positive action. A few charitable actions and good intentions shouldn't let supermarkets off the hook when it comes to challenging their wider role and impact on places. But the kind of discussions that are taking place within Asda – and some of its competitors – show that more equitable and symbiotic relationships may be possible. Common interests can become signposts to common values and a shared direction.

While some might be suspicious of Asda's motives, it is more typical for suspicion to be directed against individual civic entrepreneurs who want to improve their communities. Chris Chalkley's conviction for criminal damage for painting murals in Stokes Croft is a case in point. But here, too, is the beginning of a journey to the common good: helpful troublemakers can be the greatest builders of social capital.

The architect Malcolm Fraser speaks of the need to let some light in, invoking the spirit of Patrick Geddes:

> 'Geddes talked about conservative surgery. That means taking things out in order to keep the strength and

vibrancy of the place, and he talked about letting a little light in. I think it's an immensely powerful way of looking at urban planning in general, because it's changeable and interactive and allows us to see cities as living organisms.' (interview with the author)

We need to let light into the human as well as the built environment, taking out the shades of suspicion and cynicism. In Chapter 4 we looked at malls and supermarkets as places where humanity has gone missing. In towns and cities across Britain, a rainbow assortment of activists and entrepreneurs are rediscovering and reviving that common humanity, letting a little light into dingy places.

Hope for the future

This book has been all about hope. Not hope as a slogan, but hope that we can craft a better future for the places where we live by starting at their heart, focusing on the high streets and town centres that say so much about our shared identity and do so much to create shared value. On a practical level, this hope involves examining the way we do business and finding better and more equitable ways to do it; examining how land and property is owned and used and finding ways to open it up to new activities and local ownership; and ensuring that the way we raise and spend money creates the widest possible local benefits.

But it is also a hope rooted in recognising the cultural and social value of people and places. It is rooted in an understanding that the places we call home are more than a functional agglomeration of houses, shops and workplaces but carry memories, meanings and futures that matter.

As the Scottish experience of community ownership demonstrates, real hope involves getting your hands dirty. It requires pragmatism and compromise. But instead of the pointless pragmatism of muddling along that has served our towns so disastrously, it demands purposeful pragmatism: the knowledge that although the road to the future will twist and turn and contain all sorts of bumps and potholes, it is still worth taking.

This is the hope and determination that can save our high streets, our town centres and our wider communities. John Ruskin famously observed that there is no wealth but life. The best future for our town centres is not merely as places to buy, but as places to be; places where we live and act as citizens rather than as consumers. Then they can be places where we rediscover local identity and community, where we can be more fully alive and more fully ourselves. As many a shopkeeper has said, why settle for less?

References

ABB (Association of British Bookmakers) (2013) *The truth about betting shops and gaming machines: ABB submission to DCMS Triennial Review*, April (www.gov.uk/government/uploads/system/uploads/attachment_data/file/248922/Association_of_British_Bookmakers.pdf).

Action for Market Towns (nd, a) 'Wantage means business!' (http://premium.towns.org.uk).

Action for Market Towns (nd, b) 'Artisan market, Wilmslow' (http://premium.towns.org.uk).

Allen, K. (2013) 'Wage cuts for British workers deepest since records began, IFS shows', *The Guardian*, 12 June.

Amazon.com (2012) *2011 annual report* (http://phx.corporate-ir.net).

Arts Council England (2013) *Community libraries. Learning from experience: Guiding principles for local authorities*, London: Arts Council England.

Aspen Institute, The (2003) *Making sense: Reviewing program design with theory of change*, Washington, DC: The Aspen Institute, Washington.

Baker Associates (2010) 'The impact of pedestrianisation on Taunton town centre: A retail perspective' (www.somerset.gov.uk).

Bayley, S. (2010) *Liverpool: Shaping the city*, London: RIBA Publishing.

BBC News (2010) 'England floods in 2007 "cost the economy £3.2bn"', 18 January (http://news.bbc.co.uk/1/hi/uk/8464717.stm).

BBC News (2012a) 'Dairy farmers threaten more protests over milk prices', 12 October (www.bbc.co.uk/news/uk-england-shropshire-19917950).

BBC News (2012b) 'Wet weather set to hit UK food prices', 10 October (www.bbc.co.uk/news/uk-19893873).

BBC News (2014) 'John Lewis staff get 15% annual bonus', 6 March (www.bbc.co.uk/news/business-26462969).

BBC Radio 4 (2013) 'Desert island discs: Sir Terry Leahy' (www. bbc.co.uk/programmes/b01qdr2m).

BCSC (British Council of Shopping Centres) (2012) *Shopping centres: At the heart of the community*, London: BCSC (www.bcsc.org.uk).

Bendigo Bank (nd) 'What is a community bank?' (www.bendigobank. com.au).

Benfield, K. (2012) 'Why community-based planning works better than anything else', *The Atlantic Cities*, 26 March (www.citylab. com/design/2012/03/why-community-based-planning-works-better-anything-else/1587/).

Benford, J. and Burrows, O. (2013) 'Commercial property and financial stability', *Bank of England Quarterly Bulletin 2013*, Q1, pp 48-58.

BIRA (British Independent Retailers Association) (2013) 'Storm warning' (http://bira.co.uk).

BIS (Department for Business Innovation and Skills), LGA (Local Government Association) and Post Office (2012) *The local authority and Post Office Ltd pathfinder programme. An evaluation of strategic engagement* (www.postoffice.co.uk).

Blythman, J. (2005) *Shopped: The shocking power of British supermarkets*, London: Harper Perennial.

Bolton, P. (2010) *Key issues for the new Parliament 2010: Energy price rises and fuel poverty*, London: House of Commons Library Research.

Bookseller, The (2013) 'Dale: booksellers have publishers "over a barrel"', 8 March.

Bowers, S. (2013) 'Amazon's fees hike for third-party traders provokes fury', *The Guardian*, 28 March.

Bowlby, R. (2000) *Carried away: The invention of modern shopping*, London: Faber & Faber.

Boyle, D. (2009) *Money matters*, Bristol: Alastair Sawday's Publishing.

Boyle, D. and Harris, M. (2009) *The challenge of co-production: How equal partnerships between professionals and the public are crucial to improving public services*, London: Nesta and New Economics Foundation (nef).

BPF (British Property Federation) (2013) *Property data report 2013* (www.bpf.org.uk).

Braw, E. (2013) 'Hamburg's answer to climate change', *The Guardian*, 31 October.

Brierley Hillness Project (2011) 'My Brierley Hill' (http://brierleyhillnesstoolkit.wordpress.com).

Briggs, F. (2013) 'Town centres in Midlands and North West top shop vacancy rates, data reveals', *Retail Times*, 19 February.

Brown, L. (2012) *Full planet, empty plates: The new geopolitics of food scarcity*, New York: W.W. Norton & Company.

Butler, T. (2013) 'Independent museums, financial resilience and social impact' (http://tonybutler1.wordpress.com).

Cabinet Office (2011) 'PM's speech on the fightback after the riots', 15 August (www.gov.uk).

Cabinet Office (2012) *National Risk Register of Civil Emergencies: 2012 edition*, London: Cabinet Office.

Cabinet Office (2013) *2012-13 Community Life Survey* (http://communitylife.cabinetoffice.gov.uk).

Cambridge & Counties Bank (2013) 'Bank celebrates one year anniversary by signing up 1000th new customer', Press release, 11 June (www.ccbank.co.uk).

Campbell, L. (2013) 'Waterstones "on track" as losses are slashed', *The Bookseller*, 31 January.

CCBS (Campaign for Community Banking Services) (2012) *Branch network reduction: 2012 report* (www.communitybanking.org.uk).

Centre for Cities (2011) 'Lessons from 1980s on Enterprise Zones', London: Centre for Cities (www.centreforcities.org/40/press/articles/2011/03/24/lessons-from-1980s).

Centre for Cities (2014) *Cities outlook 2014*, London: Centre for Cities (www.centreforcities.org/assets/files/2014/Cities_Outlook_2014.pdf).

Chatsworth Road Traders and Residents Association (nd) 'Our vision' (www.chatsworthroade5.co.uk).

Christopher, D. (2010) 'Long Eaton, the town without a voice', *Press Gazette*, 8 March (www.pressgazette.co.uk).

CILIP (Chartered Institute of Library and Information Professionals) (2013) *A changing landscape: A survey of public library authorities in England, Wales and Northern Ireland, 2012-13* (www.cilip.org.uk/sites/default/files/documents/CILIP_Public_Library_Survey_Summary_Report_A_Changing_Landscape_2012-13_0.pdf).

Clarke, R. (2010) *A review of recommendations and remedies to address supermarket buyer power in the EU* (www.rogerclarke.org.uk).

CNU (Congress for the New Urbanism) (2005) *Malls into mainstreets: An in-depth guide to transforming dead malls into communities*, Chicago, IL: CNU (www.cnu.org/sites/files/mallsintomainstreets.pdf).

Co-operatives UK (2014) *The UK Co-operative economy 2014: Untold resilience* (www.uk.coop/sites/storage/public/downloads/co-operative_economy_2014.pdf).

Coalfields Regeneration Review Board (2010) *A review of coalfields regeneration*, London: Department for Communities and Local Government.

Colin Buchanan (2006) *Stokes Croft gateway enhancement project: Final report*, Bristol: Colin Buchanan.

Committee on Climate Change (2012) *Climate change – Is the UK preparing for flooding and water scarcity?*, London: Committee on Climate Change.

Competition Commission (2000) *Supermarkets: A report on the supply of groceries from multiple stores in the United Kingdom*, London: Competition Commission.

Competition Commission (2008) *The supply of groceries in the UK market investigation* (http://webarchive.nationalarchives.gov.uk/20140402141250/http://www.competition-commission.org.uk/assets/competitioncommission/docs/pdf/non-inquiry/rep_pub/reports/2008/fulltext/538.pdf).

Connell, J. and Klem, A. (2000) 'You *can* get there from here: using a theory of change approach to plan urban education reform', *Journal of Educational and Psychological Consultation*, vol 11, no 1, pp 93-120.

Conservativehome.com (2013) 'Exclusive: CCHQ declares Conservative Party membership to be 134,000', 17 September (www.conservativehome.com).

Cooper, K. (2008) 'Closing time for Living Over the Shop project', *Inside Housing*, 10 June (www.insidehousing.co.uk/closing-time-for-living-over-the-shop-project/1446809.article).

Coulthard, T. et al (2007) *The June 2007 floods in Hull: Final report by the Independent Review Body* (www.coulthard.org.uk).

Cracknell, R. (2010) *Key issues for the new Parliament 2010: The ageing population*, London: House of Commons Library Research.

Cumming, L. (2010) *2020 vision: A far-sighted approach to transforming public services*, London: 2020 Public Services Trust.

Daily Telegraph (2006) 'Who are the Notting Hill Set?', 26 February.

David, R. (2010) *The impact of the recession on secondary shopping centres*, London: British Council of Shopping Centres.

Davies, K. (2012) 'Bensham families say no but Tesco gets go ahead', *Chronicle Live* (www.chroniclelive.co.uk).

Davis, J.E. and Stokes, A. (2008) *Lands in trust, homes that last: A performance evaluation of the Champlain Housing Trust*, Burlington: Champlain Housing Trust.

Dawson, J. (1988) 'Futures for the High Street', *The Geographical Journal*, vol 154, no 1, pp 1-12.

DCLG (Department for Communities and Local Government) (2011a) 'High streets get boost from fairer parking', 1 August (www.gov.uk).

DCLG (2011b) *Lifetime neighbourhoods*, London: DCLG.

DCLG (2014) '"Convenience culture" drives high street revival', Press release, 29 July (www.gov.uk).

de Certeau, M. (1984) *The practice of everyday life*, Berkeley, CA: University of California Press.

Defoe, D. (1927) *A tour thro' the whole island of Great Britain, divided into circuits or journies*, London: J.M. Dent & Co.

Defra (Department for Environment, Food and Rural Affairs) (2012) *Food statistics pocketbook 2012*, London: Office for National Statistics.

Dellot, B. et al (2014) *Making the connection: Local post offices as community enterprise hubs*, London: RSA 2020 Public Services.

Deutrom, S. (2013) 'Listening to our customers in "real" time', Tesco PLC, 5 March (www.tescoplc.com).

Distinguin, S. (2013) *Amazon.com: the hidden empire*, faberNovel (www.fabernovel.com).

Dwelly, T., Lake, A. and Thompson, L. (2010) *Work hubs: Smart workspace for the low carbon economy* (www.workhubs.com).

Ebrahimi, H. (2013) 'Local councils "harm" high street', *The Telegraph*, 2 February.

Economist, The (2013) 'The rise of the sharing economy', 9 March (www.economist.com).

Ellen MacArthur Foundation (2013) *Towards the circular economy: Opportunities for the consumer goods sector* (www.ellenmacarthurfoundation.org/business/reports/ce2013).

Ernst & Young (2011) *The contribution made by beer to the European economy* (www.brewersofeurope.org).

ESRC (Economic and Social Research Council) (2012) *Global food systems and UK food imports: Resilience, safety and security*, Discussions from the ESRC Public Policy Seminar, 30 March (www.foodsecurity.ac.uk).

Express & Star (2013) '2,500 applications for 22 jobs at Merry Hill DFS', 13 March (www.expressandstar.com/news/2013/03/13/2500-applications-for-22-jobs-at-merry-hill-dfs/).

FARMA (2013) 'Shoppers want British post "Horsegate"' (www.farma.org.uk).

Federation of Small Businesses (2008) 'Keep trade local: parking policies for sustainable communities' (www.fsb.org.uk).

Findlay, A. and Sparks, L. (2009) *Literature review: Policies adopted to support a healthy retail sector and retail led regeneration and the impact of retail on the regeneration of town centres and local high streets*, Edinburgh: Scottish Government (www.scotland.gov.uk).

Flouch, H. and Harris, K. (2013) *The online neighbourhood networks study*, Networked Neighbourhoods (http://networkedneighbourhoods.com).

FPH (Faculty of Public Health) (2010) *Great outdoors: How our natural health service uses green space to improve wellbeing* (www.fph.org.uk/uploads/bs_great_outdoors.pdf).

Friends of the Earth (2006) 'Calling the shots: how supermarkets get their way in planning decisions', Briefing, January (www.foe.co.uk).

Frost, T. (1875) *The old showmen, and the old London fairs*, London: Tinsley Brothers.

FSA (Financial Services Authority) (2011) 'Credit creation and social optimality', Speech by Adair Turner at Southampton University, 29 September (www.mondovisione.com/_assets/files/Credit-Creation-Social-Optimality-Southampton-Uni-20110929.pdf).

Fullilove, M.T. (2005) *Root shock: How tearing up city neighborhoods hurts America, and what we can do about it*, New York: Ballantine Books.

Galbraith, J.K. (2009) *The great crash 1929*, London: Penguin.

Gehl, J. (2010) *Cities for people*, Washington, DC: Island Press.

GLA (Greater London Authority) (2011) '"Help me make Croydon great again" mayor tells investors' (www.london.gov.uk).

Glavan, H. (2013) *Inside community finance: The CDFI industry in the UK 2012*, London: Community Development Finance Association (www.cdfa.org.uk).

Godwin, R. (2013) 'Is gentrification killing Brixton Market?', *London Evening Standard*, 25 January.

Greenspace Scotland (2007) *The links between greenspace and health: A critical literature review*, Stirling: Greenspace Scotland.

Grimsey, W. (2012) *Sold out: Who killed the high street?*, Croydon: Filament Publishing.

Grimsey, W. (2013) *The Grimsey review: An alternative future for the high street* (www.vanishinghighstreet.com).

Grosvenor (2012) *Annual report and accounts 2012* (www.grosvenor. com).

Grosvenor (nd) 'Liverpool One: Delivering a step change for Liverpool's city centre' (www.grosvenor.com).

Guardian, The (2012) 'UK historic election turnouts since 1918', Datablog (www.theguardian.com/news/datablog/2012/nov/16/ uk-election-turnouts-historic).

Hall, J. and Fletcher, R. (2010) 'Planning test to safeguard competition could cost 25,000 supermarket jobs', *The Telegraph*, 1 January.

Hallsworth, A., de Kernevoael, R., Elms, J. and Canning, C. (2010) 'The food superstore revolution: changing times, changing research agendas in the UK', *The International Review of Retail, Distribution and Consumer Research*, vol 20, no 1, pp 135-46.

Hamdi, N. (2010) *The placemaker's guide to building community*, London: Earthscan.

Hardin, G. (1968) 'The tragedy of the commons', *Science*, vol 162, pp 1243-8.

Harkins, C. and Egan, J. (2012) *The role of participatory budgeting in promoting localism and mobilising community assets*, Glasgow: Glasgow Centre for Population Health.

Hess, C. (2008) 'Mapping the new commons', Paper presented at 'Governing shared resources: Connecting local experience to global challenges', The 12th Biennial Conference of the International Association for the Study of the Commons, University of Gloucestershire, Cheltenham, 14-18 July.

Hine, D. (2010) 'Space Makers at Brixton Village (aka Granville Arcade)' (http://dougald.co.uk).

HM Treasury (2011) *The Green Book: Appraisal and evaluation in central government* (www.hm-treasury.gov.uk).

HM Treasury (2012) *Accounting for environmental impacts. Supplementary Green Book guidance* (www.hm-treasury.gov.uk).

HM Treasury (2013) *Investing in Britain's future* (www.gov.uk).

Holloway, E. (1958) *How Guernsey beat the bankers*, London: Economic Reform Club.

Holyoake, G. (1907) *Self-help by the people: The history of the Rochdale Pioneers*, London: Swan Sonnenschein.

Hopkins, R. (2012) 'Totnes's victory over Costa Coffee and the true meaning of choice', *The Guardian*, 2 November (www.theguardian. com/commentisfree/2012/nov/02/totnes-costa-coffee).

House of Commons Business and Enterprise Committee (2009) *Post offices – Securing their future*, London: The Stationery Office.

House of Commons Business, Innovation and Skills Committee (2013) *Inquiry into the UK retail sector. Written evidence from the National Federation of SubPostmasters*, April (www.publications. parliament.uk/pa/cm201314/cmselect/cmbis/168/168vw20.htm).

House of Commons Communities and Local Government Committee (2009) *Market failure? Can the traditional market survive? Ninth report of session 2008-09*, London: The Stationery Office.

House of Commons Culture, Media and Sport Committee (2012) *Library closures: Third report of session 2012-13*, London: The Stationery Office.

House of Commons Scottish Affairs Committee (2012) *The Crown Estate in Scotland: Seventh report of session 2010-12*, London: The Stationery Office.

Howard, E. (1902) *Garden cities of to-morrow*, London: S. Sonnenschein & Co.

Hunt, T. (2004) *Building Jerusalem: The rise and fall of the Victorian city*, London: Phoenix.

Hunter, J. (2012) *From the low tide of the sea to the highest mountain tops: Community ownership of land in the Highlands and Islands of Scotland*, Kershader: The Islands Book Trust.

Idler Magazine, The (2005) 'Wolverhampton', 4 August (http://idler. co.uk/wolverhampton).

IFS (Institute for Fiscal Studies) (2011) *Reforming the tax system for the 21st century: The Mirrlees review*, London: IFS (www.ifs.org.uk/ publications/mirrleesreview).

ILSR (Institute for Local Self-Reliance) (2012) 'Independent businesses report strong holiday sales', 26 January (www.ilsr.org).

IME (Institution of Mechanical Engineers) (2013) *Global food: Waste not, want not* (www.imeche.org).

Inside Housing (2005) 'Closing time for Living Over the Shop project', 4 November.

Isaksen, K.J. and Roper, S. (2012) 'The commodification of self-esteem: branding and British teenagers', *Psychology and Marketing*, vol 29, no 3, pp 117-35.

ITV Wales (2013) 'What is the future for the Welsh high street?', 25 March (www.itv.com).

Jackson, M. (2010) *The power of procurement*, Manchester: Centre for Local Economic Strategies.

Jackson, T. (2009) *Prosperity without growth: Economics for a finite planet*, London: Earthscan.

Jacobs, J. (1993) *The death and life of great American cities*, New York: The Modern Library.

Jama, D. and Dugdale, G. (2012) *Literacy: State of the nation*, London: National Literacy Trust (www.literacytrust.org.uk).

Jones, S. and Flood, A. (2012) 'Kensal Rise library stripped in night of books and Twain plaque', *The Guardian*, 29 May.

Kantar Worldpanel (2013) 'Grocery market share UK – big four under pressure', 16 July, Barcelona (www.kantarworldpanel.com).

Kawano, E. (2013) *Social solidarity economy: Towards convergence across continental divides*, Geneva: United Nations Research Institute for Social Development (UNRISD) (www.unrisd.org).

Kennedy, M., Lietaer, B. and Rogers, J. (2012) *People money: The promise of regional currencies*, Axminster: Triarchy Press.

Kennedy, R. (1968) Remarks at the University of Kansas, March 18, 1968 (www.jfklibrary.org/Research/Research-Aids/Ready-Reference/RFK-Speeches/Remarks-of-Robert-F-Kennedy-at-the-University-of-Kansas-March-18-1968.aspx).

Land and Society Commission (2011) *The Land and Society Commission report*, Royal Institution of Chartered Surveyors (www.rics.org).

Landman Economics (2013) *The economic impact of fixed odds betting terminals* (fairergambling.org/wp-content/uploads/2012/11/The-Economic-Impact-of-Fixed-Odds-Betting-Terminals.pdf).

Latitude (nd) *The new sharing economy* (http://latdsurvey.net).

Lawton, J. (2010) *Making space for nature: A review of England's wildlife sites and ecological network* (http://archive.defra.gov.uk/environment/biodiversity/documents/201009space-for-nature.pdf).

Legalfutures.co.uk (2013) 'Susskind: no future for high street firms, but window of opportunity for mid-sized practices', 11 January (www.legalfutures.co.uk/latest-news/susskind-future-high-street-firms-window-opportunity-mid-sized-practices).

Lewis, M. and Conaty, P. (2012) *The resilience imperative: Cooperative transitions to a steady-state economy*, Gabriola Island: New Society Publishers.

LGA (Local Government Association) (2012) *Funding outlook for councils from 2010/11 to 2019/20: Preliminary modelling*, London: LGA.

Live/Work Network (2012) 'Business briefing 2012' (www.liveworknet.com).

Lizieri, C. (2011) *Who owns the City?*, London: Development Securities PLC.

London Planning Advisory Committee (1998) *Dwellings over and in shops in London* (http://products.ihs.com).

Macdonald, O. (2013) 'Re-think! Parking on the high street. Guidance on parking provision in town and city centres' (www.britishparking.co.uk).

Mackie, D. (2011) *Introduction to social network analysis*, (http://bit.ly/HKUAzx).

McCrone, P. (2008) *Paying the price: The cost of mental health care in England to 2026*, London: King's Fund.

McIntosh, A. (2008) *Rekindling community: Connecting people, environment and spirituality*, Totnes: Green Books.

McMillan, J. (2002) *Reinventing the bazaar: A natural history of markets*, New York: W.W. Norton.

Maas, J., Verheij, R.A, de Vries, S., Spreeuwenberg, P. et al (2009) 'Morbidity is related to a green living environment', *Journal of Epidemiology and Community Health*, vol 63, pp 967-73.

Mainstreet Australia (2014) Mainstreet News, autumn, Heidelberg, Australia: Mainstreet Australia (www.mainstreetaustralia.org.au).

Manchester Evening News (2013) 'Taking the Teenage Market into Stockport's local community', 21 February (http://blogs.menmedia.co.uk).

Mann, J. (2002) *Heroin in Bassetlaw: Report of the inquiry convened by John Mann MP* (www.johnmannmp.com).

Manzo, L. (2005) 'For better or worse: exploring multiple dimensions of place meaning', *Journal of Environmental Psychology*, vol 25, pp 67-86.

Marsden, G. (2006) 'The evidence base for parking policies – a review', *Transport Policy*, vol 13, no 6, pp 447-57.

Maxted, W. and Porter, T. (2013) *The commercial property lending market research report – Year end 2012*, Leicester: De Montfort University (www.dmu.ac.uk).

Meanwhile Project (2010) *No time to waste… The meanwhile use of assets for community benefit*, The Meanwhile Foundation (www.meanwhile.org.uk).

Met Office (nd) 'Awful August' – floods 2008' (www.metoffice.gov.uk).

Miller, D. et al (1998) *Shopping, place and identity*, Abingdon: Routledge.

Minton, A. (2009) *Ground control: Fear and happiness in the twenty-first century city*, London: Penguin.

Money Advice Service, The (2013) *The financial capability of the UK* (www.moneyadviceservice.org.uk).

Money Charity, The (2014) *Money statistics* (http://themoneycharity.org.uk).

Mumford, L. (1961) *The city in history*, San Diego, CA: Harcourt.

National Archives, The (nd) 'Round Oak Steelworks Ltd' (www.nationalarchives.gov.uk).

National Assembly for Wales Enterprise and Business Committee (2012) *Regeneration of town centres* (www.senedd.assemblywales.org).

National Economic Development Office (1988) *The future of the high street*, London: HMSO.

National Federation of Women's Institutes (2013) *On permanent loan? Community managed libraries: The volunteer perspective* (www.thewi.org.uk).

National Housing Federation (nd) 'Facts and figures' (www.housing.org.uk).

Naylor, A. (2013) *On the origins of St Botolph's* (http://commonfutures.eu).

NCVO (National Council for Voluntary Organisations) (2013) 'Counting the cuts: the impact of spending cuts on the UK voluntary and community sector – 2013 update (www.ncvo-vol.org.uk).

Neate, R. (2011) 'Costa sales boosted as UK love affair with fancy coffee continues', *The Guardian*, 21 June.

Nesta, CABE (Commission for Architecture and the Built Environment) and 00:/ (2011) *Compendium for the civic economy* (www.nesta.org.uk).

New South China Mall (2006) 'Opening of Teletubbies Edutaiment Centre, South China Mall' (www.southchinamall.com.cn).

NICE (National Institute for Health and Care Excellence) (2012) *Walking and cycling: Guidance* (http://guidance.nice.org.uk).

'No to Costa' campaign (2012) 'It's about localism, not capitalism' (www.notocosta.co.uk).

Norman, J. (2011) *Conservative free markets, and the case for real capitalism* (www.jessenorman.com).

Nottingham Radical History Group (nd) 'Damn his charity, we'll have the cheese for nought!' (http://peopleshistreh.wordpress.com).

ODPM (Office of the Deputy Prime Minister) (2005) *Learning lessons from the Estates Renewal Challenge Fund*, London: ODPM.

O'Flynn, C. (2007) *What was lost*, Birmingham: Tindall Street Press.

ONS (Office for National Statistics) (2012a) *Religion in England and Wales 2011* (www.ons.gov.uk).

ONS (2012b) *South east has biggest share of the wealthiest households* (www.ons.gov.uk).

ONS (2013) *Measuring what matters* (www.ons.gov.uk/ons/guide-method/user-guidance/well-being/index.html).

ONS (2014) Statistical bulletin: 'Retail sales, December 2013', London: ONS.

Ostrom, E. (1990) *Governing the commons: The evolution of institutions for collective action*, Cambridge: Cambridge University Press.

Ostrom, E. (2012) *The future of the commons*, London: The Institute of Economic Affairs.

Oxford Economics and University of Exeter (2012) *The economic impact of the University of Exeter's international students* (www.oxfordeconomics.com).

Parker, G. (2009) 'Live at Newlands Tavern' (http://chairmanparker.blogspot.co.uk).

Pennycook, M. and Whittaker, M. (2012) *Low pay Britain 2012*, London: Resolution Foundation.

Petherick, A. (2001) *An assessment of the housing potential of vacant commercial space over shops in Chichester*, York: LOTS Projects.

Ponsford, D. (2012) 'PG research reveals 242 local press closures in 7 years', *Press Gazette*, 30 April (www.pressgazette.co.uk).

Portas, M. (2011) *The Portas review: An independent review into the future of our high streets*, London: Department for Business, Innovation and Skills.

Power, A. and Houghton, J. (2007) *Jigsaw cities*, Bristol: Policy Press.

Quinn, I. (2014) 'Costa boss reveals new high street rescue plan', *The Grocer*, 17 February.

Ramesh, R. (2014) 'England's poorest spend £13bn on gambling machines', *The Guardian*, 28 February.

Redman, P. (2001) 'Living over the shop', Lecture at Design for Homes 'Intensive flair' Conference, June (www.designforhomes. org).

Retail Markets Alliance (2009) *Markets 21: A policy and research review of UK retail and wholesale markets in the 21st century* (http://cms.webbeat.net/contentsuite/tools/fileManagement/getfile.aspx?sit=129&guid=97487384-21bb-48b6-afad-245f783c6d71).

Richards, J.M. (1938) *High street*, London: Country Life.

Riots Communities and Victims Panel (2012) *Five days in August*, London: Riots Communities and Victims Panel.

Robinson, M. (2013) Talk at Action for Market Towns Policy Conference, London, 23 April.

Rose, C. (1986) 'The comedy of the commons: custom, commerce and inherently public property', *The University of Chicago Law Review*, vol 53, no 3, pp 711-81.

Rosenberg, J. (1998) *Against the odds: Walterton and Elgin from campaign to control*, London: Walterton and Elgin Community Homes.

Rosenberg, J. (2011) 'Social housing, community empowerment and well-being: part one – empowerment practice in social housing', *Housing, Care and Support*, vol 14, no 4, pp 113-22.

Rosenberg, J. (2012) 'Social housing, community empowerment and well-being: part two – measuring the benefits of empowerment through community ownership', *Housing, Care and Support*, vol 15, no 1, pp 24-33.

Ruddick, G. (2013) 'Jessops, HMV and now Blockbuster – is the high street dying?', *The Telegraph*, 16 January.

Savills World Research (2013) *UK shopping centre and high street bulletin. Quarter 2* (www.savills.co.uk).

Schoenborn, A. (2011) *The right to retail: Can localism save Britain's small retailers?*, London: ResPublica (www.respublica.org.uk).

Self-help-housing.org (nd, a) 'Bow Arts Live/Work scheme – a social enterprise for artists and communities' (http://self-help-housing.org).

Self-help-housing.org (nd, b) 'How does self-help housing work?' (http://self-help-housing.org).

SIBA (Society of Independent Brewers) (2013) *Local beer report 2013* (http://siba.co.uk).

Simms, A. (2007) *Tescopoly: How one shop came out on top and why it matters*, London: Constable.

Simms, A. (2008) *Nine meals from anarchy: Oil dependence, climate change and the transition to resilience*, London: New Economics Foundation (nef).

Sissons, A. and Brown, C. (2011) *Do Enterprise Zones work?*, London: The Work Foundation.

Sklar, H. (2009) 'No foreclosures here', *YES! Magazine*, Winter (www.yesmagazine.org/issues/sustainable-happiness/no-foreclosures-here).

Soil Association (nd) 'Nottingham University Hospitals Trust – saving money by going local and developing their own brand "Coffee City"' (www.soilassociation.org).

Steele, J. (2013) 'Precious buildings at risk through irresponsible ownership' (http://jesssteele.wordpress.com).

Stiglitz, J., Sen, A. and Fitoussi, J.-P. (2009) *Report by the Commission on the Measurement of Economic Performance and Social Progress* (www.stiglitz-sen-fitoussi.fr).

Streetsblog San Francisco (2013) '85 percent of people on Polk Street arrive without a car', 29 March (http://sf.streetsblog.org).

Strother, J. (2011) 'Shopping by phone at South Korea's virtual grocery' (www.bbc.co.uk/news/business-15341910).

Swinford, S. (2013) 'Motorists allowed to park on double yellow lines to help save high streets', *Daily Telegraph*, 28 July.

Ted.com (2013) '8 views of Tirana, Albania – with its bright, multicolored buildings', 8 February (http://blog.ted.com).

Telegraph, The (2014) 'No margin for error as Clarke asks investors to back turnaround plan', 25 February.

Tescopoly (2011) 'Supermarket sweep: how retailers manipulate the planning system and what you can do to challenge it' (www.tescopoly.org).

Tesco PLC (2012a) 'Earn extra Clubcard points on Facebook when you "Share & Earn"', Press release, 5 July (www.tescoplc.com).

Tesco PLC (2012b) *Annual report and financial statements 2012* (www.tescoplc.com).

Tesco PLC (2013) *Annual report and financial statements 2013* (www.tescoplc.com).

Thompson, D. (2011) '#riotcleanup' (http://mrdanthompson.wordpress.com).

Thompson, D. (2012) *Pop-up business for dummies*, Chichester: John Wiley & Sons.

Thomson, A. (2012) 'Regeneration revisited', *Public Finance*, 9 February.

Tomlinson, L. (2013) *Banks' lending practices: Treatment of businesses in distress* (www.tomlinsonreport.com).

Townsend, S. (2011) 'Blasts from the past', *Planning*, 21 April.

Transition Town Totnes (2013) Totnes & District local economic blueprint (www.transitiontowntotnes.org).

Tuan, Y.-F. (1977) *Space and place: The perspective of experience*, Minneapolis, MN: University of Minnesota Press.

Tyler, S., Semper, G., Guest, P. and Fieldhouse, B. (2012) *The relevance of parking in the success of urban centres: A review for London councils*, Haywards Heath: British Parking Association (www.britishparking.co.uk).

ULI (Urban Land Institute) and PricewaterhouseCoopers (2007) *Emerging trends in real estate Europe 2007* (www.uli.org).

UN (United Nations) Secretary-General's High-level Panel on Global Sustainability (2012) *Resilient people, resilient planet: A future worth choosing*, New York: UN.

Urban Task Force (1999) *Towards an urban renaissance: Final report of the Urban Task Force chaired by Lord Rogers of Riverside*, London: E. & F.N. Spon.

US EPA (Environmental Protection Agency) (nd) 'Heat island effect', Washington, DC: US EPA (www.epa.gov/hiri/).

Vale of White Horse District Council (2013) 'Free parking a big success in the Vale', 20 March (http://ht.ly/mCjKL).

Wainwright, S. (2012) 'Enterprise Zones: do they create or transfer value?', *Journal of Urban Regeneration and Renewal*, vol 5, no 2, pp 124-31.

Wallop, H. (2012) 'Future of High Street is not shopping, says new Dixon chief Sebastian James', *The Telegraph*, 21 June.

Watt, N. and Inman, P. (2013) 'Britain faces at least two "austerity elections" says thinktank', *The Guardian*, 7 June.

Webb, S. (2012) 'Guerilla gardener plants beautiful miniature flowerbeds in potholes blighting London's streets', *Daily Mail*, 12 November (www.dailymail.co.uk/news/article-2231849/Steve-Wheen-Pothole-gardener-creates-miniature-flowerbeds-potholes-Londons-streets.html).

Westlake, A. (2013) '25 Ten Boutique opens in Littleborough', *Rochdale Online*, 27 July.

Whitbread PLC (2014) *Annual report and accounts 2013/14* (www.whitbread.co.uk).

Whyte, W.H. (1980) 'The social life of small urban spaces' (https://archive.org/details/SmallUrbanSpaces).

Wightman, A. (2013) 'Scotland needs radical land reform', Evidence to the Land Reform Review Group, January (www.andywightman.com).

Wilder, C. (2010) 'A fresh face in South London', *New York Times*, 4 August.

Wilks-Heeg, S., Blick, A. and Crone, S. (2012) *How democratic is the UK? The 2012 audit*, Liverpool: Democratic Audit (www.democraticaudit.com/wp-content/uploads/2013/06/auditing-the-uk-democracy-the-framework-2.pdf).

Wood, Z. (2012) 'Rise of the dark store feeds the online shoppers', *The Guardian*, 30 November.

Work Shop, The (2013) *Report #01*, February (http://issuu.com/socialspaces/docs/work_shop_report_-_final).

World Bank, The (2011) 'The World Bank supports Thailand's post-floods recovery effort' (www.worldbank.org).

World Economic Forum (2013) *Global risks 2013*, Geneva: World Economic Forum.

World Economic Forum (2014) *Global risks 2014: Ninth edition*, Geneva: World Economic Forum.

Wrigley, N. and Lambiri, D. (2014) *High street performance and evolution: A brief guide to the evidence*, Southampton: University of Southampton (www.southampton.ac.uk).

Index